Designing and Managing a
Research Project

DESIGNING AND MANAGING a
RESEARCH PROJECT
A Business Student's Guide

Michael Jay Polonsky
Victoria University

David S. Waller
University of Technology, Sydney

SAGE Publications
Thousand Oaks ■ London ■ New Delhi

For information:

Sage Publications, Inc.
2455 Teller Road
Thousand Oaks, California 91320
E-mail: order@sagepub.com

Sage Publications Ltd.
1 Oliver's Yard
55 City Road
London EC1Y 1SP
United Kingdom

Sage Publications India Pvt. Ltd.
B-42, Panchsheel Enclave
Post Box 4109
New Delhi 110 017 India

Printed in the United States of America

Library of Congress Cataloging-in-Publication Data

Polonsky, Michael J.
Designing and managing a research project: A business
student's guide / Michael Jay Polonsky and David S. Waller.
    p. cm.
Includes bibliographical references and index.
ISBN 0-7619-2249-0 (pbk. : alk. paper)
  1. Business—Research—Methodology. I. Waller, David S. II. Title.
HD30.4.P65 2004
658.4′03′0072—dc22   2004003259

This book is printed on acid-free paper.

06 07 10 9 8 7 6 5 4 3 2

Acquisitions Editor:	Al Bruckner
Editorial Assistant:	MaryAnn Vail
Copy Editor:	Publication Services
Production Editor:	Diane S. Foster
Typesetter:	C&M Digitals (P) Ltd.
Proofreader:	Scott Oney
Indexer:	Teri Greenberg
Cover Designer:	Glenn Vogel

Contents

Preface to Academics

This book has been written to guide students through various aspects of research projects. Though it is recognized that projects can take various forms, as well as be of varying importance within a class, this book's focus is on research projects that have a solid academic basis, although some implications for more applied projects are also highlighted. We believe that the book would be most suitable as a support text for classes involving undergraduate research projects, some MBA assignments, and, possibly, a master's thesis. This means classes in which research assignments represent a significant contribution to the overall grade, if not the sole assignment in the class. However, the book is not designed to support PhD dissertations.

In writing we book, we envisaged that students would have taken various other research-related subjects previously, such as marketing research, business research methods, and so forth. As a result, the book is designed to supplement other texts and materials that students are presently using or may have previously used. If you are running a class in which the sole focus is on research projects, this book might be used as the primary text, as it was designed based on previous experiences in running such a research project class.

In looking through the book, the reader must recognize that it is not a research methods or advanced analysis text. It is designed, as the title suggests, to be a business student's guide to issues associated with designing and managing a research project. Chapters have been written to focus on advice to the student, rather than developing advanced theoretical understanding of issues, although various degrees of theory have been integrated throughout the chapters. Also, a unique aspect of the book is the inclusion of particular chapters on topics such as supervision, group work, ethics, and data analysis (qualitative and quantitative), which can all be very important issues for students during the research process.

The book is divided into three main parts that present a logical flow for the research project. The first part, "The Foundations," includes five chapters that give an overview of the basic issues involved in the management of the research process. Chapter 1, "Introduction," introduces the book to the student and explains what a research project is. Chapter 2, "Choosing a Topic," discusses how a student might define a topic to be examined in the project. This, of course, assumes that students are given the flexibility in a class to choose their topic; if not, you might want to skip this chapter. Chapter 3, "The Role of the Supervisor," is designed to discuss a range of issues relating to supervision that students might face while undertaking a substantial piece of research. Students frequently have not had one-to-one supervision previously, and thus clarifying the importance of this process, as well as the various roles of potential supervisors, is important. Chapter 4, "Group Dynamics and the Role of Conflict," discusses the important issues relating to group conflict, the difficulties students might face during the project, and ways to deal with these issues. This was explicitly included in the book, as we have learned from past experience that group activities can cause many students quite a lot of stress and there is usually limited guidance on the underlying issues. Chapter 5, "Ethical Considerations," outlines some of the issues involved in research ethics related to a student project. Again, past experience has taught us that students, and some staff, do not understand the complexities of research ethics. This is particularly important, as this issue has become increasingly complex and many institutions require students to complete an application for ethical clearance before a project can proceed. This chapter is designed to help students understand the main research ethics issues and assist them in completing an application for ethical clearance. Therefore, this chapter may be more in-depth than other chapters.

The second part of the book focuses on the activities involved in "Undertaking the Research." Chapter 6, "Planning the Research Process," covers many of the basic issues that need to be considered when planning a student project. Many of the topics introduced here are discussed later in other chapters. Chapter 7, "Literature Review," is next, as it is important for researchers to have an understanding of the literature to assist them in the research process. Though some researchers might have placed this chapter in the first section, as part of "The Foundations," we believe that understanding the literature is a key aspect of the research process. Interestingly, this topic is frequently not discussed in any detail in other books on research, or it does not focus on how students can actually use the literature for their research. Chapter 8, "Data Gathering," examines the basic issues associated with collecting data and should build on students' previous experience looking at research issues. Chapter 9, "Qualitative Data Analysis," discusses the reasons why a researcher can undertake qualitative research and how this fits into the broader research process. This is another unique aspect of this book. Importantly, it does not outline the complex detail of how one actually undertakes qualitative research, as this would be well beyond one text, although it does provide references to relevant literature. Chapter 10, "Quantitative Data Analysis," discusses how various quantitative techniques can be used to examine the data. More important, this is done without presenting an explanation of the underlying statistics of the techniques. The chapter is not designed to explain how to use techniques, but rather to explain why you would use a given technique to address a research question. Students will, however, need to refer to other materials (e.g., texts, statistical packages, etc.) to understand how to actually undertake the analysis. Chapter 11, "Establishing Recommendations," looks at how students can draw conclusions from their research. From past experience, we have learned that students frequently have difficulty in understanding the broader implications of their research, and this chapter was designed to give some guidance in this area.

The third part of the book focuses on "Communicating the Results." A core part of the research process is to communicate the findings, although many students do not see it this way. Chapter 12, "Presenting the Results," focuses on how students can ensure that what they found is communicated effectively to the intended audience. Chapter 13, "Writing the Report," discusses the complexities associated with writing up the results for the various target audiences. In some institutions this material may have been discussed in a business writing or business communications course, but in other institutions the material may have been discussed only briefly within marketing research courses. A practical guideline is included for students. Chapter 14, "Oral Presentations," examines a range of issues associated with oral presentations, including a checklist that students can use to improve oral presentations. Chapter 15, "Concluding Remarks," ties the book together and seeks to give students some final hints to assist them in completing their research projects.

From past experience, we have learned that the use of research projects has been an excellent educational tool that has had a positive benefit for the students, supervisors, and business partners (where one has been involved). We wish you and your students well in your courses involving research projects!

Acknowledgments

We would like to thank all those who have assisted in the writing of this book. This could not have been completed without the help of a number of people. In particular we thank Paul Keogh, Work Matters Pty Ltd (Chapter 4); Dale Miller, Griffith University (Chapter 9); and Dr. Christopher D. Hopkins, Clemson University (Chapter 10) for their contributions. Past supervisors and students who have completed the Project in Marketing and Marketing Research subjects at the University of Newcastle have been an invaluable source of information and inspiration on what can and, importantly, cannot be done in business project research. Their efforts have been greatly appreciated. The staff at Sage and associated bodies has been very supportive, which has been particularly helpful.

Finally we would like to thank our wives and families for their support in completing this book and putting up with our long hours.

PART I

The Foundations

1

Introduction

This book is designed to serve as a guide that will assist you to develop ideas systematically and be an active participant in the learning process when undertaking a research project within a business subject. Such projects frequently draw on knowledge from a range of subjects that you have studied in the past, such as marketing research, business research methods, and business report writing. This book is explicitly designed to complement the material you have previously covered in these subjects, not to replace it.

Within this book, we have highlighted a range of issues that frequently arise during the course of a research project, some of which might not be covered in courses or texts designed for other subjects. Not every issue discussed within the text will necessarily be of relevance to each type of project (these will be discussed in Chapter 6). Distinctions will be made in regard to the importance of issues to various types of projects throughout the book and when these issues are particularly relevant.

The first research project you undertake can be a daunting task, so this book provides a step-by-step guide that will assist you with undertaking the various activities associated with designing, implementing, and writing up a substantial research project within the business area. It aims to be cross-disciplinary, as it covers the general research process and discusses questions that arise when undertaking research across various research topics and business subjects.

As the requirements of each project are different, there is no way that this book could cover each aspect of every type of research project. Instead, the book should serve as a "road map" to the processes that you can follow to complete your assignment. It has been designed to provide an overview of critical issues, as well as to present some helpful suggestions for dealing with the pragmatic issues involved in actually undertaking research projects, primarily at the undergraduate and MBA levels. While the issues within this book also need to be addressed in a PhD thesis, the book is not focused on dealing with the complexities of such research.

In writing this book, we have attempted to summarize the critical issues rather than comprehensively discuss the underlying theory behind each issue.

The book will, therefore, provide a useful reference that not only explains the various steps associated with aspects of research projects but also directs you to other useful materials that examine particular points discussed within the chapters in more detail. You will most likely need to refer to a range of other materials related to the activities and issues discussed within the book.

The book has been written with you, the undergraduate business/MBA student, in mind. It tries to address issues that students regularly have to deal with when undertaking research projects in their various business subjects, including major projects, minor theses, and to some extent even business consulting reports. Hopefully this text will make your experience in preparing, undertaking, and writing a research project within these subjects more worthwhile and allow you to maximize your learning experience.

How a Research Project Fits Within Your Business Education

Why are you undertaking a business degree? While this seems like an unusual question with which to start a text, it is one that sets out the foundation for undertaking a research project. Ideally, most of you, whether undergraduate or MBA students, are undertaking your degree to learn skills that will enhance your employability and/or earning potential. Obtaining a degree is important for a range of reasons: It demonstrates that you have the ability to learn, have some core knowledge base in an aspect of business, and have obtained important skills that will allow you to assist your future, or present, employer in operating more effectively.

While these goals are all sound, you need to ask yourself the following question: What is it that employers are looking for in new employees? This question is important, as it is critical that you adopt a marketing perspective on yourself early in your career, and yes, university is part of your career. Therefore, you need to arm yourself with skills, abilities, and knowledge that make you more attractive to potential employers, that is, knowledge and skills that potential employers deem valuable. While this makes sense, it is not always easy to do, especially when you are entering the job market for the first time and do not know what is expected.

Interestingly, there are a range of global studies that look at what employers want in new business employees. These studies have generally found that the main attributes employers are looking for are in fact not an understanding of theory related to a specific discipline, but rather a range of generic managerial skills (Johnson & Pere-Verge, 1993; Lau & Rans, 1993; O'Brien & Deans, 1996). These managerial skills include the ability to communicate effectively, the ability to work as part of a team and meet deadlines, the ability to be self-directed and work without supervision, and the ability to think "outside the box" and examine alternative solutions to complex problems. This broader set of business skills enables new employees to effectively integrate into organizations and assist with solving complex business problems. While you might not use all these skills from Day One in an organization, employers want to know that you have these skills and that they can be drawn on as needed as you become integrated into the organization.

What does this mean for you when you are studying at college/university? It means that employers are frequently keenly interested in ensuring that you not only have a solid academic background (i.e., good grades), but that you have obtained a level of proficiency in skills that are not frequently the primary focus of a given subject (e.g., developing team work, critical thinking, problem solving, etc.). Research projects in various business subjects, individual or team-based, are one activity that allows you to develop these critical thinking skills. Successful completion of a research or project report can then be used to demonstrate to employers that you have the skills they are seeking (Polonsky & Waller, 1998) and, as such, might be just as important as having a strong academic record. Therefore, while not the sole reason for undertaking research assignments in your business subjects, your teacher/lecturer/professor will assign these tasks to allow you to develop skills that employers value.

Overview of the Book

As suggested earlier, all projects are different, and because of this, this book seeks to cover issues that students might need to address in a diverse range of projects. The book is divided into 15 chapters covering three main areas, and while each chapter and area has a different goal, the sequential order is important, as it draws you through the research process.

The first part of the book, "The Foundations," covers topics associated with a general understanding of some broad issues associated with research projects. These are designed to address issues associated with the broad management of the research rather than the technical aspects of the research process. There are four "Foundation" chapters in addition to this "Introduction" chapter.

Chapter 2 discusses how you go about selecting your topic. Your topic will depend on the objectives of the subject/assignment, as well as your particular interests. Ideally, you will choose a topic that not only relates to the subject you are studying but also allows you to obtain a better understanding of an issue, industry, or firm that you are interested in. This should allow you to maintain your enthusiasm for the project, as well as allow you to gain valuable insights into an area in which you might wish to seek employment, which should assist you in being able to differentiate yourself from other, less prepared applicants in your search for employment.

Chapter 3 examines the role of supervisors in the research process. The applicability of this topic will vary widely across types of research projects being undertaken. The critical issue in this chapter is to realize that there are different styles of supervision and learning, depending on the type of research project. This issue will also be raised in relation to working in groups. It is essential that you and your supervisor have a mutual understanding of each other's expectations in regard to the research process.

Chapter 4 examines the complexities of working in groups, which again may not apply to all research projects. This chapter suggests some strategies for dealing with different sets of expectations and work practices. Working in groups is difficult, especially when you are dependent on others for the successful completion of tasks. This is one area where team skills are critical, and because of this, working in teams is an important task to master. Not all research projects involve groups, and so for some students, this may not be a relevant chapter of the book.

Chapter 5 examines issues associated with research ethics. This is an issue of growing importance for both student and academic research. The focus of this chapter is on understanding where ethical issues might arise in research projects as well as issues associated with research involving "human subjects." If there is no primary data collection within your research, this chapter may not be relevant to you. This chapter discusses a range of issues that need to be considered to ensure that potential participants in your research, should they be required, are not exposed to harm. Should you be involving others as research participants (e.g., people filling out surveys, undertaking interviews or focus groups, etc.), it is important that you consider potential ethical issues that might arise and how you can deal with them. Being "prepared" is important for researchers as well as Boy Scouts. It is important to remember that all participants are helping you by participating, and so you should treat them appropriately.

The second part of the book, "Undertaking the Research," focuses on issues associated directly with the research activities to be undertaken; that is, it directs you through the various practical aspects of undertaking your research. Chapter 6 starts this discussion by examining the issue of what research is and how one undertakes the broad research process. It is our experience that students who put in more time in understanding this phase of their project tend to experience fewer problems associated with the implementation of the project. The chapter also discusses the research proposal, which sets out a "road map" that you will follow throughout the project. Because the proposal sets out the course of your project, it is a critical part of the overall research process.

Chapter 7 focuses on the role of literature within the project. While this is something that might be thought of as a "general" issue, it is something that we suggest be a core part of the research process. It is important that you understand the role of previous work related to your area. This will be used not only to gain an understanding of the issue (i.e., the background), as well as develop arguments and ideas, but also to identify issues that have been overlooked. In addition, reviewing previous literature directs you in terms of the overall research process, including research methods and "instruments" that might be used to collect data. There is no need to reinvent the wheel, and so understanding the literature in your area of interest will not only save you time but will also ensure that you do not repeat errors others have encountered.

Chapter 8 considers issues associated with data gathering. This step is critical as it ensures that you have the information necessary to answer the question that you set out to examine. You would be wise to remember the saying "garbage in, garbage out," which means that there are limited opportunities to "rescue" a project based on inaccurate or inappropriate data. Thus determining what data is necessary to assist you in addressing your research question or in terms of the business decision being made is critical.

Chapter 9 focuses on qualitative data analysis. There is an increasing amount of research relying on in-depth, nonempirical data, that is, no numbers. This data is different from empirical data and needs to be collected and analyzed in a different fashion. It does have some limitations; for example, it is more difficult to suggest generalizability of results or statistical significance of findings. These are important, but the benefits of gathering a more in-depth understanding of issues, which are usually more complex than surveys would suggest, outweighs these potential problems. That is, you can frequently gain a depth of understanding that is not possible using simple survey techniques, and in many cases qualitative research is also undertaken prior to quantitative research.

Chapter 10 overviews a range of techniques that can be used for quantitative analysis, with the focus being on understanding what techniques might be used to best examine your research issue. The object is not to explain how to use or even interpret all the techniques discussed, and the chapter provides only a sample of the possible techniques available. The objective of this chapter is to describe what kinds of techniques are needed to analyze different issues, that is, what technique is most appropriate to answer your question. It refers you to a range of sources that will expand on the statistical properties of techniques, as well as the specifics of using them. This chapter, more so than others, is designed to assist you in considering critical issues and directing you to sources in which more complex discussion of these issues can be found. Students will most certainly need to refer to the material covered as part of other subjects such as marketing research or business research methods to gain an understanding of the detailed workings of the techniques discussed.

Chapter 11 examines the role of recommendations in your research. Understanding what you have found is a critical part of the research process, but the question of what this means for business practice or theory is critical. This chapter discusses how you need to think about what can be learned from your research to enable advances to be made. The significance of recommendations will vary based on the objectives of the project and on the specific findings. This is an important conclusion to the research task, although not necessarily the end of the assessment activities.

The last part of the book, "Communicating the Results," focuses on communicating the findings of your research. The first three chapters discuss a range of issues associated with written and oral communication of information, where it is critical to communicate the value of your results. Like many things in business, how well you present your ideas often is as important as what you present. Chapter 12 discusses how you can present your results in a meaningful way. It is important that others understand what you have found, and there are a number of ways you can present this, using words, statistics, graphs, or figures. This chapter discusses each of these communication methods in regard to communicating what you have found. This is linked to material in the preceding chapters as well as those that follow. All the chapters in this section seek to identify issues of relevance to academic and more applied types of projects, although there is a greater emphasis on academic-type projects.

Chapter 13 follows on from Chapter 12 in that it discusses the actual writing process. As mentioned earlier, businesses want to hire employees with good written and oral communication skills. The written research report, therefore, serves not only as a vehicle for communicating what was done in the project (which is graded by your professor) but also serves as a tangible output that you can use to demonstrate that you have the ability and skills to deal with complex issues.

Chapter 14 discusses the role of oral communication and the presentation of your project. This is important for getting your point across to the audience. The oral presentation, should you be required to give one, provides an opportunity for you to further explain your ideas in a succinct fashion. This allows you to emphasize issues of importance, as well as address any areas of your presentation that may confuse the audience. An oral presentation, therefore, allows you to further develop your oral communication skills.

Chapter 15 provides some concluding remarks about research projects within business subjects. It identifies a few cautions that you need to consider when working on a project and ties some final issues together.

References

Johnson, D., & Pere-Verge, L. (1993). Attitudes towards graduate employment in the SME sector. *International Small Business Journal, 11*(4), 65–70.

Lau, R., & Rans, D. L. (1993). They can add but can they communicate? *Business Forum, 18*(3), 24–26.

O'Brien, E. M., & Deans, K. R. (1996). Educational supply chain: A tool for strategic planning in tertiary education? *Marketing Intelligence & Planning, 14*(2), 33–40.

Polonsky, M. J., & Waller, D. (1998). Using student projects to link academics, employers and students. *Journal of Teaching in International Business, 10*(2), 55–78.

2

Choosing a Topic

This chapter examines issues associated with selecting a topic for your research project. It is essential that you formalize your topic as soon as possible in order to ensure that you are focused. Defining a topic is the first and most important step in the research project process. According to Howard and Sharp (1998), "Until a topic has been selected the research cannot be said to be underway"; however, if the topic is poorly chosen or defined, it will adversely affect all other aspects of the research project.

Some students often want to research very broad, all-encompassing topics that involve too many different activities. We sometimes suggest to these students that they are trying "to solve all the world's problems at once" rather than focusing on one manageable issue or aspect of the problem. Doing too much in a single project is usually difficult and causes unnecessary stress on you and your research team. Broad topics involve substantially more effort and expertise than most undergraduate students can effectively manage. The focus of your topic must be narrowed into something manageable that advances your learning outcomes, but it should not be too narrow, or it will be too difficult to obtain sufficient data. The goal, therefore, is to define and concentrate on a specific, appropriate topic.

In some classes, you may be assigned a specific research topic by a teacher/lecturer/professor, or alternatively you may get to choose one for yourself. Even if a topic has been assigned to you, there may be some room for you to put your own focus on it so that the project will become your own. It is, therefore, vitally important for you to consider a number of factors before choosing a topic for your research project, which will ensure that your topic is manageable and suitable for the research assignment at hand. To begin, you must ask yourself: Has the topic been assigned to me, or must I decide on the topic for myself? From past experience, we have found that though students like to select their own topic, it is sometimes difficult for them to be able to develop something that is not too broad. This usually occurs because the student has not undertaken a research project before and thus is learning not only about his or her project, but also about the research process in general.

Has the Topic Been Assigned?

You may have no choice as to what your topic is. If this is the case, you still should not jump into the secondary or primary research until you are comfortable with the scope of the topic and know exactly what you plan to examine. Think about the type of final research paper or report you are expected to produce. You must make sure that your approach to examining the topic addresses the requirements of the assignment. Are you to write a general overview of an issue, or are you expected to undertake detailed analysis of the topic? In most cases, even if a general topic is assigned, you will have the option of determining the specific question to be researched or the focus you will take in answering the question. There is rarely one way to examine a topic. You need to make sure your topic is specific, and if it seems to be too general, you should choose a narrower subtopic to examine. Assume that the assigned topic is a very general one such as "Consumer Behavior." Even if your task is to write an overview, there are many aspects that could be considered. For example, are you looking at models of consumer behavior or comparing different approaches to examining the topic? If your objective is to write a specific analysis, a general topic such as consumer behavior is far too general. You must narrow it to something such as "Factors Influencing University Students' Purchase Behavior of Music CDs."

If you must narrow your assigned topic, it is worthwhile to continue reading this chapter to assist you in narrowing your possibilities to a manageable business project topic. It is important that you spend some time thinking about research possibilities and options, as these will direct all your research activities. Do not necessarily choose the first idea that comes into your head, because you may end up writing about something that is not really the best topic or that may not be able to maintain your interests in the long run. The best topic is the one that can successfully achieve your assignment requirements and that will keep your interest over the length of the project. Once you have determined that your topic is suitable, you can move on.

If the Topic Has Not Been Assigned . . .

If you have not been assigned a topic, then an exciting opportunity lies before you. This means that you are free to choose a topic of interest to you, which will often make your essay a stronger one. However, you need to ensure that any topic achieves the desired learning objectives set out and that you are not simply researching an "interesting" topic. Though in some classes the choice of topics available is totally up to you, there are several ways that academic staff can assist you with this activity. They might, for example, provide a list of topics that they are interested in supervising, thus linking topics with staff expertise (Polonsky & Waller, 1998). If you are determined to develop a topic on your own, below are a number of important steps to assist you in choosing a topic for a business research project. When students choose their own topics, they often complain that there is not enough direction in the literature or that the selected topic is too difficult to examine. In these cases, we always suggest that they complain to the person who selected the topic; that is, they should blame themselves. Thus, selecting the right topic for you is essential.

Steps in Choosing a Topic

Step 1: Define Your Purpose

The first thing you must do is to think about the purpose of the project you must complete. What is the overall purpose of the project? Is the project designed to pass a single course, or is it designed to be a substantial part of your degree, such as a research class assignment, an honors thesis, or even a Master's thesis? Each of these types of projects has specific requirements that must be fulfilled, and your supervisor or the institution usually specifies these requirements. For example, the length, objectives, and tasks undertaken for an undergraduate business project would be very different from those expected for a master's thesis (Phillips & Pugh, 1994; Howard & Sharp, 1998). It is, therefore, important to keep in mind the overall purpose of the project.

Second, what is the more specific learning outcome of the project? Is it to undertake an academic examination of an issue of interest, to examine some practical business-related research and communicate the findings, to explain to the reader how to complete a particular task, to give the researcher experience in using a particular methodology, or to educate the reader about a specific thing or idea? Whatever topic you choose, it must fit its assigned purpose.

It is usually important that all projects, even those that are not directly involved with a particular business, have a stated "business or managerial implication." This often will assist you in giving the project a practical purpose and focus the project to make it worthwhile to undertake and complete. One of the overall objectives of a research project is to demonstrate the ability to apply theory to practical business problems in a serious academic fashion. Of course, the specific requirements of the project will specify the importance of this objective.

You must also complete your project within your time and money constraints and given your specific level of expertise (Jankowicz, 1995). Thus, projects must have definable boundaries. There is probably a limited time schedule within which to work on your project, for example, one semester or one year. Though many topics may be potentially excellent issues to study, they may require more time or money than you would like or are able to invest in order to properly examine them. Remember, you might be free to choose the topic of the project, but you must still adequately cover the topic, no matter how much time or money that takes. A good understanding of the purpose of your project will greatly help you to complete it successfully.

Step 2: Explore Potential Topics

Once you have determined the purpose of your research, you should write down some subjects or ideas that interest you and explore the feasibility of studying these issues as a project. There may be an endless number of topics that could be suitable. The trick is to choose one that you can successfully complete and that is of interest to you.

If you are having trouble thinking of potential topics, begin by looking at issues that interest you. Are there issues of interest in your text or industries that you find interesting? There may even be interesting current events or "hot topics" that might become the subject for a good topic. For example, the issue of whether consumers will pay to download songs is one that has been recently discussed in the news as well as in academic journals. Write down all the possible ideas on a piece of paper. Don't jump in and start your research, as this topic has to be your focus for the rest of your research project.

Conversations with other members in your group or, if you are undertaking an individual project, with other students, friends, or academic staff can also be a good source of ideas. Discussing the topic with others might also help you to identify potential problems in researching a possible area. Go to a library and look at recent issues of newspapers, industry magazines, and academic journals related to the field you are studying for some inspiration and to get a feel for the type of topic that would be worthwhile for your project. Newspapers will report current developments, and magazines may give more detailed analysis of issues from an industry point of view, whereas journals may look at academic research of issues and provide a background to the issue or summarize and/or discuss past research. Citations in academic journals or textbooks can also be a good source of references for your literature review, give valuable background to your analysis, and indicate whether this topic is an area of interest that is worth further analysis. Some sources of good potential ideas include the following:

Newspapers: *USA Today*, *New York Times*, *Los Angeles Times*, and *Wall Street Journal*

Magazines: *Business Week*, *Time Magazine*, and *Marketing News*

Journals: *Harvard Business Review*, *Journal of Marketing*, and *Journal of Human Resource Management*

Electronic information sources, such as the library's online catalog, online indexes, the Web search engines, subject-based Web directories, and electronic databases can also be an important source of information and inspiration for potential topics. If you are not sure how to search these resources, you should talk to your librarian, as training is often provided. However, when undertaking an electronic search, you will have to decide on the keywords that describe your topic. If you have a general idea of the subject area, think about what words would be significant for your project. These words will become the key for searching the catalogs, indexes, directories, and databases for information about your subject.

Potential Topic:	What are consumer attitudes toward the purchasing of individual songs from record companies on the Web?
Keywords:	Consumer
	Attitudes
	E-tailing
	Music
	United States

At this stage, you are still exploring and learning about your potential topic and a possible focus for your project. Be careful that you do not spend too much time reading, photocopying, and gathering as much information as you can on the topic generally, when you have not properly defined your topic. This could result in a lot of wasted effort if you decide to focus on only one aspect of the topic area. Also, you must keep in mind Step 1, the purpose of the project, and make sure that the potential topics you may choose will match the overall purpose of the project.

Finally, while you are exploring the possibility of potential topics for your project, you should ask a number of questions:

Are you interested in the topic?

What do you already know about the topic?

Are the other group members (if any) also interested in the topic?

Will the topic fulfill the purpose of the project?

Is there enough information about the topic?

Will you be able to collect primary data on the issue, if this is required?

Do you have the skills or knowledge of the methodology to complete the topic?

Will your supervisor, or the audience, be interested in your topic?

Will the topic offend some members of your audience?

Will this topic keep your interest for the time it will take to complete the project?

If you have appropriate responses to these questions for a few potential topic ideas, there is still some important evaluation to be done, which will be discussed in the next step.

Step 3: Evaluate Each Potential Topic

If you can think of a few topics that would be appropriate (at this stage there should be only two or three possibilities, according to Phillips & Pugh [1994]), you must then consider each one individually. Think about how you feel about each topic and whether you could work on it as a project topic through to its completion. Even if a potential topic does not seem particularly appealing, it may be useful to work with it and focus on a new angle, or a "hook," that may make the topic better than you first thought. Although, if nothing about the topic interests you, then you should reevaluate whether it is indeed a potential option. To assist you in evaluating your potential topic, a number of issues should be considered:

Interest of Researcher/Audience

As mentioned earlier, your topic must be interesting to you. This is really an obvious point. The topic you choose will have to keep your interest until the completion of the project. An enormous amount of time will be spent doing your research, and a topic that does not hold your interest can easily become tiresome and result in an unsuccessful project (Jankowicz, 1995). If, on the other hand, you are interested in the topic, the whole project will be much easier to complete. Your interest will express itself by adding to your enthusiasm about the project, your confidence in analysis, and your ability to clearly write your findings. Even if your topic has been assigned to you, try to discover an aspect of your topic on which to focus the research that will make it interesting to you and motivate you to do a good job.

Similarly, the topic you choose should be of interest to your audience (Cornford & Smithson, 1996). This may include your supervisor, examiners, fellow students, or local business managers, if it is a business-linked project. Research projects should be undertaken that are worthwhile; otherwise, it could be a total waste of valuable time and energy. If the topic does not gain the audience's interest, they will easily become bored, which can result in low grades, little response to presentations, or a lack of interest from businesses that may have initially been interested in learning the results of your research, if this is the focus. Ultimately, you cannot bore an examiner/marker into giving you a better grade.

Appropriate for the Purpose

It is not enough that the topic you choose is interesting to you and your audience. As mentioned earlier, you should be clear on the purpose of your project and make sure that your topic matches its purpose (Cornford & Smithson, 1996). While you are evaluating the potential topics, you should continually confirm that the topic is appropriate for its purpose. Is the potential topic more appropriate for a PhD thesis than for an undergraduate project or an MBA assignment? You must keep in mind the size of the project. What are the requirements of your project and the amount of information needed to complete it? Does the proposed topic fulfill these requirements? Does the proposed topic relate to the overall subject of the project?

Feasibility

There are many potential subjects that you might pick that, unfortunately, do not work well as research topics for a project. It is important that the topic you choose is feasible, that is, that you are able to complete it or collect primary data (if this is required) to answer the question being asked. Remember that you have to have time to obtain enough information *and* undertake the research (Jankowicz, 1995). This is a practical issue, as there is no sense in choosing a topic if it is not going to provide a finished project. Some current topics may be too recent to have generated enough available literature in the library or might be so popular that competition from other students will make obtaining information on them difficult. Other topics may be too obscure or require too much creative thinking, which does not lend itself to project research. In all cases, you will also need to be able to access the information from respondents, if these are used, to answer your question.

Therefore, when evaluating topics, it is a good idea to spend a small amount of time to ensure that there is enough information presently available on your chosen topic or that you can obtain the required information, secondary and/or primary. Once you have begun your project, it may be difficult to change your topic to any significant degree, and supervisors often do not look favorably on major topic changes after you have committed yourself to a specific topic. In regard to secondary information, this may mean that when you go to a library to check the availability of resources, you should personally speak to a librarian and make sure that the materials you need are not only in the library catalog but actually on the shelves (i.e., they are not missing, stolen, at the bindery, etc.). Also undertake an online search to find out if important reference material is available from the Web or online databases. Some academic journals are available online or have abstracts available on the journal's Web site. If there is not enough material *available* to you to successfully complete a particular topic, then the topic should be discarded and another one should be considered.

Another issue we have already mentioned is time. Is it feasible for you to complete the project based on your chosen topic within the deadline set by your supervisor? How much time do you have to become familiar with the subject matter? How much time will you have to properly complete the literature review, data gathering, analysis, etc? You must ensure that you can reasonably complete the project within the amount of time allowed.

Topics of Other Research Projects

It is a good idea to find out the topics of past research projects that have been completed or those currently being researched by fellow students. These can be valuable when trying to determine the subject area to choose and the scope that your project should cover. Ideally, you should choose a topic that no one else is working on, so that you don't have to directly compete with others for the resources, such as books, journal articles, or respondents to surveys, if required, and that the examiners don't directly compare two projects on the same topic—examiners would much prefer a topic that is interesting and different.

Questionable Topics

Some potential topics may be interesting and you may be able to find a reasonable amount of published information about them, but if they are too controversial, you might offend some people (including those being researched) if you do not handle your research sensitively. When topics fall within the range of "questionable," students should be able to justify that they meet the desired criteria of achieving the research purpose. Some topics could result in interesting research, such as racism or sexism in business, the gay market, or nudity in advertising, but unless you can bring something new to the discussion and collect data that will not offend your audience, these types of topics should not be considered. For example, one student group wanted to examine the strategic implications of using varying levels of female nudity in jeans ads. To do this, the students suggested that they would develop their own ads. After several discussions with the students, they demonstrated that they could do this and that the materials would really be levels of bare skin rather than true nudity. They were only allowed to proceed after convincing their supervisor that they had the necessary skill, resources, and sensitivity to undertake the project they suggested. You should always consider the ethical considerations of any topic before you finally commit to it. Some potential ethical issues are discussed in Chapter 5.

Business-Linked Projects

It is generally important for research projects to discuss business or managerial implications, although this will most certainly vary with the type of project being undertaken. For some research, it will be essential to involve a business in these research projects (Browne, 1979; de los Santos & Vincent, 1989; Humphreys, 1981). At some institutions, staff proactively seek out organizations that want a given piece of "research" undertaken, which may be suitable for your research project. You could be encouraged to talk independently with businesses involved with your area of interest to seek information, input, assistance with data collection, and possibly some financing. Often there may be small and medium-size firms that would like to use student projects in this way. This might include a firm that is launching a new product and would like to examine attitudes and adoption rates, a local shop wanting to find out why local residents frequent other shops, or a firm that wishes to find out how well various management levels have adopted a service culture.

Though involving businesses gives the project more practical relevance, it is important that the business managers you work with understand that the primary focus of the process is to help you (a student) in completing your degree and that any useful information would be a positive by-product. Organizations that "hijack" a project not only potentially interfere with your independence but also may impinge on the quality of the project (this issue will be discussed further in Chapter 3). It is, therefore, vital that your professor monitor any agreement between the firm and you. Having said this, it is still possible that firms change their collective mind. For example, one student had received approval from one manager to survey employees, yet the manager left the firm before the study started and the manager's replacement was not positively disposed to having a student surveying the firm's employees.

It is also important that *all* feedback from you to the organization is carefully checked by academic staff. Students in the past have been very good at marketing their work, and have overlooked important issues and/or had errors in their analysis and interpretation. As such, this could result in organizations acting on inaccurate information. All student-based feedback to businesses needs to, at the very least, include comments from the group's supervisor to ensure that any limitations are highlighted (Polonsky, 1996).

Step 4: Finalize Your Topic

Once you have evaluated the potential topics, look at them again to focus, refine, and finalize the topic you have selected for your project. Think again about the type of research project you are expected to complete. Will your topic produce a suitable outcome? It is important to be flexible. Your topic, or its focus, may change, and you might need to revise your research strategy as you undertake your preliminary search for information. You might discover an interesting article or a newspaper item that could introduce an interesting twist in your topic. It could be worthwhile to follow this lead and reconsider your focus. Even though this could feel like a time-consuming process, it can be a valuable exercise in focusing your research, which can result in a more interesting final project.

When finalizing your topic, you should also determine whether your topic is too general or too specific. Researchers often start with a broad topic, which they must narrow to make a more focused project. A major criticism of unsuccessful projects is often that the basic idea was too vague and there was insufficient work refining it in the early stages (Jankowicz, 1995). If your topic is too broad, you may find that there is too much information that you can assimilate into the project and it will become vague, unfocused, and confusing. If your topic is too narrow, or specific, you may discover that there is not enough information available, and your project will be too detailed to fully analyze in an acceptable depth. If you realize that your topic is either too general or too narrow, you must be willing to narrow or broaden your existing topic to create your final topic.

To narrow a topic, you may choose to focus on a specific aspect of the subject area. To help you, ask yourself some questions: What do I already know about this subject? What aspect of the subject am I really interested in? Is there a time period on which I should concentrate? Is there a geographic region or country on which I should focus? How will I obtain primary data to examine the issue (if this is required)? For example,

Broad Topic:	Buying on the Internet
Interests:	Factors influencing purchase behavior, music
Time span:	Last five years
Place:	U.S.A.
Narrowed Topic:	What are local university students' attitudes toward paying for downloading individual songs from music companies?

To broaden topics, think of parallel and broader associations for your research to find a topic that will be easier to research. Sometimes a topic may be too new, and resources or knowledge of the topic might not be widely available. Again, to help you, ask yourself some questions: Are there more broad aspects of this subject area to research? Are there more broad aspects of this subject that interest me? Are there other countries or regions to include in my research? What wider issues does this topic include?

Following the process discussed in this chapter means that you will ultimately undertake the following steps:

1. Select a potential topic.

2. Survey information on the topic.

3. Locate materials.

4. Evaluate your topic, resources, and research strategy.

5. Reevaluate your topic.

6. Revise and edit.

7. Finalize your topic.

If you have any difficulty in finding or refining your research topic, make sure that you talk with your supervisor before spending too much time and effort on the project (Jankowicz, 1995). Your supervisor would have more experience with research projects and may suggest alternative approaches or recommend important sources of information to assist you.

Step 5: Begin Your Research

Once you have determined that your topic will be suitable and achievable, and you are committed to it, you can move on. Go on to the next step to establish your research objectives. Chapters 6 will discuss the planning of your research. Before undertaking the research, it is important to discuss issues associated with the research, such as defining the role of your supervisor (Chapter 3), issues associated with working in groups (Chapter 4), and understanding ethical considerations (Chapter 5). Those of you undertaking an individually based minor research project that is part of a course might wish to skip chapters that are not relevant, although these chapters may serve as valuable resources for future research assignments.

References

Browne, W. G. (1979). Using corporate sponsored marketing management projects. *Journal of Marketing Education, Nov.,* 39–47.

Cornford, T., & Smithson, S. (1996). *Project research in information systems: A student's guide.* Basingstoke, UK: Macmillan.

de los Santos, G., & Vincent, V. (1989). Student research projects are gaining in popularity. *Marketing News, 23*(1), 3.

Howard, K., & Sharp, J. A. (1998). *The management of a student research project.* Aldershot, UK: Gower.

Humphreys, M. A. (1981). Client-sponsored projects in a marketing research course. *Journal of Marketing Education, Fall,* 7–12.

Jankowicz, A. D. (1995). *Business research projects.* London: International Thomson Business Press.

Phillips, E. M., & Pugh, D. S. (1994). *How to Get a PhD: A Handbook for Students and Their Supervisors.* Buckingham, UK: Open University Press.

Polonsky, M. (1996). Making student research more ethical: A preliminary examination. In E. J. Wilson & J. F Hair, Jr. (Eds.), *Developments in marketing science* (pp. 74–75). Coral Gables, FL: Academy of Marketing Science.

Polonsky, M. J., & Waller, D. S. (1998). Using student projects to link academics, business and students. *Journal of Teaching in International Business, 10*(2), 55–78.

3

The Role
of the Supervisor

I n all cases, research projects undertaken by individuals or as part of a group are designed to provide enhanced student learning. However, what is to be learned will differ with each project. Learning outcomes for an undergraduate research project might be to better understand how to collect industry information or develop a research proposal, to conduct self-directed learning on a research topic of interest, or to understand how an organization applies theory. Depending on the type of project, these goals could equally apply to some MBA or other graduate research projects. However, there may be higher-order learning outcomes, such as advancing a body of knowledge, that are more often associated with a PhD dissertation, which is not the focus of this text.

You may not have previously undertaken a research project similar to the one presently being completed. In some research projects, you will require extensive one-on-one assistance from your teacher/lecturer/professor in his or her capacity as your academic supervisor. This chapter will examine this supervisory role from your perspective. That is, while the academic wants you to learn as much as possible from the research process, you will want to get as much assistance as possible, or at least as much as you require.

The problem with a supervisor–student relationship is that, like all service encounters, it varies depending on a number of factors, and the expected outcomes may also affect how much assistance is provided. Your supervisor's individuality will determine how he or she likes to operate within this relationship, and, of course, your own personal characteristics will affect the relationship as well (Mead, Campbell, & Milan, 1999). Thus, many of the issues dealing with groups discussed in the next chapter, Chapter 4, will also be applicable to dealing with your supervisor. Understanding the supervisor's potential role, expectations, and method of operation will allow you to work with him or her in the most effective fashion and, hopefully, bring about the best learning outcome.

Understanding Your Supervisor

Given that each supervisor is different, it will be difficult, if not impossible, to describe all supervisors' styles. In fact, it is highly likely that one supervisor will deal with different students in different ways, depending on the student's level of understanding of the task, as well as the student's perceived motivation. For example, some supervisors tend to spend more time with students, or groups of students, who appear to be really interested in their project. In these cases, the academic is consulted so regularly that he or she may almost seem to become a group member, and both the students and the supervisor learn from the process (Elton & Pope, 1989). In other cases, a supervisor may be likely to give more assistance to students who are having difficulties but can demonstrate that they have tried to understand the issues causing these difficulties. Alternatively, students who simply ask for help but who have clearly not attempted to solve the problem themselves may be less likely to receive in-depth assistance from a supervisor.

Unfortunately, supervisors are not experts on every theoretical issue, but they will, one hopes, be more than happy to help students on any research topic. However, they will most likely get more involved in projects that cover an issue of interest to them or topics that are something they have expertise in. For example, if a student asks a professor to act as his or her honors supervisor, the academic might decline or grudgingly accept if he or she only has passing interest in the student's topic. In this case, the supervisor's limited knowledge in the area might mean he or she will not be able to provide as much detailed theoretical advice as the student may need. Even after discussions to refocus the topic, the student might be better off with a supervisor who is more interested in the student's area of study, and thus the students' learning outcome would possibly be increased.

Academics do not attempt to discriminate against one student or another, but like all people, rather tend to be more "interested" in students who have demonstrated that they are willing to put in the effort or are examining topics of particular interest to the supervisor. Unfortunately, students who expect a supervisor to guide their every step, and who have no desire to actively participate in the learning process, will usually receive less supervisory input. A supervisor is not the giver of knowledge or solver of all problems. In reality, students and supervisor are working together to solve a common problem (Elton & Pope, 1989). This does not mean that the supervisor is working simply to help you to complete a research project, but to ensure that you, the student, learn as much as possible from the project and process. Later in this chapter, issues relating to selecting a supervisor will be discussed, which does need to be taken into consideration if you have the chance to choose a supervisor.

What Is the Role of a Supervisor?

Your supervisor can play many roles in relation to your research project. In many cases, these roles are integrated or overlap, although in some cases they may be separate. Below are five of the key roles that supervisors can fulfill.

Information Source

As we mentioned earlier, your supervisor ideally has a range of research experiences that can be referred to and that will assist you in the completion of your project. On the most basic level, your supervisor will be able to tell you where you can find information for your topic, or at least give you some direction as to where you might obtain relevant information. This role is not restricted to your formal supervisor. Other individuals, such as librarians, might also be able to guide you to useful information sources. As will be discussed in Chapter 7, there are many types of information. We hope that your supervisor will be able to steer you in the direction of recent or seminal works in the area. Your spervisor may also be able to identify industry information sources.

You need to be careful in relying too heavily on your supervisor as your sole information source. First, overdependence, if allowed by the supervisor, prevents you from learning as much as you could from the project (Kam, 1997). Second, it will potentially influence how your supervisor deals with you in later stages of the project; that is, if your supervisor believes he or she helped you too much in the early stage of the research, he or she may be hesitant to provide more important help later. Last, supervisors might believe that you are not making an appropriate effort and thus, once again, be less likely to assist you at more critical phases of the assignment. Using supervisors as a source of information is valuable, but overreliance on them may ultimately harm you more than it may help.

Sounding Board

Often, one of the most important roles of a supervisor is to act as a "sounding board," that is, someone whom you can bounce ideas off and who focuses your thinking. In many cases, you will not have extensive experience with undertaking research, whereas your supervisor will probably have this experience. As such, they act as guides of sorts. Using the term "guide" might be a bit misleading, as in many cases supervisors attempt to keep you on track and thus prevent you from losing focus.

This guiding role is important in a number of areas. When selecting a topic, your supervisor will hopefully be able to help you decide if the topic is too broad or narrow. Supervisors may suggest that you look at your problem/ issue from another perspective, which may allow you to focus your topic. For example, one group of students wanted to look at why people give gifts; after directing them to do some reading and discussing their goals, it was decided to redefine the topic into the following: Why do young males, 18 to 25, give Valentine's Day presents?

Your supervisor will be able to assist you in shaping the scope of the work, as well as, defining the critical issues that will be examined in detail. Once again, he or she may do this by having you undertake additional reading and then discussing issues with you. In other cases, your supervisor may play the "devil's advocate," whereby he or she asks tricky questions that force you to rethink issues or clarify your thinking on a topic.

Educator

Though undertaking a research project is a learning process, much of your learning comes from your efforts in the research process or the efforts of other group members. There is also a role for your supervisor to act more directly in bringing about your learning. This frequently takes place in one of two ways. First, your supervisor may explain difficult material. In some cases, he or she may ask you to read more material on the topic. However, if it is clear that you need assistance, your supervisor will frequently work through the material with you. In some cases, your problems might relate to understanding theory; for example, you may not understand why variables should be related in a given way. Your problem might relate to dealing with analytical issues (i.e., how do you undertake an analysis or what does the analysis mean)? Alternatively, your supervisor might assist you with understanding the implications of research, especially when there are contradictory or counterintuitive results.

Second, your supervisor might facilitate learning through formalized classes. For example, in some cases projects are embedded within a course and, students work through their project as part of the class (Polonsky & Waller, 1998). In this way, examples are drawn from various students to teach the class about aspects of the research process. This latter approach is usually integrated into the research project process.

Motivator

Your supervisor will ideally also take on a role as motivator and keep you progressing through your project. This is often the most difficult role, especially if you lose interest in the project. If you lose interest, it is very difficult for your supervisor to reinvigorate you. One approach that he or she might try is to have you work through the importance of the project. If you can see the "real" benefits, or unique aspects, of your project, you sometimes can gain a renewed interest.

Ensuring that you keep on track can be difficult, as it is not something that your supervisor can control—it is usually up to *you*. There are several ways that your supervisor may keep you motivated. One way is through establishing a timetable for the project and then reviewing it at regular meetings. This approach at least lets you identify if you are falling behind and can encourage you to put in extra energy if you start falling behind the planned schedule. However, in some cases it will be clear to both you and the supervisor that the initial schedule was overly optimistic, and if this is the case, you may need to revisit the research proposal and modify activities to be more realistic. In all our years supervising student projects, there has never been a student or group in this situation that has not been able to refocus the work and achieve a reasonable outcome.

Depending on the type of project, your supervisor might ask you to keep a journal identifying the major developments, obstacles, and learning outcomes (Yeatman, 1995). This type of tool is used both to facilitate learning and to keep you motivated. With a journal, it is often easy to see how much progress has been made, and thus see how you are progressing. If you experience numerous problems, it might seem to suggest that you are not progressing, which might be traced through your learning journal. This learning journal process is often focused more on learning about the research process than on the topic being researched. Dealing with problems is an important part of the process.

Evaluator

In many cases, your supervisor will also be responsible, or partly responsible, for evaluating your research, that is, giving you a grade. From a supervisor's perspective, this is often the most difficult part of the process, as supervisors frequently get so involved that they feel they are part of the research. In some cases, though, research projects are also evaluated by others not involved in the process, i.e., independent examiners who may be within or external to your university. Independent examiners are usually used only for more substantial pieces of research, such as honors or masters' theses.

In thinking about those who evaluate your project, supervisor or independent examiner, it is important for you to clearly understand the specific criteria that they will use. As with all issues, this will vary based on the objectives of the project. For example, how important is the learning process associated with the project? If this issue is important, then you will most likely be evaluated using some measure of your progression through the process, such as the evaluation of reflective journals or peer assessment if you are working in groups. If the objective is to better understand business practices, then one of the assessment components might be the implication for practice. In some cases, you may even have an industry supervisor who evaluates this aspect. In other cases, the issue might simply be how well you actually answered your research question. (This is, in fact, different from advancing the body of knowledge, which is beyond the scope of most undergraduate or even MBA research projects.) When supervisors evaluate research projects, they should make sure that students actually tie material back to their questions and do what they said they would do.

The critical issue is to ensure that you clearly understand the criteria on which you will be evaluated as well as how this will be assessed. This understanding will at least allow you to be aware of what aspects or issues are most important.

Selecting a Supervisor

Depending on the project, you may have the opportunity to select your supervisor. Choosing a supervisor who is right for you is critical, as he or she will be assisting you with the research process and have substantial input into the project. There are a number of issues that you need to consider when selecting a supervisor. In many cases, one supervisor may have several of the "skills" you require, but it may be rare to find someone who has all these characteristics (Kam, 1997). Picking the right supervisor for *you* is the critical factor, and thus a good supervisor for one person is not necessarily a good supervisor for another (Hammick & Acker, 1998).

Topic Expert

You may want to identify a supervisor who has expertise in the topic being researched. The benefit of your supervisor having knowledge in your topic area is that you will be able to get strong direction from your supervisor and he or she will be able to discuss issues specific to your topic in detail (i.e., act as a sounding board). Your supervisor will also be able to undertake the role of a teacher if there are complex issues that you are unsure of.

Methodology Expert

Some academics are exceptionally strong in designing research projects or have skills in specific analytical techniques. Therefore, if you believe that this is an area where you will need extensive assistance, you may wish to try to find a supervisor whose strengths lie in this area. While such a supervisor is indeed useful, selecting such a person means that you already have an idea as to what you wish to examine and thus have spent substantial time developing a broad topic and research question. Past experience suggests that most undergraduate and MBA students undertaking research projects do not have the experience with research to be able to develop their ideas completely alone. So, looking for a supervisor with methodological expertise might be something that is more appropriately emphasized when undertaking very advanced research projects.

Process Expertise

In some cases, supervisors have a very structured approach to supervising students, which ensures that students complete their project within the time constraints (Beer, 1995). For example, one of our colleagues has very structured processes for supervising higher degree research students. His structure ensures that students complete their research on time and usually have few changes required by examiners. It should be noted that a set process does not necessarily work for every student, as each of you is different. Thus, looking for a process-focused supervisor assumes that you are willing to work to their process.

Motivational Expertise

In some cases, having a structured process, as just mentioned, can keep you motivated, as there are clear targets to be achieved that allow you to reach the finish line. Some supervisors may be able to keep you motivated with your project using these targets. In other cases, the supervisor gets excited about his or her student's work, which tends to excite the student as well (Elton & Pope, 1989). Some supervisors may put in a structured meeting process that keeps you on track, although you might not be excited about the work (Beer, 1995). Not everyone works well with such supervisors, especially if you like a lot of freedom and flexibility. Thus, as will be suggested in Chapter 4, your personality will have an impact on the type of supervisor that is best for you.

Types of Supervisors

As was discussed earlier, supervisors fulfill several different roles as well as have different types of expertise. Though in most cases you will have one academic supervisor who is a member of staff, this is not always the case. Two other types of supervisor situations will now be discussed, business supervisors and multiple supervisors, both of which may have unique challenges.

Business Supervisors

If you have an applied industry research project, you may have a supervisor for your research who is based in the organization you are examining (Polonsky & Waller, 1998). Such supervisors can be extremely valuable, as they are usually experts in their business and have a strong understanding of the complexities associated with their business and thus the issues associated with your project. They may also have access to extensive information about the business, which might not normally be accessible without their assistance (e.g., confidential, historical, or "not documented" information).

There are various potential problems that can arise with business supervisors. One of the main problems is that they sometimes forget that you are undertaking the project as part of your degree, and they see the project as "free consulting" designed to assist them. In this situation, business supervisors sometimes try to redirect the project away from your original focus.

They might have very strong views, which could make them less open to objective results. In this situation, they may not agree with anything that is inconsistent with their view of the organization.

In other situations, industry supervisors may want the answer yesterday and do not understand why your research needs to take so long to complete. They may not understand the educational purpose of the project process. To address this problem, it might be possible to give them something based on preliminary work as you progress with the main parts of the project. Though this is beneficial, it does frequently require additional time and energy, which may distract you from your research goals. It is critical that you do not alienate your business supervisor, as his or her support (i.e., access to information) is often critical to the completion of the project.

Another problem is that in some cases, business supervisors do not fully understand the implications of academic theory. In these cases, they may not understand why you are doing something a given way. In some cases, business supervisors may not even have academic degrees. For example, one group of students had a business supervisor who wanted them to look at why people don't consume a snack food he produced, namely, beef jerky. What the students felt was appropriate was a positioning study of this snack food verses others. Though this examined the core problem, they discovered that consumers in this market did not perceive beef jerky to be a snack food, and they suggested a shift in the organization's activities. The business supervisor simply wanted to know how to get people to eat beef jerky, and thus, the results were not as helpful as he had anticipated, especially given that he did not want to change his focus.

Another potential problem comes from the fact that business supervisors' expectations of how involved they will be in the process may vary. In some cases they don't understand or want to take on all the required supervisory roles. In some cases, they simply let you proceed as you see fit, and though this independence is exhilarating, it can be a problem if you need to actively engage the business supervisor as you would any other supervisor. When this problem happens, it often is because the business supervisor feels that the project is taking up too much of his or her time. On the other hand, a supervisor may want to be actively involved in every step of the project. This is not problematic if you and the business supervisor clearly understand where the project is heading. However, if the business supervisor has somewhat different views, his or her involvement may slow down the process. For example, one student undertaking an honors degree was looking at focusing her project on one organization. When she showed her business supervisor her survey, he asked if an additional section could be added looking at a tangential issue. While including the section would not be problematic, there was an expectation that the student would also evaluate this tangential information for the organization, and thus take her attention away from focusing on her research project.

Multiple Supervisors

In many ways, having multiple supervisors is an ideal situation, especially if you have a team of supervisors who have expertise in different areas. In this case, the supervisors complement one another and thus increase the likelihood that you will maximize your learning outcomes, as well as undertake a solid research project. For example, having a business supervisor with industry expertise who is complemented by an academic supervisor with theoretical expertise will provide a strong basis for the project. However, the situation of having multiple supervisors usually does not occur in most undergraduate or graduate research projects.

The biggest problem with multiple supervisors arises when you receive conflicting advice or information. This can arise when the supervisors are looking at your research from different points of view, which might suggest that your research question and objectives are not clear to all those involved. The bigger problem arises when you have supervisors who disagree on an issue or have different philosophical approaches to a topic. This type of problem is, unfortunately, extremely difficult for you to address, especially when one supervisor tells you that you are wrong for following another supervisor's advice. If this problem arises, it is essential that you have the supervisors discuss the matter directly rather than undertaking a debate through you. This type of conflict is often difficult for a student to deal with, and it might be possible to involve an independent person to assist in solving the conflict. The main concern is that you do not want their disagreements to negatively affect on your progress. This can easily happen if you are being directed in two different ways.

In dealing with "disagreements" between yourself and your supervisor(s), it is important to remember that the research is yours, but the various parties have a vested interest in the project as well. Ideally, if you are able to clearly put forward a point of view and defend it, logic will prevail; unfortunately, this is not always the case, and you may need to bring in an independent person, which is usually less than ideal (see Chapter 4). If you believe that what you are doing or need to do is more appropriate than what is suggested by a supervisor, you should be able to put forward a coherent argument based on evidence (often the literature). Though it might seem that you should not have to justify yourself to your supervisors, this process will enable you to justify your approach within the report and thus convince those evaluating the work as well. Therefore, it is a valuable activity and adds to the research process.

Ground Rules and Expectations

Most of what has been discussed in this chapter is about clearly establishing the ground rules and expectations of both you and your supervisor. Many universities have a code of practice relating to the supervising of students, but these frequently don't deal with the day-to-day operation of the student–supervisor relationship. Because of this, it is essential that you not only know what each of you expects from the other, but you should also ensure that you at least discuss how you believe the relationship should operate. If you each have different expectations, conflict will arise (Connell, 1985). For example, what are the roles that you want your supervisor to fill, and what do they expect from you? As was mentioned earlier, if your supervisor expects you to undertake your project following his or her process, but you want a more flexible approach, there will most likely be problems in the relationship. This means that you either selected the wrong supervisor or you did not clearly establish how you wanted the relationship to work.

Some supervisors design contracts with their students that clearly specify the roles and responsibilities of both parties. We do not suggest that this is the best way to manage a student–supervisor relationship, but it does ensure that the roles are clearly defined.

One of the biggest problems for you will be deciding what to do if your supervisor is not fulfilling the role you anticipated he or she would fill. There are several ways to deal with this issue. First and foremost, it is essential that you discuss this with your supervisor early on. At times, students have complained that there have been problems with their supervisor that have gone on for months. These often could have been easily addressed if the issues were discussed earlier rather than later. Unfortunately, discussing problems associated with how you are being supervised is often difficult, especially for students who usually feel that that they have minimal power in the relationship.

After repeated attempts to rectify the situation with the supervisor, you should talk to an independent academic to see if he or she can assist. Many students will do this, instead of discussing the issue with their supervisor. Though other academics are usually more than happy to help, you do need to be proactive and try to address the matter yourself.

In *all* cases, one of the most important things to remember is that you need to try to be as calm and objective as possible. In most cases, problems happen as the result of a misunderstanding on the part of you and/or your supervisor. The sooner these misunderstandings are clarified, the better it is for the process. It is important that you remember that your supervisor is human as well, and a range of factors might affect how he or she interacts with you on a given day, just as they might affect how you interact with your supervisor.

Conclusion

This chapter discussed a range of issues associated with the role of your supervisor. One of the themes that was discussed was that you need to have some idea of what you expect from the student–supervisor relationship, as there are many roles, skills, and requirements that could be anticipated by either party. The more experienced you are with research, the better able you will be to define what you are looking for. Each research project might require a different set of supervisory needs, and thus there is no one ideal supervisor.

Given that both you and your supervisor are human, it is essential that there is communication early on in the research process to explain each party's expectations of the other. Without such discussion, it is easy for you or your supervisor to incorrectly understand what you expect and what he or she expects. Once this has been clarified, your supervisor will be able to provide you with the most appropriate guidance, and therefore your learning will, hopefully, be maximized.

References

Beer, R. H. (1995). Guidelines for supervision of undergraduate research. *Journal of Chemical Education, 72*(8), 721–731.

Connell, R. W. (1985). How to supervise a PhD. *Vestes, 28*(2), 38–41.

Elton, L., & Pope, M. (1989). Research supervision: The value of collegiality. *Cambridge Journal of Education, 19*(3), 267–276.

Hammick, M., & Acker, S. (1998). Undergraduate research supervision: A gender analysis. *Studies in Higher Education, 23*(3), 335–347.

Kam, B. H. (1997). Style and quality in supervision: The supervisor dependency factor. *Higher Education, 34*(1), 81–103.

Mead, G., Campbell, J., & Milan, M. (1999). Mentor and Athene: Supervising professional coaches and mentors. *Career Development International, 4*(5), 283–290.

Polonsky, M. J., & Waller, D. (1998). Using student projects to link academics, employers and students. *Journal of Teaching in International Business, 10*(2), 55–78.

Yeatman, A. (1995). Making supervision relationships accountable: Graduate student logs. *Australia Universities' Review, 38*(2), 9–11.

4   Group Dynamics and the Role of Conflict

This chapter will discuss one of the more difficult aspects of student research: the complexities of working in groups. This chapter is one of those that may be of benefit to you in many courses throughout your degree, especially if these courses involve group activities, and thus has the advantage of also applying to nonresearch projects as well. Given that this issue is one that may not have been discussed extensively within other research courses, broader discussion of issues is provided in this chapter to allow you to understand group dynamics and how they may affect research activities, as well as some potential approaches to deal with any conflict that does arise.

A group project sometimes brings together students who do not know one another, but who are asked to work together, as a team, to examine a common research problem. Working as a member of a team is made even more difficult given that you and your fellow students often have diverse educational, social, and cultural backgrounds, skill bases, knowledge bases, and experiences, as well as expectations in terms of outcomes. There are a variety of approaches that can be used to integrate such diversity, and the approach taken might affect the outcome; that is, the research project's success.

Though in an ideal world groups should meld seamlessly together, this is sometimes not the case, and conflict among group members might arise. As will be discussed in this chapter, not all conflict is bad. Conflict can be a dynamic force that creates positive tensions and adds a constructive energy to the work practices of you and your group members. On the other hand, if conflict is left unchecked, it could, in extreme cases, destroy the team's ability to work together and substantially harm the research outcomes.

It is important to note that you and your team members have some choice in regard to how conflict is managed; a group can choose to allow conflict to exist, manage it, or ignore it. This raises two important questions about conflict: (a) Do you think you really have such a choice at all? and (b) If you do believe you have the choice as to how it is managed, what

Authors' Note: The authors gratefully acknowledge Mr. Paul Keogh of Work Matters in Newcastle, Australia, for writing this chapter.

determines how you and the others in the group decide how to deal with it?

Conflict can be defined in a number of ways:

- "Conflict involves direct confrontations between groups or individuals usually arising from situations where each side perceives that the other is about to frustrate (or already has frustrated) its major interests" (Baron, 1986, p. 377).
- Conflict is the "perceived incompatible differences resulting in some form of interference or opposition" (Robbins, Bergman, & Stagg, 1997, p. 626).
- Conflict is "a process that begins when one party perceives that another party has negatively affected, or is about to negatively affect, something that the first party cares about" (Robbins, Millett, Cacioppem, & Waters-Marsh, 1998, p. 475).

The common threads of these definitions are that conflict is a matter of perception, and that these perceptions focus on notions of frustration, interference, opposition, or negative effect. It is important to remember that though perceptions are reality, perceptions are also manageable. In this way, different members of a group may perceive frustration, interference, opposition, or negative effect in different ways. This is important in your group, as one member may think things are working fine, but another perceives that there is a major problem.

You and your group have the ability to decide how to respond to any conflict that might arise. You will need to reflect on how you define conflict and what you think about conflict. In many cases, this relates to your individual background and includes how conflict was dealt with when you were growing up. Is conflict and conflict resolution tied in to cultural differences of group members? Should conflict be viewed as "inherently bad and to be avoided at all costs"; "part of the way the world operates and accepted as such"; or was it viewed as "a positive dynamic that helps create constructive tensions that cause me to question things and spur me to action"? Yes, conflict can even sometimes be thought of as a positive aspect of teamwork.

Group Work and Conflict

Many of you will dislike group work and will prefer to work on your own. This might be because you feel that you are not in control of your grades, that you have to rely on others to achieve desired levels of performance, or have had less than satisfactory past experiences. You might find it easier for you to individually plan how to address a problem, find the necessary resources, and decide upon your own schedule without concern or reference to any other students. Though working in groups is frequently more complex than working on your own, there are a number of reasons that you need to develop team skills:

- Group and teamwork is becoming the norm in organizational life (Kolb, 1998). Project teams, manufacturing teams, management teams, autonomous and semiautonomous work groups, functional groups, research and development groups, and quality management teams represent just some of the groups and teams that now constitute modern organizational work practice.

- As group work and teamwork can involve conflict, it is important that you initially face the pressures of that conflict in a supportive environment. The educational environment is focused on you learning from the successes and the failures you may experience while practicing group- and teamwork, and so there is a great opportunity to make mistakes, to even initially fail in that practice. These successes, mistakes, and initial failures become important learning opportunities.

- Last, and putting aside the purely educational aspects, group and teamwork at the college/university level is a great networking device. It is through such work that you get to meet other students that you may not have normally had a chance or opportunity to meet and work with. Other team members might be thought of as the first people in your wider business network, as you can be almost assured that within the first three years of full-time employment you will need some form of advice, business leads, or contacts from both within and outside your profession, industry, firm, or country.

You have the opportunity to see group work as fraught with negative aspects, *or* you can see it as an opportunity to develop yourself, others, and your personal network. The conflicts you may experience while doing such work are a small price to pay for these advantages, particularly when you take into account that some of the conflict is positive anyway, and even when it is negative, it is something that can be learned from. You should not let this opportunity slip by but should take full advantage of all aspects when working through issues in your group.

Positive and Negative Conflict

As we have mentioned, conflict can be both a negative and a positive aspect of group work. Given that you may have one type of view or the other about conflict, it is important to at least try to understand both the positive and negative views relating to conflict. There are three general views of conflict (see Table 4.1) and each suggests that the beliefs will affect actions taken. This is important, as it will determine how you and others in a group deal with issues.

Table 4.1   Alternative Viewpoints on Conflict

Beliefs	Reactions
Traditional Viewpoint	
• Conflict is unnecessary. • Conflict is to be feared. • Conflict is harmful. • Conflict is a personal failure.	• Immediately stop conflict. • Remove all evidence of conflict, including people. • Pretend that the conflict never really occurred.
Behavioral Viewpoint	
• Conflict occurs frequently in organizations. • Conflict is to be expected. • Conflict can be positive, but, more likely, it is harmful.	• Immediately move to resolve or eliminate conflict. • Attempt to learn something from the conflict. • Try to prepare for conflict.
Interactionist Viewpoint	
• Conflict is inevitable in organizations. • Conflict is necessary for organizational health. • Conflict is neither inherently good nor bad.	• Manage conflict to maximize its positive outcomes. • Manage conflict to minimize its negative outcomes.

SOURCE: Adapted from Robbins, Bergman, and Stagg (1997).

The traditional view of conflict states that conflict in groups is a negative aspect and suggests that conflict should be immediately eliminated. The rationale for assuming it is "bad" relates to people seeing conflict as destabilizing groups and preventing them from working together effectively. This perspective assumes that people who do not agree on all aspects of an issue cannot cooperate to solve a problem, which is not necessarily the case. There is an assumption that conflict should be removed, which might result in someone "giving in" to the group's view or the group discounting valuable input that is inconsistent with the general view.

The behavioral view of conflict acknowledges that conflict frequently occurs and should therefore be expected. It is unreasonable to anticipate that individuals will always agree, although this view also generally holds that though conflict can be a positive characteristic, it is most often a negative characteristic and should be resolved or eliminated as quickly as possible. This might mean that the group spends a lot of time developing a process to manage conflict, rather than trying to understand why the conflict occurs and how it might be used in the task at hand.

The interactionist view of conflict contends that conflict is neither inherently good nor bad, but rather it is the manner in which conflict is managed that is most important. Conflict is inevitable and might, in fact, be a sign of a group's health, as members are always questioning what they do and seeking to improve activities. This perspective involves reflection on issues as conflict arises and allows the group to question what it is doing, which should improve processes.

General Causes of Conflict

Conflict usually arises at different times because of a number of reasons that exist within a particular group. Being aware of these reasons will also help you to understand the other members of the group and, it is hoped, allow you to deal with the cause of conflict as well as the consequences of any conflict. As will be discussed next, there are a large variety of causes of conflict, some of which are related to the research process and others which are the result of personality differences. The following seven subsections summarize the main factors that might cause conflict to arise. Each of these have subareas; however, given that this is only one chapter of the book and one that might not be relevant to all student projects, only the most frequently experienced factors will be covered.

Competition

Though individuals, units, and organizations who work together might be striving to achieve one goal, they also often compete for resources such as money, time, additional people, promotions, raw materials, superiors' favor, and so forth. Competition for these limited resources can become quite fierce. At one extreme, this competition can degenerate into personal duels or vendettas. For example, group members might disagree over the selected organization of the project, which results in those who "lost out" being less helpful, or even disruptive, in the project undertaken. On the other hand, competition within a group might be constructive, as it means that people raise their performance level. For example, in selecting a topic for study, it might mean that ideas are more thoroughly developed so that one individual can convince the other group members that this topic is the one worth examining.

There is also competition for an individual's time that might be considered. Though some people in the group may be full-time students (aged 18–24 years old) who live at home and work part-time, others may be mature students (i.e., not straight out of high school) who are balancing more complex demands of education, family, and full-time employment. Thus, competition is not just about the issues associated with the project, but there are also competing demands placed on members of your group in regard to managing various aspects of life. This might mean that some students in your group have different constraints placed on them, which in turn influences on other aspects of how they participate in the project process.

Differences in Objectives

Individuals might have different objectives in terms of the assignment being undertaken or broader educational outcomes. For example, some students might want to undertake projects that help them with their current jobs, whereas others might want to undertake projects on topics related to some personal interest. If the topic selected does not fulfill both parties' objectives, there will most likely be some conflict, which might translate into different levels of enthusiasm or performance. There are, of course, other objectives that might differ in a group as well. For example, one group member might want an "A" grade, whereas others might want to just pass. Alternatively, some might want to undertake a more complex project that maximizes learning, whereas others might want to undertake a less complex project that can be undertaken quickly.

Another possible level of conflict in regard to objectives relates to the overall focus of a project. In many cases, your project is designed to achieve several objectives, develop group skills, understand practice, apply theory, and so forth. However, the proportion allocated to each aspect might not be clearly identified by your lecturer/professor. Thus, your group might disagree as to whether the research is theoretical or applied in focus. As a result, if the group has differing views on what the overall objective(s) of an assignment is, then conflict can also result. Unfortunately, this type of conflict might only arise after tasks are completed and your group identifies that there are problems with how one member has interpreted or undertaken his or her assigned tasks.

In addition, the opportunity for differing objectives increases as the number of members increases. Group members frequently do not ask one another what their objectives are, which might at least ensure that expectations are clear, even if members have different objectives.

Differences in Values and Perspectives

Each member of the group will bring his or her own values and perspectives to group work. Values and perspectives become even more complex when one also considers that group members' cultural background and gender may also affect how they each view things. In terms of values, one member may value group harmony above all other issues, whereas another member might value autonomy rather than collective decision making. These differences will affect the operation of the group and the management of conflict.

Group members may also hold different perspectives on the significance of group work in education, the worth or importance of the subject within which the group work is taking place, or the contribution that they or others are making to the group. For example, a person who feels forced to undertake group work will have a very different view on the project than does a student who chooses to take a course because it contains the opportunity to undertake group work.

Disagreements About Role Requirements

Everyone in your group will bring different skills and abilities to a group, and this needs to be realized early on. Conflict arises from individuals feeling that they are not given opportunities or that they are pressured into taking on tasks that they are uncomfortable with. For example, simply deciding on who should be a group's leader or coordinator might cause conflict if two people want to take on the role, and then the one who missed out may feel disadvantaged or rejected. Alternatively, if no one wants to take on the role, the one chosen may feel forced to do something that he or she is not comfortable with. Consider, for example, a situation in which a lecturer/professor appoints one group member as the team leader because he or she wants to assist that individual in developing leadership skills. In this case, the individual might not be comfortable with the role, and other group members might feel that they deserved to be leader. Thus, conflict potentially arises from all sides.

The same sort of issues might arise in terms of allocation of other group tasks as well. One or more members might believe that another member is not carrying his or her weight, which might occur because the concerned members believe that that their tasks are more difficult than others. This might occur simply because they do not understand the complexity associated with others' tasks or they believe that the others are not doing the task as they would, thus linking back to perceptual differences. Alternatively, it might occur because the offending group member has never worked in a group and does not understand the expectations others have.

One question that is sometimes raised here relates to the effectiveness of undertaking roles as distinct from the efficiency of undertaking roles. It might be efficient to share activities equally, but this might mean giving tasks to people who may not have the best skills in an area. In this case, you will need to consider how to best use the skills of the people in your group. Unfortunately, this might mean letting go of some key tasks and/or changing your expectations of outcomes. It is, after all, a group project, in which each member contributes to the greater whole.

One must also consider the fact that there are many ways to address a task, and each person will deal with a matter differently. The critical group issue is that the information and input is correct and in a format that can be integrated into other aspects of the project. Again, conflict arises because one individual addresses an issue in a different way than others would. Does this mean it is less correct or valuable? The answer is frequently no, but it does mean that other members of the group need to broaden their thinking about how issues are dealt with. The more important issue in this regard is making sure that the expectations of what information is needed is consistent across the group. In some cases, groups might want to provide more concise objectives for each aspect of the research, but this does require much more management of the process. If there are differences in what you and other members of your group see as important, conflict will arise because of these role disagreements.

Disagreements About Work Activities

Conflict or disagreement can occur in regard to how the group is managed or how individuals undertake tasks, and this can be further described as disagreement about work activities. These include the following areas:

1. What Specific Work Elements Need to Be Performed?

The members of the work group may have different views on how the overall work assignment should be broken down into its key subassignments. For a group assignment, some members may feel that it is best to break the research question down into its component parts and have individual members address each of those parts. Other members may feel that the best way of breaking down the work is to address the question as a whole but divide the work into key activities such as coordination, research, writing, proofreading, and collation.

2. What Priorities Should Be Given to Those Work Elements?

Group members may agree on the work activities but disagree about which of the work elements have priority or even if priorities should exist at all. For example, one of the members may be given the work task of coordinating the assignment. They may feel, quite genuinely, that if the assignment is to be completed satisfactorily, their particular task is central (and therefore a priority) to the overall project. This may not be a feeling shared by other members, but the conflict only surfaces after a substantial number of tasks have been completed.

3. Who Is to Perform the Elements and Why?

Decisions about who is responsible for what task, and why, can cause conflict. Returning to the points mentioned earlier about skills and knowledge sets, some members may want to take on a work element that utilizes their current strengths so that they can build on those strengths and do the work quickly and efficiently. Others may want to take on work elements that lie outside their current skills and knowledge sets so that they give themselves an opportunity to learn something new. For example, some international students may want to be actively involved in an oral presentation to develop their presentation skills, whereas other members may be concerned that potentially poor communication will harm their grades. The group is caught between deciding whether it is more advantageous to get the assignment done in the quickest and most efficient manner by assigning the work to those currently most skilled to perform the work tasks or to be skilfull or knowledgeable. The final decision may not please everyone.

4. What Are the Interrelationships and Dependencies Between the Work Elements?

Some members of the group may not appreciate the way in which the individual work elements relate to, or are interdependant on, each other. This may be particularly acute if external pressures affect the work deadlines being faced by individual members. For example, if one member of the group is taking only one course during the semester, then the pressures on him or her to complete work may be decidedly less than those on another student who is taking four or five courses that semester. The group may inadvertently assign work such that the second student is depending on the work output of the first. The first student completes his or her work at a leisurely pace commensurate with his or her work commitments and pressures, whereas another student might want to clear this assignment away so that he or she can concentrate on other subjects quickly and becomes frustrated and attempts to force the pace of the first. Though this may be done in a sensible manner, it may be interpreted as unreasonable or unnecessary pressure. Conflict may potentially result.

5. How Are the Work Elements Best Coordinated?

The manner in which the work is to be coordinated becomes the source of conflict. Some members of the group may feel that it is best to appoint someone to head the group or assignment. This person leads the overall work project and makes decisions about how the work is to be carried forward. Naturally, such a role would require someone with good coordination and interpersonal skills. Other members of the group may feel that the coordination is best done via committee rule. In this case, the group as a whole makes key decisions along the way to completing the assignment. The group meets regularly, and coordination decisions are made by majority vote. Each of these approaches, as well as others, has advantages and disadvantages. Unless the group has considered them, made a decision on the best approach to take, and satisfied themselves why the decision is the best, conflict can easily be generated.

Disagreements About Individual Approaches

In many cases, the conflict shows its head when one group member makes comments such as "this is how I would have done that" or "why did you do it that way?" Such questions allow for a healthy discussion of issues, although they might lead to conflict if asked or taken as criticisms.

You and your group members may agree about what work actually has to be done, but the disagreement arises over how you believe it should be done and the way in which others in the group believe it should be done.

Table 4.2   Influence Dimensions

Dimension	Continuum		
1	Conceptualizer	← — — — — — — →	Detailer
2	Rapid	← — — — — — — →	Gradual
3	Exaggerator	← — — — — — — →	Understater
4	Initiator	← — — — — — — →	Responder
5	Other evaluator	← — — — — — — →	Self evaluator
6	Lateral	← — — — — — — →	Linear

SOURCE: McPhee-Andrewartha (1997, p. 13).

People have alternative approaches to the way they work. For example, the consulting group McPhee-Andrewartha (1997) has suggested that there are variations on at least six different work dimensions that can vary when undertaking a task (see Table 4.2).

Some members of your group might approach the project by focusing on the broad conceptual issues, making rapid decisions, exaggerating the successes and/or failures, initiating work patterns and tasks, evaluating the performance of others before evaluating their own, and thinking laterally about the project, its issues, and problems, whereas others might concentrate on the details of the assignment or project, make decisions more slowly and judiciously, understate the issues and problems that they confront, be more comfortable following the lead of others, evaluate their own performance before that of others, and think more linearly about the project and its issues. Still others may be somewhere in between, or use a combination of views.

It is not important that everyone have the same approach, and, in fact, McPhee-Andrewartha (1997) has suggested that a mix of perspectives is important to the successful operation of a group. The critical issue, as with most of the areas in conflict, is to realize that differences exist and accept them, rather than expect everyone to operate as you do. Remember, they might be equally frustrated that you do not operate as they do. Conflict will most likely arise when these differences are either not respected or not appreciated for the strengths they can be.

Breakdown in Communication

The issue of group communication is something that could be written on extensively, and there are many texts on this topic (e.g., Bovée, Thill, & Schatzman, 2003; Hartley & Bruckmann, 2002). Group communication can break down because of problems with verbal communication, written communication, or nonverbal communication.

Communication, or lack of communication, is not only important in terms of causing conflict, but is also critical in dealing with conflict. Unfortunately, during times of conflict (arising out of any of these or any of the previous sources mentioned), the chances of misunderstandings or breakdowns in communication are heightened. This means that the best avenue for resolving conflict—good communication—is often the very first casualty of that conflict.

Communication issues are made more complex given the increasing diversity (cultural, gender, religious, ethnic, geographic, etc.) within groups. Each group has its own norms of communication and behavior. For example, in some cultures, disagreeing with colleagues or even asking questions might be seen as "losing face" and something that is to be avoided. For this reason, it might mean that some group members, if they are from different cultures, are not as clear on tasks or activities, and do not voice their uncertainty. In this case, it would not be surprising to later find that they might not have completed the task as required, or as was expected. As you can see, communication can break down very quickly if the group has little appreciation of such dynamics.

It is, therefore, essential that when conflict arises, you explain what the problem is clearly in a way that does not make things worse. For example, telling someone that his or her work is not up to standard without explaining the deficiencies or how it can be improved is of limited benefit. You need to remember that no matter what you say, in many cases, your group members will most certainly take criticism personally, even if it is not meant in that way. Thus, you need to be extremely careful that you focus communication on discussing what the problem is and how it can be addressed.

Conflict Stimulation

As mentioned earlier, conflict is not always negative, especially if it is effectively managed. Thus, your group might want to think about stimulating positive conflict. There are a number of circumstances in which this would be valuable:

- The group is suffering from unproductive "groupthink," that is, there are no new ideas being developed.
- The group is seeking to define minimal performance levels of members that are above "just passing."
- There are one or two very dominant group members, and other members are not actively participating.
- Group members are afraid to extend themselves into new areas.

Robbins (1987) established five strategies for stimulating positive conflict that can move the members of a group out of their respective comfort zones.

1. *Bring in an outsider* who introduces new perspectives, ways of doing things, and/or alternative ways of thinking. In bigger projects, your supervisor might be willing to take this role.

2. *Change the rules under which the group or individuals operate.* For example, ask people to prepare brief reports on their tasks prior to meetings rather than simply turn up and discuss what they are up to (or not up to).

3. *Change the group structure.* Reassign tasks and roles to different members of the group.

4. *Change team leaders.* Let someone else coordinate the project or aspects of it. This might be for a short time to give others a different perspective, or might be an ongoing change.

5. *Encourage competition within the team.* This may be done through the setting of deadlines, work quality parameters, and so forth, that the members are striving to best one another on. Alternatively, the competition may be between groups to gain outcomes such as highest group mark, best impression, best individual performances, and so on.

The stimulation of conflict can have several benefits, but it is not something that necessarily has to be focused on, and like all issues discussed, it will depend on the group and the project. One benefit is that it might allow the group to begin thinking about issues in different ways, as there are usually a range of alternatives available, and the direction selected might not necessarily be the best. If no one questions the approach taken, alternatives will never be considered. Stimulating conflict might also allow members of the group to begin looking at things from others' perspectives. For example, when taking on the role of team leader, a group member might begin to appreciate the difficulties of the role. Stimulating positive conflict might, therefore, be valuable in some situations.

Managing Conflict

Now that you know what conflict is and why it occurs, how do you manage it? Unfortunately, while there is no magic answer to this question, there are a variety of techniques and processes that might be able to assist you in dealing with it in your group work.

Analysis of a Conflict Situation

In a situation in which there is some conflict within the group, it is important to understand why the conflict exists. To do this, you will need to ask three questions:

1. *Who in the group is in conflict?* There may be a conflict between two group members; alternatively, the group might be in conflict with one member, possibly even the team leader. The solution needs to target those involved and should not unnecessarily involve others in the group.

2. *What is the source of the conflict?* As was discussed earlier, there are many reasons why conflict will arise. In many cases, this occurs because of differences in perceptions, which are less difficult to address, as expectations can change. On the other hand, conflict is much more difficult to address if conflict arises because an individual is not contributing (or interested in contributing), or if he or she does not have the ability to contribute. In these cases, there will most likely need to be some intervention from your lecturer/professor. In any case, conflict will not be effectively dealt with if the source is not correctly identified.

3. *What is the level of the conflict?* This question will affect the strategy used to deal with the conflict. For example, if one person refuses to contribute, this is much more difficult than deciding on which of two members should be assigned with a desirable task.

General Approaches for Dealing With Conflict

In looking at conflict, it is important to realize that there will be a range of possible responses. These have implications for the successful operation of the group and, in some cases, only delay conflict becoming excessively disruptive. Some of the ways individuals and groups deal with conflict are as follows:

In the case of *avoidance*, individuals seek to ignore conflict. This might occur by members giving in to the views of individuals even though they do not agree. Alternatively, this could occur when group members do not tell one member that his or her work is not up to standard, as they do not want to upset the individual. Avoidance means that conflict does not arise, but in many cases this might cause more serious problems later on. For example, those giving in may become increasingly frustrated with the fact that their ideas are not considered, or, in the case of the underperforming member, the other group members will potentially need to do extra work to make up for this member's deficiencies. In most cases, it is better to address the problem early, when corrective action is most likely to be successful.

Compromise is a situation in which parties reach some agreement or a middle ground. Though this approach seems to be positive, it might result in a suboptimum solution. For example, if there is disagreement over two different topics to be studied in a project, the group might decide to select a third topic that is not aligned to anyone's interests. The problem then may be that no one has the commitment with this compromise option to contribute to the team effectively. However, you should consider the possibility that this approach would result in a reasonable outcome.

Collaboration is a consensus approach in which all members seek to work together to find the most appropriate solution. It is more than individuals compromising, as the ultimate outcome is one that everyone agrees will bring about the best outcomes. This approach requires that you and your group members have open minds, and while you may have strong views about issues, you need to be able to see the bigger picture. A collaborative process will be less effective if there are any individuals who are unwilling to modify their views or have radically different perspectives. For example, if in discussing the desired grade, one member is adamant he or she wants 90% or better, whereas others are more flexible in their expectations, there may be a limited chance of reaching a consensus solution to this conflict.

Confrontation is a process in which the conflict is addressed as it happens. This approach may get the issue out in the open and thus can be positive. It is, however, critical that any discussions remain civil and constructive. In this way, the issue is dealt with openly and fairly. However, in some cases, confrontation is designed to be aggressive and thus to push one individual's agenda. In this situation, it causes other problems, although it addresses the specific instance of conflict at hand. For example, an individual may be bullying the group and forcing it in a direction that members are not comfortable with. In this case, there is no real attempt to address the underlying issues of conflict; the approach is designed to solve a problem, but it does so in a way that might escalate the underlying issues.

Appeals to superordinate objectives is an approach in which you and your group members to step back and ask yourselves what the best outcome is in regard to the wider project goals. For example, in dealing with the best way to address a project, the question could be asked, What approach will allow us to achieve the best outcome? Such an approach has the benefit that the overall goals of individuals serve as the main resolution tool. This does, however, require that all members of the group be clear as to the objectives to be achieved. If there is disagreement on this front, then there will be differing views as to which approach will best allow you to achieve the goals. In many ways, this is a collaborative approach, as the group systematically evaluates what is the best way to deal with issues.

Third party resolution might be another approach to managing conflict. Within group research assignments, this most frequently means seeking input from your lecturer/professor. His or her willingness to intervene will vary, but in most cases he or she will expect that the group has already tried a range of solutions to deal with the conflict. In some cases, he or she will in fact be the only one who can deal with issues. For example, if one member is not contributing at all, it is frequently beyond the group's ability to fire that member from the group (although this will be discussed later). In other cases, your lecturer/professor will be less interested in intervening. For example, he or she may not want to preside over disputes related to which topic you should choose. Seeking external assistance with conflict has immense student appeal. However, it might be suggested that this is simply an avoidance strategy in which others are asked to sort out the problem.

Each of these general approaches takes a particular tack in dealing with conflict. In different situations, a group may need to use different approaches, and thus, there is no one best approach. The choice of a particular strategy is contingent on the situation, the people involved, and the time frames associated with the issue being examined.

Peer Assessment and Varying Grades

In some cases, the reason for conflict relates to the quality, value, or even amount of contribution made by various members. Many of you may have been in a group in which most of the members felt that someone did not make an equal contribution, greater or less, and thus did not feet that the individual's grade should be the same as other members of the group.

In some cases, the grading process for the project will allow for varying grades within the group (Dyrud, 2001). In other cases, this will not occur, but there is nothing to stop you asking your lecturer/professor if the group can voluntarily implement such a process. While peer assessment does not necessarily allow you to overcome conflict, it may allow the impact of conflict to be taken into consideration and thus is discussed here in this regard.

What peer assessment means is that group members evaluate one another in regard to their contributions. Many aspects of an individual's involvement in the project can be evaluated in this way. These aspects might relate to the process, such as the fact that each member attends meetings and performs tasks on time. Alternatively, it might relate to higher-order activities such as whether members identify alternative solutions to problems or take on leadership roles in regard to tasks. Or the measures might reflect an overall evaluation in terms of the individual's contribution (this implicitly assumes that there are other things being measured).

Should peer evaluation be part of the research project, either as a requirement of the lecturer/professor or something the group initiates, it is critical that there be discussion early on regarding what the evaluative criteria to be used are and what is expected in regard to each criterion. For example, working as a team member might mean more than simply coming to meetings and performing assigned tasks; it might mean providing feedback to others, occasionally taking a leadership role, and so forth. Thus, even if members agree on the criteria, they might not agree on how they are measured.

Perceptions of tasks will vary, and thus, clarifying roles and responsibilities early on is critical. It is also important for all members of the group to realize that peer evaluation is a serious task. Frequently, students say, "I did not think that it really counted"; on the other hand, some students have said, "We really don't want to mark the person down." If a peer evaluation is to be effective, it needs to be something that everyone understands and takes seriously.

Peer assessments tend to be operated in several ways. In some cases, students individually complete the evaluation of other group members anonymously, and the lecturer aggregates the results. This, unfortunately, makes it too easy for you and your group members to ignore issues of conflict both during the project and at the evaluation stage, as you may not be forced to openly discuss issues of concern with relevant group members. This approach also means that an individual who is being criticized by his or her colleagues does not have the chance to respond to accusations, true or false.

Alternatively, the peer review process can take place as an interactive group activity. This approach means that the group has to openly discuss each individual's performance, and that the individual has the opportunity to respond to comments raised. Such an approach is sometimes difficult for students, and they feel uncomfortable raising issues of conflict. Unfortunately, not doing so often means that the student or students whose performance was deficient may in fact not be aware that there was a problem. For example, in one group, three of the four members believed that the fourth student's work was not of an appropriate standard, but the group never discussed this with the individual. Though the student could be marked down in a peer evaluation, there was little opportunity for the student to respond during the project process (i.e., improve performance), given that no feedback was provided throughout the process. The conflict the three students feared was simply delayed, and given that it was not addressed during the project, the other students needed to do more work, the outcome might have suffered, and the student who needed to improve was never given the opportunity to contribute fully.

Adopting a peer review process might be effective in dealing with issues after they have occurred. Unfortunately, it might only delay conflict, as there is a limited chance to resolve conflict at the end of the project in a way that benefits all students and the group process. Thus, ongoing discussion of the evaluative criteria throughout the project is essential, rather than simply evaluating each other at the end.

A Group Contract

There are even more formal mechanisms for attempting to deal with the management of the group in an attempt to control conflict. One such process is the development of a group contract. Though this includes aspects of a peer assessment, the key objective is to clearly articulate the rights and responsibilities of all group members. In this way, it ensures that all members have a clear understanding of what is expected, and thus, perceptions are openly discussed early on in the project. Many students will see the development of a group contract as overkill, and it may be, especially for short projects that are not research based. However, if your research project is the only assessment for the course, a contract may be something that is worth developing.

The complexity of group contracts can vary based on the group and the project, as the contract outlines expectations of members for the satisfactory completion of activities. If it is to be binding to members, it should be agreed on and signed by all group members and, if possible, should also be signed by the group's supervisor. Given that the objective of the contract is to set out expectations in an attempt to reduce conflict later, it might need to cover a range of issues. Many of these issues relate back to those identified earlier in regard to where conflict can arise:

- The desired outcome, in terms of a result. This makes it clear to all group members what type of effort is expected.
- How many hours per week each member is to contribute to the project. This might be specified, especially if the project is one that will last over a long duration, although it might not be needed.
- What the expectations are in terms of individuals' contributions, which may relate to standard of work or communication with other group members.
- There might be an inventory of each member's skills (and relevant resources), which is then used to assist in distributing tasks and responsibilities.
- There might be definitions of the responsibilities of specific group roles, such as group leader or group secretary, should these roles exist.
- There may be a process for resolving conflict. This might involve using one of the approaches identified earlier. For example, it might mean there is a secret ballot to resolve disagreements in regard to aspects of the project.
- There may be clearly defined processes for dealing with members who consistently fail to contribute, which might include a mechanism for removing students from a group or adjustments to grades.
- There might be some processes for managing meetings to ensure that there are no dominant or overly quiet group members.
- There may also be a proposed timeline, which can serve as a formal schedule or a guideline.

The degree of detail used in a contract will vary across groups and research projects. In our experience, some groups have a half-page contract that addresses all the issues identified above. In other cases, groups have produced several-page contracts. The key role of a contract is to clarify expectations and ensure that perceptions of members are the same. Groups that have contracts are usually more willing to discuss issues of conflict that arise, and thus, a contract might also allow the group process to become more open because of the clarity of rights and responsibilities.

A word of caution: if you do use a group contract to deal with conflict, you will also need to make sure that there are records or a diary in regard to activities and meetings. For example, if a group wanted to expel a member for not contributing, the lecturer may only allow this to happen if the group can support its reasoning with group notes demonstrating that the person had repeatedly not completed tasks, even after extensions were given. Group and individual note-keeping does have the added benefit that there are then records of past discussions, should the group want to refer back to material. For example, a group was able to reconstruct important material that was lost based on the individuals' notes. A contract also forces you and your group members to reflect more on various aspects of the project and thus may improve broader learning outcomes.

Conclusion

This chapter has sought to raise a number of important issues that surround working in groups and the conflict(s) that inevitably arise when a group of students come together to perform a major assignment or a student research project. Ideally, you will not see the occurrence of conflict as a failure, because conflict is an almost natural consequence of drawing together different people with multiple perspectives on an issue, who have a range of competing demands on them, many of which are unrelated to the project (see Figure 4.1). The important thing to consider is how the conflict has been dealt with and whether the outcome has improved the overall process.

You should remember that you can choose to view conflict as inherently bad and therefore something that must be eliminated at all costs, or you can choose to see conflict as having both positive and negative aspects and outcomes and attempt to weave a path through them. Or, still further, you can choose to view conflict as an inevitable aspect of group work and one that can, if handled properly, be a largely positive and constructive aspect of group dynamics. How you view conflict will bias how you will deal with it.

It is the responsibility of each group member to appreciate the diverse demands placed on other members and thus be able to actively deal with conflict when it arises. Given that conflict can arise from any number of sources, it is the case that one source of conflict can accentuate another. For example, a group member may be having problems in the area of family and social relationships, and this then affects his or her group work. Because many outside factors may affect an individual's performance in a group, you must be flexible as well as understanding when dealing with others in the group.

Each member of the group must appreciate that whatever action he or she takes in the face of conflict (e.g., compromise, avoidance, collaboration, etc.), will have consequences for the group, the individual, and the outcomes. For instance, you cannot take an avoidance approach to conflict and then claim later that you didn't participate, contribute, or actively involve yourself in

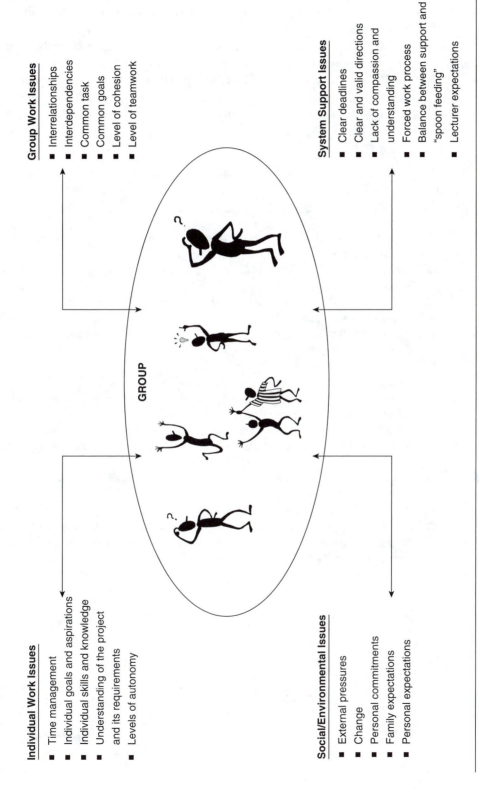

Individual Work Issues

- Time management
- Individual goals and aspirations
- Individual skills and knowledge
- Understanding of the project and its requirements
- Levels of autonomy

Group Work Issues

- Interrelationships
- Interdependencies
- Common task
- Common goals
- Level of cohesion
- Level of teamwork

GROUP

Social/Environmental Issues

- External pressures
- Change
- Personal commitments
- Family expectations
- Personal expectations

System Support Issues

- Clear deadlines
- Clear and valid directions
- Lack of compassion and understanding
- Forced work process
- Balance between support and "spoon feeding"
- Lecturer expectations

Figure 4.1   Issues Surrounding Group Work and Conflict

the conflict. The avoidance strategy may contribute to the conflict dissipating to some degree, remaining at a particular level, or becoming latent only to flare at even worse levels at some time in the future.

Ideally, the more everyone views the project objectives, goals, and processes in the same way, the less the likelihood of conflict occurring. While processes such as a contract might assist in developing a shared understanding, in other cases this will only eventuate as the group moves through the various steps of the project, thereby developing increased trust in each other's abilities to perform, which in turn tends to improve outcomes as well (Porter & Lilly, 1996).

References

Baron, R. A. (1986). *Behavior in organizations: Understanding and managing the human side of work*. Boston: Allyn and Bacon.

Bovée, C. L., Thill, J. V., & Schatzman, B. E. (2003). *Business communication today*. Upper Saddle River, NJ: Prentice Hall.

Dyrud, M. A. (2001). Group projects and peer review. *Business Communication Quarterly, 64*(4), 106–112.

Hartley, P., & Bruckmann, C. G. (2002). *Business communication*. London: Routledge.

Kolb, J. A. (1998). The relationship between self-monitoring and leadership in student project groups. *The Journal of Business Communication, 35*(2), 264–282.

McPhee-Andrewartha. (1997). *Influence Dimensions Workbook*. Kent Town, Australia: McPhee-Andrewatha.

Porter, T. W., & Lilly, B. S. (1996). The effects of conflict, trust, and task commitment on project team performance. *International Journal of Conflict Management, 7*(4), 361–377.

Robbins, S. P. (1987). *Organization theory: structure, design, and applications*. Englewood Cliffs, NJ: Prentice Hall.

Robbins, S. P., Bergman, R., & Stagg, I. (1997). *Management*. Sydney: Prentice Hall.

Robbins, S. P., Millett, B., Cacioppem, R., & Waters-Marsh, T. (1998). *Organisational behaviour: Leading and managing in Australia and New Zealand*. New York, Sydney: Prentice Hall.

5 Ethical Considerations

The consideration of ethics in research, and in general business for that matter, is of growing importance. It is, therefore, critical that you understand the basics of ethical research and how this might affect your research project. This is especially important if your research involves interaction with businesses or members of the general community who serve as participants (i.e., respondents) in your research. There are a range of interactions in your research that might occur, including in-depth interviews, focus groups, surveys, or even observing people's behavior.

Though all researchers (student, professional, or academic) are well intentioned, there is the possibility that interaction with participants may inadvertently harm them in some unintended way. This could include

- Psychological harm—for example, researching the use of nudity in advertising may show participants images that offend them.
- Financial harm—researching unethical behavior within a given firm may provide management with information on individual employees that results in an individual getting fired, or undertaking industry-based research may inadvertently share sensitive information with a firm's competitors, resulting in financial harm to the organization.
- Social harm—researching how lifestyle affects consumption may unintentionally disclose a person's sexual orientation when that person wanted to keep this confidential.

It is your responsibility to consider whether any type of harm could occur when you plan your research and to ensure that mechanisms are instituted to remove it. It is, therefore, essential that you carefully evaluate the *potential* for harm to arise and ensure that you (a) behave according to appropriate ethical standards; (b) consider how your research *might* negatively affect participants; and (c) protect yourself, your supervisors/teachers, and your institution from being placed in situations in which individuals could make claims of inappropriate behavior, resulting in public criticism or even your being sued.

Unfortunately, there is an increasing amount of litigation in the world and many universities have processes in place for vetting research to ensure that it is undertaken in an ethical fashion. This ensures that the participant is protected and also ensures that the students, staff, and university undertaking the research are protected.

In covering the topic of ethics, we are not trying to change your values, but rather we want to make you more aware of potential ethical issues that might arise when undertaking your research. To do this, some questions will be asked that, if appropriately answered, will ensure that potential ethical problems are avoided.

This chapter is designed to discuss a range of ethical issues. Many of these issues are broadly covered in the various business and marketing ethics texts (for example, Smith & Quelch, 1992) as well as marketing research texts (for example, Churchill, 1991). These texts tend to look at research ethics from a client-agency perspective; that is, where the researcher is working for a client. The following material will try to broaden this view by also considering general social research ethics (Homan, 1991), covering a range of data collection approaches such as participant observation (Bulmer, 1982) and surveys/experiments (Sieber, 1982).

What Is Human Intervention?

In the context of this chapter, human intervention is defined to encompass a broad range of activities, including interviews, review of corporate records, focus groups, experiments, oral histories, or surveys. It basically involves the researcher having access to information that is not in the public domain. *If* your research involves accessing information that is readily and publicly available, such as a content analysis, meta-analysis, or literature review, it is unlikely that much of the material discussed within this chapter would apply, although some issues, such as academic fraud and plagiarism, would apply to *all* types of research.

Some examples of student research that would be less likely to involve human intervention would include the following:

- Content analysis of information contained in advertisements
- A multiple-regression study that uses data from publicly available databases, such as Predicast
- An examination of a data set that was collected for another purpose, assuming that the participants had already given their prior permission for others researchers to access this data

Codes of Ethical Conduct/Practice

There are various ethical codes of conduct that regulate researchers' behavior. These codes discuss many issues that potentially might arise in your research, as well as other issues associated with professional practice (Beauchamp & Bowie, 1997). For example, the American Marketing Association's code of conduct (AMA, 2003) touches on research-related issues and specifically states that members must "not knowingly do harm." It also specifies other issues of particular interest to professional marketers, such as the issues relating to the development of safe new products or the prohibition of price-fixing activities, and so forth (see Appendix 5.1).

Ethical issues are also examined by the European Society for Opinion and Marketing Research's (ESOMR, 2003) Code of Practice, which sets out researchers' broad responsibilities (see Appendix 5.2). ESOMR provides more detailed codes and guidelines for a range of different activities, ranging from broad-based activities such as a "Guide to Opinion Polls" to more specific guidelines on "Mystery Shopping" and "Interviewing Children" (see Exhibit 5.1). The codes are, of course, not static, and there are also specific detailed discussions of ethical practice relating to new technologies such as the Internet (AMA, 2003; ESOMR, 2003).

Exhibit 5.1   Index of ESOMAR Codes and Guidelines

All ESOMAR members and the management of the marketing research companies listed in the ESOMAR Directory have undertaken to comply with the ICC/ESOMAR International Code of Marketing and Social Research Practice which is applied by over 100 associations world-wide.

1. ICC/ESOMAR International Code of Marketing and Social Research Practice
    – ESOMAR Notes to interpreting the ICC/ESOMAR Code
    – Annexe to the Code Notes regarding European Union Data Protection requirements

2. ESOMAR/WAPOR Guide to Opinion Polls

3. ESOMAR Guideline on Maintaining the Distinctions between Marketing Research and Direct Marketing

4. ESOMAR Guideline on Customer Satisfaction Studies

5. ESOMAR Guideline on How to Commission Research

6. ESOMAR Guideline on Interviewing Children and Young People

7. ESOMAR Guideline on Mystery Shopping

8. ESOMAR Guideline on Tape and Video-Recording and Client Observation of Interviews and Group Discussions

9. ESOMAR Guideline on Pharmaceutical Marketing Research. Endorsed by EphMRA

10. ESOMAR Guideline on Conducting Marketing and Opinion Research Using the Internet

11. The ESOMAR Arbitration Service

12. The ESOMAR Disciplinary Procedures (PDF file)

Ethical guidelines are not limited to the marketing discipline, as psychologists also have detailed guidelines regulating research involving human intervention. As can be seen in Appendix 5.3, the American Psychological Association's (APA, 2003) *Ethical Principles of Psychologists and Code of Conduct* covers a diverse range of research issues, many of which relate to business research as well. For example, there is a whole section dealing with privacy and confidentiality (Section 4 of the APA's code).

Many universities have also developed guidelines for conducting ethical research (Polonsky, 1998). In Australia, all universities have agreed to have all research comply with one set of ethical guidelines for *all* types of human intervention. These guidelines were developed by the National Health and Medical Research Council (NHMRC, 2003a) and apply to all types of research. In addition to the guidelines, the NHMRC also produced the *Human Research Ethics Handbook,* "which is the primary guideline for ethics committees and researchers alike" (NHMRC, 2003b).

Within some universities, researchers, students, and staff must complete detailed applications to be reviewed by an independent ethics committee (sometimes called a human subjects committee or human research ethics committee) before research can be undertaken (Polonsky, 1998). These committees apply basic ethical principles to all research and seek to ensure that all ethical issues are considered and appropriately addressed. Though not all the issues in every code of practice will apply to your research, reviewing these codes will give you some idea of the complexity of the issues that need to be addressed when planning your research project. Some of these issues will be described in more detail later in this chapter.

Ethical Philosophies

Within the ethics discipline there are a number of different approaches for examining ethics and values. Two philosophical approaches that relate closely to the discussion of student research ethics are deontological and teleological philosophies. To assist you in getting a better understanding of where harm may arise, a number of approaches will be briefly discussed.

According to Skinner, Ferrell, and Dubinsky (1988), "deontological philosophies focus on the *factors* or *means* used to arrive at an ethical decision. These philosophies emphasise moral obligations or commitments that should be binding or necessary for proper conduct" (p. 213). To put it quite simply, a deontological approach means that you should *not* harm participants in any way, no matter what the potential benefit. On the other hand, "teleological philosophies emphasize the *consequences* that result from an action. In other words, they deal with the moral worth of the behaviour as determined totally by the consequences of the behavior" (p. 213). This approach asks you to evaluate whether the benefits of the research outweigh the cost to participants; if so, the research would be considered acceptable.

A teleological approach is frequently used in medical research, where the research needs to weigh up the potential harm to participants versus the harm from them not participating. For example, when testing a new drug, it is determined that there is a 0.01% chance of some negative side effect occurring, but the chances of getting the disease the drug is trying to prevent is substantially higher, e.g., 10.0%. Thus, the potential harm from the research is outweighed by the potential benefit of the research. It is suggested that a teleological approach is inappropriate for your research, as you and other students would be unskilled in weighing up the associated costs and benefits.

Alternative ethical perspectives are also put forward in the ethics literature. For example, Kantian ethics suggest that "persons should be treated as ends and never purely as means" (Beauchamp & Bowie, 1997). Thus, any practice you might want to undertake that does not consider how the situation affects the individual would be unethical. This is a more stringent perspective than a deontological approach, as an individual would not have to be harmed for a breach of the Kantian perspective to occur. Other ethical perspectives put forward include common morality theory, rights theory, virtue ethics, feminist theories, and ethics of care, but these will not be discussed here, as they are less frequently applied in research associated with business practices (see Beauchamp & Bowie, 1997, Chapter 1 for a discussion of these). For our discussion of research ethics in relation to your project a deontological approach will be adopted; that is, any practice that causes any harm to an individual should be avoided.

Ethical Issues to Consider

The goal of your research project is to facilitate your learning through a better understanding of research and how it influences practice. However, in undertaking your research, you will frequently be required to seek information from individuals who are not normally part of the educational process (e.g., average consumers, managers, employees, etc.). You will need to ensure that no harm occurs to these voluntary participants and that all participants have made the decision to assist you with full information as to what is required *and* what, if any, potential negative consequences may arise from such participation. Those who choose not to participate must also be given the same information on which to make their decision not to be involved.

There are a diverse range of research methods and research contexts potentially available to you, and each carries its own specific ethical considerations, which makes it difficult to provide one global set of ethical issues. It would be impossible to construct a composite list of all potential problems. For example, Table 5.1 lists a set of potential ethical problems relating to researching consumers. This listing is not comprehensive, and similar lists could be developed in relation to research involving employees or managers.

There are six broad ethical areas that need to be considered in your research. In this chapter, we will discuss voluntary participation, informed consent, confidentiality and anonymity, the potential for harm, communicating the results, and more specific ethical issues. These six areas are interdependent, and, as such, the following discussions will overlap a bit. It should be emphasized that you need to check whether your university has processes or procedures that must be followed and that may differ from those described here. You should also identify the relevant deadlines for presenting any required documentation to the ethics committee. The discussions in the following subsections are designed to ensure that you understand the ethical issues associated with each area, as well as provide some processes for addressing the issues if they arise.

Table 5.1 Potential Ethical Problems Relating to Researching Consumers

Ethical Issue	Right Violated	Compensation Available
Preserving participants' anonymity	Right to privacy	
Exposing participants to mental stress	Right to safety	Right to be heard Right to redress
Use of special equipment and techniques	Right to privacy Right to choose	Right to redress
Involving participants in research without their knowledge	Right to be informed Right to privacy	Right to redress
Use of deception	Right to be informed	Right to be heard Right to redress
Use of coercion	Right to choose	
Selling under the guise of research	Right to be informed	
Causing embarrassment, hindrance, or offense	Right to respect	Right to redress

SOURCE: Smith and Quelch (1992, p. 162).

Voluntary Participation

Participation should be voluntary in *all* research, and there should be no coercion or deception (this latter issue will be discussed in the subsections titled "Informed Consent" and "Other, More Specific Ethical Issues"). For the most part, you should not be in a position to force respondents to participate, but there are some situations in which could potentially occur. You should remember that participants are assisting you, and they should be *invited* to participate, with a clear understanding that they are under no obligation to do so and that there will be no negative consequences for them if they do not assist you in your research.

The potential for coercion varies depending on whom you are seeking assistance from. For example, if you are undertaking an intercept-type activity involving surveying fellow students in the university parking lot, it is unlikely that potential participants would be unduly pressured by you asking for a few minutes of their time. This assumes that you do not hound them until they agree to participate. Even when dealing with peers, there is a slight potential for coercion to occur, as you might exaggerate the importance of participants' assistance or of the study. For example, you might say something like, "I need you to fill out this survey or I will fail Subject X."

Such a statement would be inappropriate, as it places unnecessary social pressure on potential respondents.

In some circumstances, the target sample group might have unique characteristics or needs, and if this were the case, they would require special treatment. For example, consider the case in which a student was undertaking research involving a group with limited English capabilities. In this situation, respondents might not understand what they are being asked to do and, equally important, might not understand that the activity is voluntary (Davidson, 1995). Thus, you should ensure that any vulnerable groups are protected, even from unintentional harm.

The issue of voluntary consent can also arise when students undertake research of employees within an organization. This might occur if you were to arrange for a firm to allow you to research the organization's activities and/or employees, and it is especially of concern when you research your own workplace.[1] In these situations, it should be made clear to participants that (a) the organization has allowed you to investigate the specified activities; (b) any involvement is voluntary; (c) there is no penalty for not participating; and (d) specific information from the research will or will not be given to their employer.

Confidentiality and anonymity are potentially even more important when you are researching other staff within your own organization. How can you, who may be in a managerial position, indicate that participants will not be harmed if they don't participate in the study? One way to overcome this potential problem is to separate yourself from respondents, so that responses are confidential/anonymous. For example, in a group project, it might be possible for a member of the group who is not affiliated with the firm to collect and code the data. It would then be impossible for you to know who participated.

Another solution, in the case of survey research, might be to have the organization distribute the surveys and then have employees return them confidentially/anonymously to you. In this way, neither you nor the firm can identify who participated. For other data collection techniques, there are other approaches for addressing this issue. For example, if you want to conduct interviews with employees, the organization could write to employees and invite them to contact you or simply show up at a predetermined appointment. However, if you work within the firm, you may still be able to identify the individual. As will be discussed in other subsections, knowing the people who participated is not necessarily problematic but needs to be considered, and participants may need to be protected.

Informed Consent

Another important issue in student research involving human intervention is to ensure that potential participants fully understand what they are being asked to do and that they are informed if there are any potential negative consequences of such participation. The most effective way to address the informed consent issue is through the use of an information sheet, which is provided to all those who are invited to participate. If possible, this should be on official university letterhead, as this not only has been shown to increase the response rate but also informs respondents that this is an official university activity. In situations in which there *is* a potential for participant harm to occur, participants should be given the invitation sufficiently in advance to enable them to carefully consider whether they will participate.

Appendix 5.3 provides a sample information sheet, as well as a range of alternative information that could be included depending on the type of research involved. It is important that the information included be sufficiently clear so that your target group can understand what they are being asked to do. The level of complexity will vary based on the project and targeted respondent. For example, you may need to describe the study differently if you are examining CEOs than if the participants are high school students.

What information should be included in the information letter? The issues should be sufficient for individuals to make an informed decision as to whether they will participate. The letter should tell them who you are and why you are doing the project. For example, "I am an Information Science student at University X and I am undertaking a research project as part of a Systems Design course."

The letter should also tell participants what the project is about and the desired outcomes. For example, "This project is designed to examine Human Resource Managers' attitudes toward the outsourcing of recruitment, to see if they believe that these services are effective." There should also be a brief discussion of how and why the participants were selected. For example, "For this study we are interested in the views of local accountants and have contacted all firms listed in the local yellow pages under accountants."

Once you have explained who you are, and broadly what you are doing and why, it is essential that you explain what you are asking them to do. For example, "We would like you to complete the attached survey, which should take approximately 15 minutes to complete and is being administered with the permission of your firm. When finished, you can place the survey in the collection box in the lunchroom." *If* information is being distributed back to an organization, it is important that this is clearly stated. For example, "We will be providing the finance manager with a copy of the final report and will be quoting individuals who have given us permission to do so." In this way, individuals can hopefully identify the negative implications of participation, and if such consequences exist, they should be explicitly stated. For example, "Though we will not quote individual respondents, given the focus of the research and small number of respondents, it may be possible that individuals could be identified by their comments." A statement such as this clearly identifies that some harm *could possibly* arise depending on the topic. There are other situations in which respondents might need to be warned about the focus of the study. For example, "We will be showing participants copies of advertisements containing female nudity similar to those in magazines such as Cosmopolitan. If you are offended by such advertisements, you may want to decline participation." In this latter case, the students have explicitly tried to protect the respondent from the potential of harm.

The information sheet should also discuss how respondents would be provided feedback, if at all. It should also include contact details of your supervisor(s). In some instances, it might need to include a complaints mechanism, although this will vary by institution and may or may not be required (see the bottom of Exhibit 5.2). Last, though this is not an ethical issue, students should not forget to provide a deadline for responding, as this ensures they get the information requested in a timely fashion.

Exhibit 5.2   Example of an Information Sheet

<Italic material should be filled in for the specific project.>
<UNIVERSITY LETTER HEAD>

<Supervisor's/Lecturer's

Contact Details>

Dear Potential Participant,

As part of *<SUBJECT X>* I/We am/are undertaking a research project entitled *<TITLE>*. The project examines *<1 or 2 sentences describing what the project is about and outcomes>*. *<Explain why they were chosen and how>*.

We would like you to *<1 or 2 sentences explaining what you want them to do>*. This will take approximately *<X minutes>*. Your participation is completely voluntary [for employees of an organization it would be beneficial to inform them that this was achieved] and there will be no negative consequences to you for not participating.

[If there are audio or videotapes of interviews it might be appropriate to allow participants to review tapes or transcripts. If you use these, it is also beneficial to say:] During the interview, you will have the opportunity to edit the tape and/or stop the interview at any time. Prior to beginning the interview we will ask you to sign a consent form.

[If using a survey you can say:] Please return the survey to *<Name of person collecting responses>* by *<Date>*. Your completion and return of the survey is taken as an indication of your consent to participate.

[You can also say (more than one may be applicable):]

1. We will be providing *<X>* with a copy of the final report; however, data will be aggregated such that individuals cannot be identified.
2. We will be providing *<X>* with a copy of the report and will be quoting individual comments with your permission.
3. We will be providing a copy of the results to your organization, which will make the results available to you.
4. If you would like a summary of results, they will be available from our supervisor after *<Date>*.

Thank you for considering participating in this study. If you have any questions in relation to my/our study, please contact my/our supervisor at the above address.

[ALL Students Sign.]

[Your university may also require you to include a complaints mechanism, such as the following:]

The university requires that all participants are informed that if they have any complaint concerning the manner in which research is conducted, they may direct it to the researcher, or if an independent person is preferred, they can contact *<X at Phone and Address>*.

Confidentiality and Anonymity

Within the information sheet, you may have mentioned that you will keep respondents' answers confidential and/or anonymous. These issues have been mentioned earlier, but they should be discussed further. You need to understand the difference between these two issues, as they are often confused.

Anonymity requires that you do not know who the participants are. This could be achieved through random phone surveying or having an organization distribute a survey on behalf of the student. Confidentiality means that you know who the participants are, but that their identity will not be revealed in any way in the resulting report. As we mentioned earlier, confidentiality is very important especially when you are examining situations within a firm in which you will give managers a copy of the report. It could also be important when undertaking an industry-based study, and the final report will be distributed to all participants, who may be competitors.

You must consider how to protect your participants, and if there is any possibility that they will not be protected, this must be clearly stated to potential respondents in the accompanying information letters and consent forms (discussed in more detail later in this chapter). If individuals clearly know they will be identified and that the report will be distributed to managers or competitors, there is no ethical problem associated with responses not remaining confidential or anonymous.

There are several ways that anonymity and confidentially can be protected. As mentioned earlier, if the researcher does not know who replies, individual confidentiality and anonymity are usually protected. However, it may be possible that individuals could still be identified based on the level of analysis. For example, how many 45-year-old female senior managers in the Finance Department are there within one organization? If the answer is one, then that individual *could* be identified if the analysis is too detailed. Therefore, you need to be careful as to how detailed and/or segmented your data is.

Potential for Harm

There are a number of ways in which participants can be harmed: physical harm, psychological harm, emotional harm, embarrassment (i.e., social harm), and so on. It is important for you to identify any potential for harm and determine how this potential for harm could be overcome. Ideally, your research should have minimal, *if any,* potential for any harm to occur. This issue is frequently one of the most difficult for students to address, as it requires them to place themselves in the other person's shoes. The question is *not* whether you believe harm could occur, but whether participants or potential participants believe that harm could occur.

There are some topics in which it could be expected that some harm might arise. For example, what would happen if you were to examine sexual harassment in the workplace, which might identify respondents who are either presently being harassed or where harassed in the past? Ideally, projects that examine issues in which there is a high likelihood of participant harm should not proceed *unless* a supervisor was actively involved and ensures that processes were in place to address any harmed individuals. One possible way to address the harm in such a project would be to provide participants with information on counseling services or appropriate support bodies dealing with the issue. Such materials should be distributed to all respondents with the information sheet, so that those who need assistance can seek it. In this way, you will have at least provided a mechanism to assist any harmed individuals and thus undertake a duty of care in regard to participants. While the research per se did not harm the individual, it may cause additional distress, and thus it is your responsibility to address the issue.

In other situations, there could be more direct harm to participants. For example, a study looking at staff drinking on the job could result in someone being fired if the study identified that they had a problem. As mentioned earlier, even showing participants advertisements used in the media may embarrass or offend some segments of the community. Thus, you must identify any potential harm to participants and seek to ensure that the potential is minimized within the study as well as that participants are clearly informed of the potential for harm.

Though not a mechanism for preventing harm, in cases involving interviews and/or focus groups, it may also be beneficial to have respondents sign consent forms in addition to receiving an information sheet. This makes it clear that individuals have agreed to participate; however, given that individuals should always be given the right to withdraw at any time, this may provide less protection than anticipated (consent forms will be examined in more detail in the subsection titled "Other, More Ethical Issues Specific Methods"). The real answer to minimizing harm is to select topics and methods that preclude any harm arising.

Communicating Results

There are three broad issues that you need to be aware of when completing your research project report and communicating results with your lecturer/professor/supervisor and with clients, should they exist: plagiarism, academic fraud, and misrepresenting results.

Plagiarism

The first issue of plagiarism relates to all student work; that is, you need to be very careful that you do not misrepresent someone else's work as your own. The appropriate techniques for referencing others' ideas are discussed in the chapter on Literature Reviews. There may be a temptation to "cut and paste" others' work to form new ideas. This is unfortunately getting easier with the use of electronic databases and information on the Web. Do *not* be tempted to simply cut paragraphs (or more) out of other documents. *If* you do, make sure you appropriately cite this material. In most universities, plagiarism is a breach of the student code of conduct and can result in failure of the subject/class or even expulsion from the institution. Therefore, you need to be very careful when using material from others to ensure that it is adequately referenced.

Academic Fraud

Once students begin undertaking research involving the collection, analysis, and interpretation of data, there is also the possibility of what is known as academic fraud, which in most cases is perceived by universities as bad if not worse than plagiarism. Academic fraud involves the intentional misrepresentation of what has been done. This would include making up data and/or results from the data or purposefully putting forward conclusions that are not accurate. Students may be inclined to commit academic fraud for a number of reasons. For example, they may have difficulty accessing the correct people to survey and so make up data. In other cases, students may find that their results are inconclusive and think that they need to find *something* in order to receive a good grade.

The temptation to commit academic fraud should be avoided. As you need to realize, most research projects have "hiccups," and, in fact, many academic journal articles include a limitation section that identifies unforeseen problems. To ensure that you will be able to get the data needed, think about the project in advance and come up with contingencies should problems arise. For example, one group of students wanted to undertake a random telephone survey of 18- to 25-year-old males by randomly calling people until they obtained 100 responses. After they called 100 people, they found that they received only one response. On looking at the census data, they found that this group (18- to 25-year-old males) represented only 5% of the population; thus if they were lucky, they would only have had five respondents from their 100 calls. The group decided that they would rather survey male students in the university cafeteria in this age category. As this example shows, a data collection problem forced the students to modify the design and refocus the question, which in this case was fine and still satisfied the assignment requirements.

In regard to research results, you may get concerned if your findings are inclusive or are inconsistent with existing literature. Many researchers undertake studies that don't find the expected outcomes; unfortunately, you will find fewer of these works published, as journals don't often want to say that nothing interesting was found. However, for your research, this should not be a problem, and in many cases there might be sound reasons that no result was found. For example, the instrument may have been imprecise, the sample problematic, the context of the study different, an so forth. In most cases, your projects are evaluated on the process, rather than the outcomes, although the criteria to be used to evaluate the research need to be clarified with your individual instructor.

Misrepresenting the Results

The last issue, misrepresenting the results, is especially important for students undertaking their project for a client. In many situations, you will be so good at marketing your work that businesses may forget that these are student projects, which frequently have substantial limitations. In the second place, students are just that, students. You are learning about the application of research to solve business problems and, as such, may make conclusions and recommendations that are inconstant or incorrect based on what you found. On occasion, some students (not you, of course) may purposefully misrepresent their work to impress their business client. Academic supervisors, on the other hand, will frequently identify these exaggerations and mark the work down accordingly.

The problem of overclaiming is often difficult to overcome without the assistance of your lecturer/professor/supervisor, who, as an objective expert, will be able to determine if there are any substantial errors or omissions. If you do have a client, you should make sure that any report to clients clearly specifies what was done and what limitations exist. In addition, we recommend that your instructor provide some objective feedback that is passed on to the client with any final report.

Other, More Specific Ethical Issues

The issues discussed so far have been applicable to a wide range of research projects. There are, however, a number of ethical issues that may arise in specific situations or when using specific types of research techniques. A number of these issues will be discussed in the following subsections, but once again these are in no way comprehensive in terms of other ethical issues that could arise, and these are meant only to be a guide.

Conflicts of Interest

This issue arises when you or one group member is an individual employed in the industry you are researching and you do not inform all respondents of this fact. While the research may be a good opportunity to gain competitive information, such action would be ethically inappropriate. It is always surprising how much competitively useful information a business will give student researchers. The easiest way to overcome this problem is to not place yourself or your group in this position to start with; that is, if you work in one firm in an industry, don't try to look at your competitors. However, if you do, it would be imperative that you make your dual status as researcher and competitor clear in the information sheet.

Focus Group Participant Identification

When conducting a focus group, the researcher is not the only one involved, as there are other participants in the focus group, and its dynamic nature is one of the benefits of its use (see Chapter 9 for a discussion of focus groups). However, this means that the information discovered within the group becomes common knowledge among all those in attendance. Therefore, it is important that members of the focus group sign appropriate consent forms in situations in which this information might be used against the person who said something or a third person who was discussed. The consent form could include a statement regarding participants keeping the information discussed confidential. This method is, of course, not foolproof, as it is unclear that any penalties for breaching the agreement could be imposed, but at least you are undertaking due diligence to protect participants and others.

Deceit

In some cases, that telling respondents your true intent might modify their response or behavior. For example, if your group were undertaking an experiment to determine whether an interviewer's attire or gender influence respondents, you would not want to tell respondents this, as it would most likely bias the results. However, for the most part deceit should be *avoided* at all times. This is one of the situations in which researchers might be tempted to apply a teleological ethical view; that is, does the benefit of misleading the respondents outweigh any potential harm to participants.

In some cases, the deceit may be minor; for example, in examining the impact of health labels on alcohol, respondents are told it is a study of factors affecting alcohol consumption. However, in other cases, such as the one related to collecting competitive data under the guise of student research, it is more substantial. Deceit should only be used if no other method of researching the issue is available and the students' instructor is well aware of what is happening. In addition, at the conclusion of the intervention, for instance, at the end of the survey in the first example, participants should be informed (i.e., debriefed) of the study's real purpose and be given the right to have their information withdrawn (i.e., not used). In extreme cases of deception, the debriefing may need to be more detailed and structured, although student researchers should generally not undertake studies requiring excessive deceit.

Observation

Another ethical issue that may arise when undertaking projects involves the observation of participants. This becomes an ethical issue especially when you are observing people in a public or quasipublic place. For example, what if you want to examine how respondents behave in the ice cream section of a food store (i.e., how much time they spend there, what products they look at, etc.)? In this situation, it is likely that asking to observe people will modify their behavior, and therefore, researchers may not want to explicitly ask each person if he or she can be watched. One solution to this issue is to have notices placed at the entrance of the store indicating that researchers will be operating in this area at these times. Individuals not wishing to participate could then avoid this area at these times. Should you wish to videotape these encounters, it may also be advisable to seek permission using a consent form to use the information after the participant has been taped, even if a notice is used (if someone declines, you should erase this person's data). Broader covert observation, such as hidden cameras in work areas without employee awareness (and possibly consent), should be avoided, and it is not only usually inappropriate but often illegal as well.

Permission From Organization/Location

One ethical issue that students frequently overlook relates to getting written permission from the organization in which the research is being undertaken or the location in which the data is being collected. Students have been ejected from shopping malls simply because they did not have written permission to be there. In one case, the person who gave them oral permission had simply not passed this information on to those responsible for security. In another case, the students' contact suddenly left the organization, and since the students did not have permission in writing, they were not allowed to proceed.

When getting written permission, it is also important that the person you talk with has the ability to give that permission and that your activities are organized well in advance. For example, one group had been planning for several months to examine employees in one organization, assuming that getting permission would be easy, and waited until the last minute. Unfortunately, they discovered that their request would have to go through several levels within the organization and, therefore, would take more time than they had.

Video/Audio Taping

In a number of situations, you may wish to audio record or videotape the specific intervention. This can be done for a number of reasons, such as to ensure that no verbal information is missed in a focus group or interview. Alternatively, you may be attempting to capture nonverbal information, such as body language. Taping of participants has been discussed earlier, but the ethical issues associated with it should be reinforced here as well. It is essential that when taping participants, you clearly state in the information sheet and consent form that you will be doing so. You should also allow participants to have some ability to edit the tape, and as with all activities, allow participants to withdraw, even during the taping process. You should tell participants what will happen to the taped material after it has been analyzed, and in some cases it may be worthwhile to offer the tape to the participant. In most cases, the tapes will be erased after the data has been transcribed. We also recommend that you obtain consent forms from participants when taping activities. Though participants can withdraw at any time, this still provides some evidence that participants initially agreed to participate.

Consent Forms

Whenever interviewing (other than a researcher-administered survey), audio/videotaping, or conducting a focus group, we strongly suggest that you not only use an information sheet but have the respondent sign a consent form as well. You should keep the consent form as an indication of informed consent by the respondent, should any question arise. However, you need to remember that a person who signs an informed consent form can still rescind their consent (i.e., it is not a binding document) for any reason, and you must not use the information they provided.

For the most part, the information contained in the consent form should be similar to the material in the information sheet, but there is more emphasis on what the respondent is agreeing to do and that they understand any potential negative consequences, as described in the information sheet. Exhibit 5.3 provides an example of a consent form. Some specific information that should be included relates to whether the participant agrees to be quoted in the final report and what happens to any tapes of the interview/focus group that might exist. As discussed in the focus group section, there is also a clause related to keeping any information discussed during the focus group confidential, which is designed to protect the other participants in the focus group discussions.

Exhibit 5.3   Example of a Consent Form

<Italic material should be filled in for the specific project.>
<UNIVERSITY LETTER HEAD>

<Supervisor's/Lecturer's

Contact Details>

CONSENT FORM

<Title of Project>

I, (please print) _____ have read the information on the research project *<Title of Project>* that is to be conducted by *<Student name(s)>* from the University of *<X>*, and all queries have been answered to my satisfaction.

I agree to participate in this investigation, which involves *<X>*. [If this consent form is for a focus group, students may wish to include a statement such as: I agree to keep all information confidential and not discuss it with individuals other than the student researchers.]

I understand that I can withdraw from this project at any time without reason or penalty. My responses will remain confidential and any documentation, including audio/visual tapes, will be destroyed once the project is completed. My identity will not be revealed without my consent to anyone other than the investigator conducting the project. [This clause would state that they had given their consent to be quoted if they had.]

<Signature>

<Date>

Conclusion

As has been discussed in this chapter, there are various potential ethical issues that you should carefully consider when planning your research. Though the discussion in this chapter can be used as a guide, it is important that you determine what the appropriate rules within your institution are. The objective of these guidelines is to ensure that potential respondents have full information before voluntarily participating in your research. In addition, you need to put yourself in the participant's position and determine if there is any reasonable possibility of harm arising. It is your responsibility to eliminate, or at least minimize, this possibility. Addressing the potential for harm might require a modification of the research design or of the specific questions asked. For this reason, it is important that this issue be considered when designing the study rather than once the project has substantially progressed.

Note

1. The instances of students researching their own workplace may increase as part-time and/or mature student enrollments increase.

Appendixes

Appendix 5.1   AMA Code of Ethics

Members of the American Marketing Association are committed to ethical professional conduct. They have joined together in subscribing to this Code of Ethics embracing the following topics:

Responsibilities of the Marketer

Marketers must accept responsibility for the consequences of their activities and make every effort to ensure that their decisions, recommendations and actions function to identify, serve and satisfy all relevant publics: customers, organizations and society.
Marketers' Professional Conduct must be guided by:

1. The basic rule of professional ethics: not knowingly to do harm;

2. The adherence to all applicable laws and regulations;

3. The accurate representation of their education, training and experience; and

4. The active support, practice and promotion of this Code of Ethics.

Honesty and Fairness

Marketers shall uphold and advance the integrity, honor and dignity of the marketing profession by:

1. Being honest in serving consumers, clients, employees, suppliers, distributors, and the public;

2. Not knowingly participating in conflict of interest without prior notice to all parties involved; and

3. Establishing equitable fee schedules including the payment or receipt of usual, customary and/or legal compensation for marketing exchanges.

Rights and Duties of Parties in the Marketing Exchange Process

Participants in the marketing exchange process should be able to expect that

1. Products and services offered are safe and fit for their intended uses;

2. Communications about offered products and services are not deceptive;

3. All parties intend to discharge their obligations, financial and otherwise, in good faith; and

4. Appropriate internal methods exist for equitable adjustment and/or redress of grievances concerning purchases.

It is understood that the above would include, but is not limited to, the following responsibilities of the marketer:

In the area of product development and management:

- disclosure of all substantial risks associated with product or service usage;
- identification of any product component substitution that might materially change the product or impact on the buyer's purchase decision;
- identification of extra cost-added features.

In the area of promotions:

- avoidance of false and misleading advertising;
- rejection of high-pressure manipulations, or misleading sales tactics;
- avoidance of sales promotions that use deception or manipulation.

In the area of distribution:

- not manipulating the availability of a product for the purpose of exploitation;
- not using coercion in the marketing channel;
- not exerting undue influence over the reseller's choice to handle a product.

In the area of pricing:

- not engaging in price fixing;
- not practicing predatory pricing;
- disclosing the full price associated with any purchase.

In the area of marketing research:

- prohibiting selling or fundraising under the guise of conducting research;
- maintaining research integrity by avoiding misrepresentation and omission of pertinent research data;
- treating outside clients and suppliers fairly.

Organizational Relationships

Marketers should be aware of how their behavior may influence or impact the behavior of others in organizational relationships. They should not demand, encourage or apply coercion to obtain unethical behavior in their relationships with others, such as employees, suppliers, or customers.

1. Apply confidentiality and anonymity in professional relationships with regard to privileged information;

2. Meet their obligations and responsibilities in contracts and mutual agreements in a timely manner;

3. Avoid taking the work of others, in whole, or in part, and representing this work as their own or directly benefiting from it without compensation or consent of the originator or owner; and

4. Avoid manipulation to take advantage of situations to maximize personal welfare in a way that unfairly deprives or damages the organization or others.

Any AMA member found to be in violation of any provision of this Code of Ethics may have his or her Association membership suspended or revoked.

Appendix 5.2   ICC/ESOMAR International Code of Marketing and Social Research Practice

Introduction

Effective communication between the suppliers and the consumers of goods and services of all kinds is vital to any modern society. Growing international links make this even more essential. For a supplier to provide in the most efficient way what consumers require he must understand their differing needs; how best to meet these needs; and how he can most effectively communicate the nature of the goods or services he is offering.

This is the objective of marketing research. It applies in both private and public sectors of the economy. Similar approaches are also used in other fields of study: for example in measuring the public's behaviour and attitudes with respect to social, political and other issues by Government and public bodies, the media, academic institutions, etc. Marketing and social research have many interests, methods and problems in common although the subjects of study tend to be different.

Such research depends upon public confidence: confidence that it is carried out honestly, objectively, without unwelcome intrusion or disadvantage to respondents, and that it is based upon their willing cooperation. This confidence must be supported by an appropriate professional Code of Practice which governs the way in which marketing research projects are conducted.

The first such Code was published by ESOMAR in 1948. This was followed by a number of Codes prepared by national marketing research societies and by other bodies such as the International Chamber of Commerce (ICC), which represents the international marketing community. In 1976 ESOMAR and the ICC decided that it would be preferable to have a single International Code instead of two differing ones, and a joint ICC/ESOMAR Code was therefore published in the following year (with revisions in 1986).

Subsequent changes in the marketing and social environment, new developments in marketing research methods and a great increase in international activities of all kinds including legislation, led ESOMAR to prepare a new version of the International Code in 1994. This new version sets out as concisely as possible the basic ethical and business principles which govern the practice of marketing and social research. It specifies the rules which are to be followed in dealing with the general public and with the business community, including clients and other members of the profession.

ESOMAR will be glad to give advice on the implementation of this Code; and also offers an arbitration and expert assessment service to help resolve technical and other disputes relating to marketing research projects.

Other aspects of marketing—in particular Direct Marketing and Advertising—are covered by separate International Codes of Practice published by the ICC. Copies of these may be obtained from the ICC Secretariat in Paris.

Appendix 5.3 Contents of the APA's Ethical Principles of Psychologists and Code of Conduct

TABLE OF CONTENTS
INTRODUCTION AND APPLICABILITY
PREAMBLE
GENERAL PRINCIPLES

Principle A: Beneficence and Nonmaleficence
Principle B: Fidelity and Responsibility
Principle C: Integrity
Principle D: Justice
Principle E: Respect for People's Rights and Dignity

ETHICAL STANDARDS

(Continued)

Appendix 5.3 (Continued)

10. Therapy
10.01 Informed Consent to Therapy
10.02 Therapy Involving Couples or Families
10.03 Group Therapy
10.04 Providing Therapy to Those Served by Others
10.05 Sexual Intimacies With Current Therapy Clients/Patients
10.06 Sexual Intimacies With Relatives or Significant Others of Current Therapy Clients/Patients
10.07 Therapy With Former Sexual Partners
10.08 Sexual Intimacies With Former Therapy Clients/Patients
10.09 Interruption of Therapy
10.10 Terminating Therapy

References

American Marketing Association. (2003). *AMA code of ethics*. Retrieved December 14, 2003, from http://www.marketingpower.com/live/content435.php.

American Psychological Association. (2003). *Ethical principles of psychologists and code of conduct*. Retrieved February 28, 2004, from http://www.apastyle.org/elecref.html.

Beauchamp, T. L., & Bowie, N. E. (1997). *Ethical theory and business*. Upper Saddle River, NJ: Prentice Hall.

Bulmer, M. (Ed.). (1982). *Social research ethics: An examination of the merits of covert participant observation*. London: Macmillan.

Churchill, G. A., Jr. (1991). *Marketing research: Methodological foundations*. Orlando, FL: Drydon Press.

Davidson, D. K. (1995). Targeting is innocent until it exploits the vulnerable. *Marketing News, 29*(19), 10.

European Society for Opinion and Marketing Research. (2003). *ICC/ESOMAR international code of marketing and social research practice*. Retrieved December 14, 2003, from http://www.esomar.org/index.php.

Homan, R. (1991). *The ethics of social research*. London: Longman House.

National Health and Medical Research Council. (2003a). *Ethical conduct in research*. Retrieved December 14, 2003, from http://www.nhmrc.gov.au/issues/researchethics.htm.

National Health and Medical Research Council. (2003b). *Human research ethics handbook*. Retrieved December 14, 2003, from http://www.nhmrc.gov.au/publications/synopses/e42syn.htm.

Polonsky, M. J. (1998). Incorporating ethics into business students' research projects: A process approach. *Journal of Business Ethics, 17*(11), 1227–1241.

Sieber, J. E. (Ed.) (1982). *The ethics of social research: Surveys and experiments*. New York: Springer-Verlag.

Skinner, S. J., Ferrell, O. C., & Dubinsky, A. J. (1988). Organizational dimensions of marketing research ethics. *Journal of Business Research, 16*, 209–223.

Smith, N. C., & Quelch, J. A. (1992). *Ethics in Marketing*. Homewood, IL: Irwin.

PART II

Undertaking the Research

6 Planning the Research Process

After laying the foundations of your research (i.e., going through the issues discussed in the first five chapters), you can commence undertaking the research, which is the topic of this part of the book. However, before you physically do the research, it is important to be aware of various issues and problems that could arise during the process and that your specific research plan takes into account these potential pitfalls. This section of the book will discuss a number of areas, including an overview of the research process (Chapter 6), the literature review, which can be a core part of the research process (Chapter 7), issues relating to data gathering (Chapter 8), the analysis of qualitative data (Chapter 9) and quantitative data (Chapter 10), and, finally, establishing recommendations from your research (Chapter 11).

This chapter will provide an overview of the process used to complete a research project. Research can be exciting and educational, as you discover new things related to your research topic. Undertaking a research project, however, can also be a daunting prospect if you try to do too many things all at once. For a research project to be successfully completed, it will be helpful if you follow a structured process. This process will take you through a number of steps with one step leading you to the next. However, there are a number of potential pitfalls that you may encounter that will also be discussed. The layout of a research proposal will also be presented, as this is the communication of what you plan to do.

Importance of Planning

Before discussing each step of the research process, it is important to mention that you need to properly plan your research project. This means determining what specific tasks you are going to do, who will do them (if you are working in a group), how they will be done, and when they will be completed. By taking the time to plan your activities, you can effectively manage your time, improve your morale and attitude toward your research, and provide a sense of security about your future research effort (Sherman, 1991).

According to Sharp and Howard (1996, p. 51), the main purposes of planning are to:

1. Clarify the aims and objectives of the researcher

2. Define the activities required to attain these aims and the order in which they take place

3. Identify various critical points or "milestones" in the research at which progress can be reviewed and the research plan reassessed

4. Produce estimates of times at which the various milestones will be reached so that progress can be clearly measured

5. Ensure that effective use is made of key resources, particularly the researchers themselves

6. Define priorities once the research is under way

7. Serve as a guide for increasing the likelihood of successful completion on time

Clearly, it is important for *any* researcher to plan. Unfortunately many, especially students and other new researchers, do not adequately plan the various steps, as they may feel that it is too time-consuming, takes too much effort, or is too restricting, or they do not know how to plan their research project (Sherman, 1991). As planning increases the likelihood of completion, it is believed that the benefits of planning will outweigh any disadvantages, especially if the project is being undertaken by a group of students. To assist in the planning of your research project, we recommend that you:

1. Draw up specific goals and put them in writing

2. Make sure your activities are achievable, especially in a given timeframe and within the limited resources available

3. Prioritize your activities so that those that are most urgent or important are given the highest priority

4. Make a commitment to your group and/or the plan and the completion of the research project with a clear timetable

5. Keep the project moving and keep writing, even if it is rewriting the literature review while waiting for the primary research to be completed

6. Be flexible—even the best plans may have to be varied to take account of unexpected changes, and replanning may be necessary

7. Focus on producing the best research project you can

If you properly plan, it will make it easier for you to complete each step of the research process and also ensure that any potential problems are considered before they eventuate.

The Research Process

As a researcher, you will need to understand the basic research process so you can clearly follow the steps to complete your research project (Page & Meyer, 2000). Although a number of authors suggest slightly different models of the research process, the basic process is the same and includes six basic steps (see Model 6.1).

When undertaking a research project, you should first define the main problem that you want to answer through your research (problem definition) and establish clear, measurable objectives to assist you in answering your problem (research objectives). You have to decide in what way you will do your research (research design) and then obtain the data (data gathering). Once you have obtained the data, you must work out what it means and interpret it to answer your objectives and the overall research problem (data analysis and interpretation). Finally, you must write up your findings and communicate them to your audience (presenting the results).

If you follow this basic process, step-by-step, you will be guaranteed to complete your research project. To better understand this process and how

Model 6.1   Six-Step Research Process

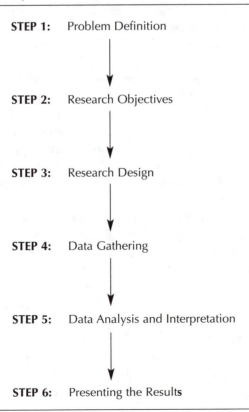

STEP 1:   Problem Definition

STEP 2:   Research Objectives

STEP 3:   Research Design

STEP 4:   Data Gathering

STEP 5:   Data Analysis and Interpretation

STEP 6:   Presenting the Results

it relates to the rest of this book, the following will discuss each step of the process.

Step 1: Problem Definition

The first step of the research process is to define the problem that is to be answered by the research. This involves "a broad statement of the general problem and identification of the specific components of the market research problem" (Malhotra et al., 2002 p. 49). This is the most important part of the process, as it provides a focus and direction for the project. If the problem is unclear and poorly defined, the result could be a lot of time and resources wasted on gathering potentially useless information and data. There is a saying in research that "a problem well defined is a problem half solved" (Churchill, 2001).

It is important to note that there can be different types of business problems, from (general) managerial problems to (specific) research problems. For example, a problem for management could be: "Should the current advertising campaign be changed?" The more specific research problem, however, would be "How effective is the current advertising campaign?" This makes the research process easier to undertake, as the problem directs the research: if, after analyzing the current advertising campaign, you find it to be effective, the campaign should *not* be changed. On the other hand, if the campaign is *not* effective, then the campaign most certainly should be changed. Therefore, when defining the research problem, it is important that the final statement allow the researcher to obtain the information needed to address the management problem and be a guide in formulating the research design (Malhotra et al., 2002, p. 63).

To assist you in defining your problem, some preliminary information gathering should be undertaken, such as interviews with industry experts, secondary data (i.e., reading the literature), and discussions with your lecturer/professor/supervisor (see Chapter 2 for more on defining the topic). Problems can occur if the research is too broad or the guidelines for the intended research are not clear, or the research is too narrow and will not provide enough information to answer the management problem. For example, in the management problem above—Should the current advertising campaign be changed?—a broad research problem might be to define the elements of successful advertising, whereas a narrow research problem might be how Monty Python humor can be used successfully in our next advertising campaign.

These research problems would most likely not be able to provide clear answers for your management problem; therefore, it is important to carefully word your research problem, even if you have to undertake some preliminary data gathering to make sure that your research problem is well defined. When the problem is clearly defined, you can then begin the next step, in which you will establish the research objectives for the project that will guide the project and assist in answering your research problem.

Step 2: Research Objectives

The second step involves the establishment of research objectives. These objectives will further assist in guiding your research project. As you will not have the time or resources to study every single aspect relating to your research problem, it is more effective for you to focus on specific objectives for the research at hand. These research objectives are the specific components of the research problem that you will be working to answer or complete in order to answer the overall research problem (Churchill, 2001). It is, therefore, important that the research objectives are clear and achievable, and that they will directly assist in answering the research problem.

Students and academics frequently use the following three terms to define their research: research question, research objectives, and research hypotheses. These terms need to be considered as different levels of detail associated with the project. The critical issue for you is to make sure that you have thought about each of these, although in a given project all three might not be used. For example, in an exploratory research project, if you are looking at what various factors might make businesses switch suppliers, you may have only a broad research objective, rather than a specific question or testable hypothesis. However, in some cases, your project may have all three.

In considering what is needed for your research, the most important point is to realize that all of these—research question, research objectives, and research hypotheses—can be used to guide your research. As you progress in your research, you should be able to use each of these (question, objectives, and hypotheses) to direct you to examine the particular issue. Therefore, though many interesting points and issues can be included in a research project, revising the question, objectives, and hypotheses will ensure that you do not include material that is not necessary to your project. This will unnecessarily use up your valuable time and energy, and may distract the reader, thus detracting from the work. Focus is the key, especially given that reviewing tangential issues or collecting related information uses valuable resources (time and possibly money).

The research question is focused and allows you to identify the specific information you will look at in the project, for example, what organizational policies can be implemented to reduce employee turnover. In this way, the research question is more specific than the broad research objective.

The research objectives are different, as these set out what your research will examine and what issues the project will cover. This statement is frequently broad, but needs to be sufficiently focused to provide you with direction. The objectives should be written as a statement regarding an action you are about to undertake, using the word "to" (e.g., "to discover . . . ," "to determine . . . ," "to ascertain . . . ," "to establish . . . ," etc.). This can be applied to the evaluation of whether a company's current employment practices should be changed in the following way: "The objective of the research is to determine why employees are leaving the firm."

Research hypotheses are even more focused. They provide the specific answers to questions that the research will examine often in an empirical way. You will ultimately demonstrate that the research hypothesis is rejected or not rejected (one cannot prove that relationships exist). Your hypothesis might, for example, be that employees will leave the firm if they believe there are no internal advancement opportunities. Hypotheses are particularly useful in quantitative research, where there is statistical analysis, such as surveys or experiments, and where the researcher has a good knowledge of the variables and wants to determine any relationship between the variables.

You need to clearly understand which type of activity—research question, research objectives, or research hypothesis—you are focusing on in your research project, as it will direct your activities. It is also critical that whichever you are using—objectives, questions, or hypotheses—that this is clearly communicated to your reader, so they will understand exactly what your project is attempting to achieve and that at the end of the project you will be able to clearly state your findings as an answer to the project's objectives.

Step 3: Research Design

The third step involves deciding on the correct research design for the project. The research design is the "framework or blueprint" for collecting the information needed for your project in the best possible way (Malhotra et al., 2002). The correct design will save resources and is also essential in allowing you to undertake valid and reliable research (Hedrick, Bickman, & Rog, 1993). There are three main designs: exploratory, descriptive, and causal research.

Exploratory research provides insights into, and an understanding of, the problem confronting the researcher. Often, this is used when the researcher does not have enough information on a topic and wants the flexibility to explore the issue. Methodologies include secondary data and qualitative research, such as expert interviews and focus groups.

Descriptive research "describes" certain characteristics, or functions, that management is likely to be interested in, such as market conditions, customers' opinions, purchase behavior, and so forth. The researcher often has some prior knowledge of the topic and uses a fairly structured approach to gather the information. Methodologies include surveys, diary panels, and observation.

Causal research is designed to examine the cause-and-effect relationships of certain variables that affect the problem. These are quite structured in their design, and the researcher would have a very good knowledge of the variables and the issues involved, and, therefore, the skills needed may be more advanced than those possessed by some undergraduate students. The primary method of this type of research is experimentation in which hypotheses are tested (Churchill, 2001).

We believe that there may also be a fourth type of research: definitional research. This type of research seeks to define the domain of issues and is frequently used in developing ways to measure a given phenomenon. For example, when researchers examine service quality, they frequently undertake a preliminary phase of research to identify how service quality should be measured in a given service experience. The first phase is thus to define service quality, and the information from this definition is then used as a variable in the study (Zeithamal, Parasuraman, & Barry, 1990). In other works, developing definitions is the sole purpose of the study, and some empirical techniques, such as factor analysis or even reliability testing, are concerned with defining variables of interest. It is unlikely that your research will focus on developing definitions, but definitional research may be a key part of the research process.

The decision of which design to use can totally depend on the nature of the research project or what is expected by your lecturer/professor/supervisor. For example, if you want to know customers' opinions of your brand, a descriptive design is used with a survey being distributed to customers. In other cases, you may use multiple approaches with one serving to redefine those following later. For example, Churchill's (1979) seminal research paradigm suggests that exploratory research might be needed before descriptive or casual research is undertaken. Once you have decided on which research design to undertake for your project, you can then develop the collection method and gather the data.

Step 4: Data Gathering

The fourth step is the gathering, or collecting, of the data. The procedures used to obtain the data vary depending on the research design chosen and the source of the data. This step is a key part of the research process and often represents the biggest cost of the research (Weller & Romney, 1988). This issue is covered in depth in Chapter 8. There are two main sources of data:

1. Primary data (data originated by the researcher for the specific purpose of addressing the research problem)

2. Secondary data (data collected for some purpose other than the problem at hand)

It is very important that secondary data be undertaken first, as this can provide invaluable background information that can be used to define the project, develop objectives, and specify the correct methodology. This data can be accessed internally (within an organization) or externally (from private organizations and the government in the form of published materials, computer databases, and syndicated sources) (Malhotra et al., 2002). Secondary data will be discussed further in Chapter 8. With the assistance of secondary data, primary data can then be gathered.

Primary data can be qualitative or quantitative. Qualitative research methods are "techniques involving small numbers of respondents who provide information about their thoughts and feelings that are not easily projected to the whole population" (Dillon, Madden, & Firtle, 1993, p. 134). These include in-depth interviews, focus groups, projective techniques, and observational methods. Qualitative methods effectively allow the researcher significant insights into the feelings of individuals who are in their sample group, but the drawback is that results are not projectable (qualitative data analysis is discussed in more detail in Chapter 9). Quantitative research methods, on the other hand, are techniques that are designed to generate information using statistical analysis that can be projected to represent the population as a whole. These include surveys (personal, telephone, electronic, and mail), observation, and experimentation. Quantitative data analysis is discussed in Chapter 10.

When it comes to gathering data, the two main objectives are (a) to maximize the relevant information and (b) to minimize errors (Luck & Rubin, 1987). Though all data collected may be valuable in some way, certain collection methods are more suitable in particular situations than others. Often, it will depend on the research problem as to exactly what type of data should be collected and analyzed. As has been mentioned previously, data gathering and the issue of errors in research will be discussed in Chapter 8.

It is important to note that data gathering is crucial to the research process and the success of your research project. All of the research and planning effort so far is of little use if the data is incorrectly collected or the respondents fail to cooperate. One educational reason that a research project is assigned to you is so that you can develop practical skills in data gathering. The next step in the research process is to analyze and interpret the data.

Step 5: Data Analysis and Interpretation

The fifth step is the analysis and interpretation of the data that was gathered. Again, the procedures used to analyze the data will vary depending on the research design chosen and the data gathered (Churchill, 2001). Analysis of data from qualitative research is very different from the more statistical analysis of quantitative data (see Chapters 9 and 10). You will most likely not be expected to have a complete understanding of *all* the possible techniques for analyzing the data for your project, but it is expected that you can logically and competently analyze and interpret the data that you have gathered with appropriate techniques. The interpretation of the analysis will bring out the meaning of the data and convert the data into useful information. This will give you the information to answer your research objectives and overall research problem (and satisfy the requirements of the project). Once the data has been analyzed, clear recommendations can be established based on the current research (see Chapter 11). To communicate the whole process you must be able to present your research findings, the final step in the research process.

Step 6: Presenting the Results

The sixth step of the research process is the presenting of the results of the research. You may have done an excellent job in planning your research, gathering your data, and analyzing the data, but all your work can be wasted if you cannot effectively communicate your research results (which is the focus of the third part of this book). Again, this is a key skill to be developed during the course of your research project (Page & Meyer, 2000). The results can be presented in a written form, in a report, or in an oral form, in a presentation. Reports are particularly important as they (a) present the results in an organized and permanent form; (b) reflect the quality of research; and (c) increase the likelihood of action (Luck & Rubin, 1987). You need to develop effective communication skills to ensure the research has been properly completed and the results are understood by the targeted audience (i.e., your lecturer/professor/supervisor or the business you are undertaking the project for). Discussions regarding written reports and oral presentations are presented in Chapters 13 and 14.

Once these steps have been followed, the result should be a completed research project, but it may not be as easy as it seems. Things may change—resources may become unavailable, data may be inefficient, group members may disappear, and so forth—so it is vital to keep an eye on the situation and effectively manage the research process. The following chapters in this book will provide some detailed assistance to help you to the successful completion of a research project. To assist you in the planning stage of your project, it is important to prepare a research proposal, which sets out a plan of your research project.

Research Proposal

When you have decided on the overall research process for your project, a research proposal discussing each step should be written. This presents the planned activities for the project in a written form and serves as a contract or agreement between the researcher and the client, the researcher and the supervisor, or the individual members in the research group. It describes what is planned for each part of the project's research process and includes proposed costs and time estimates. One way to think of the proposal is that it is a road map of the research process that you could give to someone else for them to be able to effectively complete the project. The layout of a research proposal includes the following:

1. **Title page:** A clear title page is important for any business report. This should include a title that clearly summarizes your research project, the name(s) of the researcher(s), the name of supervisor or client, and the date the proposal was submitted.

2. **Introduction:** This introduces the reader to the proposal by justifying the overall research project, setting the scope of the project, and explaining each section of the proposal report to the reader.

3. **Research problem/objectives:** As the research problem is the first, and most vital, step in the project's research process, a clear statement of the research problem must be presented. A clarification of components of the statement may be added to assist in the understanding of the problem and the approach the project will take. Statements presenting the objectives and/or hypotheses should also be made, as well as an explanation of how answering the objectives will then answer the overall research problem.

4. **Prior research/background:** Though a detailed literature review will be prepared later for the project's report, some preliminary reporting of areas of secondary data should be made. This may include a general background of the topic, main articles/books on the topic, and specific research studies that may influence how the present research will be undertaken.

5. **Methodology:** The proposal must clearly set out what method you are going to use to gather and analysize the data. You should discuss the techniques that will be used to collect the data in the project (e.g., personal survey, content analysis, etc.) and include an explanation of why this is the most suitable method to answer your research problem/objectives. In some cases, there will be two different methodologies, as the project may involve qualitative data collection that is followed by quantitative data collection.

6. **Data analysis:** To assist in the planning of your project, it is critical that you consider how you will analyze the data and interpret it (some people may put this material in methodology). The approach used will differ significantly depending on whether the data is qualitative or quantitative, and on the type of questions that may be presented to people. Discussion of the analysis techniques serves several purposes: (a) It ensures that you collect the right kind of data, and (b) it allows you time to learn about the techniques used. In many cases, it has been found that students collect data and then do not know how to use the techniques they identified in their proposal. The analysis section may also discuss why the approach selected is most appropriate.

7. **Time and cost estimates:** A common issue with research projects is the complaint that there is not enough time or money to complete it the way the researcher would like. In the proposal, there should be definite (and achievable) statements on the time and costs it will take to satisfactorily complete the project. This should include a tentative timetable (sometimes referred to as a Gantt chart) presenting the various activities and by whom and when they should be undertaken.

This forces you to carefully consider what needs to occur and when. One trick for developing this timetable is to work backward, that is, begin with the data that is needed for the research to be completed, and then give yourself time to write the report, and so forth. Unfortunately, it sometimes becomes apparent that you are trying to do too much within the allocated time, and so you may have to reconsider your activities or the time allotted for particular activities.

It is also important to develop a budget for the project. There are various costs that are often not considered, and you need to think about costs such as travel, phone calls, photocopying, and printing. For a group project, an agreement, preferably written, should be made for payment of any expenses to be spread among group members equally.

8. **Conclusion:** The proposal should conclude with a basic summary of the project and a statement to keep to the plan set out in the proposal. This section will indicate an intention to complete the project as planned. In some group projects, individual members have signed at the end of this section to indicate that there is an agreement among all members that they will do their best to complete the project as planned in the research proposal (see Chapter 4 for a discussion of the group contract).

9. **Bibliography:** The full details of all sources of information (e.g., books, articles, reports) that were directly referred to in the body of the proposal, such as in the Prior Research or Methodology and Data Analysis sections, should be presented in the bibliography. References should be made in a consistent and correct manner (see Chapter 7). In some cases, your lecturer/professor/supervisor will want you to list other materials that will be used as well, thus broadening the scope of the bibliography.

Conclusion

This chapter has looked at the importance of planning your research for a successful completion of your project and presented a six-step research process. This process simply shows the sequence that should be followed when undertaking a research project. The progression of steps is as follows: problem definition → research objectives → research design → data gathering → data analysis → presenting the results. Many decisions have to be made throughout the course of this process and they must be managed carefully, taking care to ensure a successful completion of the research project with a clear, logical written report.

The following chapters will discuss some of the issues mentioned in this chapter in more detail and guide you on your way to successfully completing your research project.

References

Churchill, G. A. (1979). Paradigm for developing better measures of marketing constructs. *Journal of Marketing Research, 29*(1), 23–38.

Churchill, G. A. (1991). *Marketing research: Methodological foundation.* Chicago: Dryden Press.

Churchill, G. A. (2001). *Basic marketing research.* Chicago: Dryden Press.

Dillon, W. R, Madden, T. J., & Firtle, N. H. (1993). *Essentials of marketing research.* Homewood, IL: Richard Irwin.

Hedrick, T. E., Bickman, L., & Rog, D. J. (1993). *Applied research design: A practical guide.* Newbury Park, CA: Sage.

Luck, D. J., & Rubin, R. S. (1987). *Marketing research.* Englewood Cliffs, NJ: Prentice Hall.

Malhotra, N. K., Hall, J., Shaw, M., & Oppenheim, P. (2002). *Marketing research: An applied orientation.* Sydney: Pearson Education.

Page, C., & Meyer, D. (2000). *Applied research design for business and management.* Sydney: Irwin/McGraw-Hill.

Sharp, J. A., & Howard, K. (1996). *The management of a student research project.* Aldershot, UK: Gower.

Sherman, J. R. (1991). *Productive planning: How to get more done.* London: Kogan Page.

Weller, S. C., & Romney, A. K. (1988). *Systematic data collection.* Newbury Park, CA: Sage.

Zeithamal, V. A., Parasuraman, A., & Barry, L. L. (1990). *Delivering quality service: Balancing customer perceptions and expectations.* New York: The Free Press.

7

Literature Review

This chapter will discuss how you can use literature within your research project. The level of literature input, like most things discussed within this book, will vary based on the focus of your specific research project. Substantial pieces of research will usually require the incorporation of more literature than smaller research projects. However, even applied research projects may require a review of the relevant industry literature.

It is important to define what a literature review is before discussing issues associated with developing one. Cooper (1989) suggests that there are, in fact, two different types of literature review. The first type is an integrated research review, which examines the previous work in the area and identifies the existing relationships among variables, which leads to identifying issues that have not been considered. The second type of review is a theoretical review that examines the various theories that have been put forward and puts forward an argument as to which is most relevant. It might also be suggested that there is also a more general background review of the literature as well, which will give insights into the issue or industry being examined. What is clear from all types of review is that you should examine what has been written previously and learn from the earlier work in the area. As will be discussed later in this chapter, literature can provide you with valuable insights into a number of aspects of your research.

What Is a Literature Review?

In almost *all* cases, there has been extensive previous work related to your research area/topic. If this is not the case, then you may be trying to research something too innovative, at least in terms of a student research project. There will usually be earlier industry and academic material written that will be directly related to your topic. For example, if you are looking at consumers' adoption of new technology, there are many studies that consider this issue. However, there will also be a substantial amount of literature that is tangentially related to your project. For example, work related to individuals' level of risk adversity might reveal an influence on whether they adopt new technology and, therefore, might have some relevance to your project.

In many cases, there will not be an exact fit between what has been written in the past and your research. This does not mean that there is no relevant literature, but rather that you may be applying ideas from areas in a slightly different way. For example, a group of students examining males' motivations for gift giving at Valentine's Day found literature on gift giving, but none of this related specifically to Valentine's Day. Many links could be drawn between the students' area of interest and the previous literature, even though there was not anything exactly related to their topic.

One of the most critical steps in *any* process of a literature review is to define what areas of the literature should be examined. Sharp and Howard (1996) suggest that you should design a relevance tree for research. Such a diagram allows you to visually map out how issues relate to one another. It allows you to (a) identify all the relevant issues or theories associated with your project; (b) visually present how issues relate to one another; and (c) prioritize areas requiring further examination. This last stage is important, as there may be some areas that only need to be briefly discussed in a project, and so you do not need an extensive review of all literature within the area. A relevance tree, therefore, gives you the ability to maintain focus and ensure that your project does not encompass too much.

There is one other question that you will have to ask yourself in relation to your literature review: How much literature is enough? This question can be complicated and, like most issues in this book, depends on the focus of your research project. On a pragmatic level, you need to ask yourself how many references you need to cite. There is no simple answer, as you need to ensure that your literature clearly covers all relevant issues. This frequently requires that you have all the recent material on the topic as well as the seminal (i.e., leading) historical material. For example, if you are looking at the globalization of the marketing mix, there are many relatively recent articles on this topic. However, it might be appropriate to include Ted Levitt's (1983) seminal work in this area, as he is often credited with popularizing the idea of globalization.

In determining when you have enough literature, refer back to the specifics of the assignment. If this is not specified, you might ask your professor/lecturer, who may simply suggest that your coverage should be comprehensive, that is, that it should cover all important topic areas. In this case, you might focus on the most recent material (say the last 5 years) as well as selectively incorporate important earlier works. One way to identify if something is important is to see how many of the recent references refer to it. That is, if everyone refers to Levitt (1983), then you might want to incorporate it, indicating that it is included because it is an important piece of work. You need to be careful that you do not confuse being comprehensive (i.e., citing the relevant literature from appropriate areas) with being exhaustive (i.e., citing everything written on a given topic). There are very few situations in which an exhaustive review would be required for a student's research project.

Another issue that needs to be addressed is the type of balance should you achieve between academic and business/popular references. One simple way to distinguish between the two is that academic works traditionally use references, but the more important identification of an academic text is usually that it has been reviewed by others within the area. This does not mean that academic works have to be purely theoretical. For example, the *Harvard Business Review* or *Sloan Management Review* both publish material concerning applied business practices and would usually be classified as academic, whereas *Marketing News, Advertising Age,* or the *Wall Street Journal* would be considered more popular or professional in nature. Referencing of popular/ professional publications can be very useful, especially for providing examples or generating ideas to research. However, in most student research projects, these popular/professional materials should not be the sole source of materials on which you develop your research project, unless your topic concerns applications of practice. Even in this case, however, you should be able to find some academic material related to your topic as well.

As will be discussed in Chapter 13, "Writing the Report," you should clearly state early on in the discussion of the literature exactly what you are going to do, that is, tell your teacher/lecturer/professor, as well as external readers, how you have selected the literature you have. In this way, they will better understand why some things are included and why other things are not included. One must be very careful because it may be easy to get information overload (i.e., by trying to be exhaustive). Citing too much literature, especially if you try to cover all related issues, *can* sometimes become confusing for you and the reader. Therefore, it is important to ensure that the material is focused and relevant to your project.

How Can Literature Be Used?

Many types of reports will have a section specifically discussing literature related to your project. However, literature can, in fact, assist you with many different parts of your research project (Cooper, 1989). These will be discussed in the following subsections.

Selecting a Topic

In some cases, you will have the opportunity to select a research topic that is of interest to you. Some students in this situation have difficulty deciding what to look at. One way to overcome this problem is to look through the literature or business press and identify a topic that is of interest and meets the requirements of your assignment. For example, if you are having trouble thinking of a topic, you might read recent journals, business publications, or even your textbooks, looking for issues or questions that you think are worth investigating further. Reading the recent academic literature might identify issues that are popular in the academic arena. However, the popular or professional press might also identify issues that are particularly relevant for businesses currently. Though these issues are often very applied in nature, they are sometimes too new and thus don't necessarily have sufficient academic literature to support them. For example, in the early 1990s, some students might have seen the growing interest in e-commerce as an opportunity for research, but the limited academic literature in the area would have made this a difficult one for most undergraduate research projects.

Background

There are two ways in which literature can be used in discussing the background of a project. First, the literature can set the rationale for examining the issue, whereby you would draw on previous literature identifying the area as warranting further examination. In doing this, you *may* be more likely to draw on the practitioner or popular literature, with the framing of the issue to take place in a Background or Introduction section.

Second, a Background can also overview the previous literature in the area (i.e., a traditional literature review). In doing this, you would identify and discuss the relevant literature, focusing on the body of academic work in the area. This discussion can be lengthy and would vary depending on the issues being covered and the depth required, as previously discussed in relation to a literature review tree. In focusing on literature in this way, you would tend to pull together the arguments, theories, and results as discussed in the literature and summarize them. It is also beneficial to identify any gaps in the previous works. These could identify that some issues or variables have not been fully considered. In this way, you tell the reader what has and has not been done in the literature, and where your research will fit in this body of knowledge.

Setting Research Questions and/or Hypotheses

You might also use literature to develop your research question and/or hypothesis. This would build directly on the evaluation of the literature in the Background section and may, in fact, appear in an earlier section to be justified within the Background section. The literature will suggest that various relationships should (or should not) exist, and you should not be surprised if in many cases the literature is inconclusive. Thus, you can use the literature to suggest that in a given situation the relationships will (or will not) exist and even specify factors that may affect or moderate any relationships. In using the literature in this way, the research questions or hypotheses are created out of the discussion. For example, "given the previous inconsistencies in the literature, this research will examine if these relationships exist when evaluating students at one university."

Methodology

One of the most useful roles of a literature review is to identify how previous researchers have examined an issue, although this is frequently overlooked in student research. There is no need to "reinvent the wheel," and using methods, instruments, or processes that have been used before is often considered to add validity to the results, although this is not always the case. In some situations, for example, in a marketing research project, you might be explicitly expected to develop a survey instrument to examine your area of study. A methodological review of the literature is, therefore, a worthwhile task and might even be a separate component of your overall review (i.e., a separate branch on your review tree). Using the literature to support the research approach used frequently is expected and provides a strong justification for undertaking the project in a given way.

It might also be useful to examine the literature in relation to components of the methodology, although this might be more applicable for substantial research projects than for minor works. For example, there is extensive literature available on techniques for improving survey responses, including the effectiveness of monetary incentives (Gunn & Rhodes, 1981), different colors of paper (Jobber & Sanderson, 1983), different types of contact (e.g., telephone or mail) (Shosteck & Fairweather, 1979), and a range of other factors including techniques associated with Internet surveys (Chittenden & Rettie, 2003). There is also available literature examining specific types of procedures or analyses, which should be considered particularly with more complex/substantial projects. For example, when using content analysis, there are several procedures to determine whether judges agree (Perreault & Leigh, 1989; Rust & Cooil, 1994). These materials will assist you in ensuring that any research undertaken considers critical issues.

Analysis

Once you have undertaken the analysis developed in the methodology section, you can use the literature to assist in interpreting the results. Are your results as expected? Were hypotheses accepted or rejected? In this section, literature can be especially helpful if the results are inconsistent with previous findings. This does not mean that your work is incorrect, but the literature may in fact suggest reasons to justify why your results differed from those anticipated. For example, there are many situations in which researchers use a survey instrument developed in one country and within a second country they find that the results differ. This might simply mean that the instrument and/or relationships are not generalizable across countries. In examining differences between the countries in more detail, there may be many cultural reasons that this occurs (Polonsky, Donoho, & Cohen, 1996).

Of course, if your results are consistent with the previous literature, this may strengthen the discussion and implications of your work. Depending on what relationships or issues you are examining, this may lend support to the argument that the results are generalizable across time, industries, segments, or countries, which provides more support for the relevance of results, although this type of discussion would apply more to academically focused research than to applied research.

Where to Obtain Literature

Previously, it was mentioned that there are a number of different types of sources for literature. Many of the items identified are fairly straightforward, and you will be well aware of all relevant issues. One area, electronic literature, is of particular interest, and there will be more time spent discussing its use, as well as potential problems associated with it.

Books and Journals

There are vast numbers of books and academic journals available to you. It is sometimes quite amazing how much has been written on a given topic. There are highly academic books and journals, and there are more applied books and journals. At the most basic level, there is your textbook, which refers to a diverse range of other materials. In most cases, it is inappropriate to rely solely on your textbook for your research, especially when these books frequently refer to an extensive amount of other literature.

Technology has made finding relevant books and journals substantially easier. For example, most universities have computerized card catalogs that allow students to locate relevant books on a topic based on a few keywords that they input. There are a number of similar electronic systems that allow students to search journals as well. One such system is called ABI/Inform. It allows students to search using a range of keywords or author names. It also allows students to limit their searches to keyworks or titles and to combine searches. These systems provide references, abstracts, in some cases the full text of the article, or even a "picture" of the article (i.e., a .pdf file).

Students sometimes suggest that one of the greatest limitations of these systems is that they frequently include references for articles that are not available in their full text, but only appear in hard copy, and that the journals referred to are not held in the their university's library. The inclusion of an increasing amount of full-text material overcomes this problem to some extent. However, in some cases, more recent works have time-based embargoes (i.e., the latest materials are not available for 6 months to a year).

In some cases, materials on electronic databases do not include pictures, figures, diagrams, and so forth, although .pdf versions of these materials would.

Another useful database that can be used in undertaking a literature review related to academic journals is the *Social Sciences Citation Index*. This index has several parts, two of which are particularly useful. One provides a list of references used in articles from journals included in the database. If you want to see what articles Smith referred to in a particular work published in the year xxxx, you look up Smith (xxxx). If this work was published in one of the indexed journals, it will tell you all the references Smith used. Alternatively, if you are looking for people who have referenced Smith (xxxx), there is another part of the index that will tell you who has referred to this work. This latter listing is very useful, especially if you want to see how others have applied one author's work.

Electronic Databases

The range of electronic databases available today is indeed mind-boggling. There are databases that focus on very narrowly defined topics and others that cover a wide spectrum of materials across disciplines. Just as the databases vary, so do the materials, which can include academic journals, conference papers, books, professional magazines, governmental reports, industry association reports, newspaper stories, current events magazines, and even abstracts of PhD dissertations.

Each institution will subscribe to a different range of databases, which students and staff usually access freely or for a nominal charge. In other cases, it is possible to actually search some databases and pay for what you want to read (i.e., a user-pays system). Databases are growing in popularity as a range of sources are realizing that the material is valuable. For example, for a price, one can search through the archives of the *New York Times* and pay to read/download older materials of interest.

Government and Industry

One important tool for undertaking a literature review is the use of government and industry reports. These materials are usually especially useful for identifying statistics about various issues. It is truly amazing how much information is available freely from these sources, although some reports are sold at a nominal price. Finding what reports exist is, in itself, a somewhat complex task. In some countries, governmental printing offices have catalogs of their materials. In some cases, these are also included on larger databases, or the bodies may have databases of their own on the topics. There are also a number of international governmental bodies that produce a range of information freely or at low cost. These include the United Nations, World Bank, International Monetary Fund, and Organisation for

Economic Co-operation and Development (OECD), not to mention all the various private associations and foundations that provide information on issues. It should be noted that in many cases, these bodies provide only summaries of reports for free, and individuals have to purchase complete reports, which are sometimes very expensive.

One of the problems with using associations is that it is sometimes difficult to track down the relevant associations, although in many cases these can be located using the Internet. In addition, many governmental bodies and associations provide a list of other relevant bodies; therefore, one group may lead you to another. The use of the Web has made finding associations and governmental bodies much easier.

The Internet

As has been mentioned earlier, the Internet has made secondary research material much easier to locate. Most of you will have searched the Web using one of the many available Web search engines, such as Yahoo, Netscape, or Lycos. These tools are in many ways quite simplistic, that is, they search a directory of Web sites and look for the use of key terms that Web designers assign to the sites in the meta-text associated with the site (a discussion of meta-text is well beyond this book). "Many information professionals suggest that it may be necessary to use as many as 12 key terms to sufficiently limit a search to a manageable amount of information" (Kent, 2001, p. 26). Therefore, though there is extensive information on the Web, finding the right information is not necessarily an easy task.

An overreliance on the Web alone is inappropriate for undertaking a literature review, although it may be a useful support device. It seems that students sometimes forget that anyone can set up a Web page and say anything they want within the relevant legal limits. Identifying the appropriateness of information on the Web is thus a difficult problem that needs to be dealt with. You should always question the extent to which the source is credible and whether the information presented has any inherent bias. For example, an article on sustainable business practices on Greenpeace's Web page might have a very different perspective from one using the same data that appears in an academic article. There are several problems with using Web-based material. These include the following:

1. Information overload—too much information may be identified in the search and, in many cases, much of it will be tangential to the topic.

2. Information accuracy—anyone can put anything on the Web; thus, there may be a question of its accuracy, or in the case of corporate-based information, it may be biased to represent a given perspective. This problem is often overcome with academic journals, as they have been peer reviewed in an attempt to provide the most accurate information.

3. Limited breadth of coverage—much academic and professional information will be overlooked, unless you explicitly search one of the various databases, as one undertaking a word search on Google or Yahoo will most likely miss important articles.

4. Information moves or sites change—as distinct from an article in a journal or trade publication, the information on the Web often changes quickly. For example, a very useful Web report may cease to be accessible. Thus, it is difficult to refer back to the information unless the individual has a hard copy of it. This causes unique referencing problems, which will be examined below.

You must use the Internet with caution, especially when you are basing an entire research project on Web-based information, which does not include specific database searching. Of course, this is not to suggest that all information on the Internet is inappropriate. The Internet provides an extremely useful research tool in conjunction with other types of information.

How to Write a Literature Review

All the material in this chapter has been designed to explain the role of a literature review. One question often asked is "how do I actually write a review?" This question will now be addressed. As was mentioned earlier, literature can be used in several places within a research project. The focus in this section will be on discussing how to write a review in which the research questions/hypotheses are developed.

The goal of this type of review is to identify the critical issues in the literature. In many cases, you will not only identify how arguments have developed within the area, but you will also discuss how different authors' works complement one another, as well as how they can disagree. Doing this is not an easy task; many students (and academics, for that matter) frequently report on divergent studies without drawing links between authors' works. For example, if you were looking at sponsorship literature, it would be important to identify how various authors define sponsorship and what the differences in definitions mean. This demonstrates an understanding of material and that some synthesis has taken place. One flaw that is often seen in students' work is that they simply list definitions without linking them together. Thus, no deeper understanding of the previous works occurs, which is ultimately part of the aim of most research projects. Providing extensive references or quotations does not add value on its own; it is the interpretation and linkages that add the value.

It is also usually important to present alternative views and/or discuss disagreements in the literature. For example, in discussing the development of corporate responsibility, you would need to discuss varying perspectives, including the idea that "the business of business is business," and thus corporations should not be responsible unless there is direct measurable return to the firm. Presenting the fact that some people do not believe an issue is relevant is essential in demonstrating that you have read widely on the topic and also that views on the topic are not universally accepted. Further, it is imperative that you somehow justify which perspective you believe to be the most appropriate one or at least why you are selecting the one that you plan to use. In doing this, you are basically developing an argument using the literature.

One very useful tool to assist in developing your literature review is to put together a table of the relevant pieces of work. These tables can be quite complex, depending on the issue you are examining. You might want to provide a listing of how your topic has evolved. In this case, you might simply list the author(s), year, and key arguments/findings (for an example of this, see Mitchell, Agle, & Wood, 1997). It may be possible to use this table of literature to identify themes (for example, see Cornwell & Maignan, 1998). There are, of course, a range of other structures tables could take to identify different methodologies used or to look at different relationships that were examined in the previous literature. The use of a table adds some structure for you and the reader. However, if you do choose to use a table to structure your literature or part of the literature, it is essential that you explain the structure to be used, how articles were selected (as you will most likely never be able to include everything), and the years that this is designed to cover. Setting these parameters ensures that your reader understands exactly what you are doing and why.

As indicated at the start of this section, the focus is on writing a literature review that develops the research's focus, as well as hypotheses, if these exist. All relationships to be examined should be readily apparent in your literature review. For example, if there are competing views on an issue, you might suggest that your research will examine which is most appropriate in your situation. The literature might suggest that there are moderating variables that have not been considered previously and that you will look at these. In this case, you are looking at a gap in the literature. Whatever your research focus, the literature provides some justification that what you are looking at makes sense and that this is not simply unfocused research (sometimes called a fishing trip), unless that is the objective of the project.

Referencing

It is essential for you to appropriately reference others' ideas, that is, to give credit where credit is due. This means citing and quoting people within the body of the report as you refer to their work and providing a comprehensive list of materials referenced. Referencing of material serves several purposes. As was mentioned earlier, it can be used to assist in supporting your arguments. It also acknowledges the ideas of others and allows the reader to refer back to the original source, should they want to. Because of this, when providing references, it is important that as much relevant information as possible is provided.

Though there are a number of different referencing styles available, all of them provide information on the author, year the material was published, title of the work, title of publication, volume and issue of the publication, and page numbers. Other information *may* also be provided depending on the material being referred to. For example, an edited book would also contain the name of the book editors, the publisher, and the place of publication. The specifics of the various styles (i.e., ordering of information and punctuation used) vary, although the same information is presented consistently across different reference styles. Though you may think that the references are not important, in some cases those grading your research will look at the references before they even read your paper to see what body of literature you have based your work on. Also, poor referencing reflects a poor effort in report writing to the reader, and readers may then begin to question your ideas as well.

There are several systems for organizing and presenting references, and we will mention several of these briefly, as well as refer to specific style guides or other relevant sources that are commonly used. There are two issues related to references: (a) how to acknowledge the ideas of others within the body of the paper, and (b) compiling a comprehensive list of references. The answers to these problems vary depending on whether you are required to have a Reference section or a Bibliography at the end of the project, *or* if you have to use footnotes.

When dealing with material in the body of your project, it is important to identify others' contributions. Therefore, if you are referring to the components of Sheth's (1973) model of Industrial Buying Behavior, you might say the following:

- Within Sheth's (1973) model of industrial buying behavior, there are four major components.
- In some models of industrial buying behavior, there are a number of influencing factors (Sheth, 1973).
- Sheth (1973, p. 50) has suggested that . . .

In some cases, you might not include author names within the text of the paper but rather refer to authors in footnotes or use numbers that refer to materials included in the references. For example, in some models of industrial buying behavior, there are a number of influencing factors.[1] The superscript would refer to a footnote/endnote or to a citation in the references, and the details of the material would be expanded on in the footnote or citation. For the above example, this would state:

1. Sheth, J. N. (1973). A model of industrial buying behavior. *Journal of Marketing, 37*(4), 50–56.

While the footnoting format is often taught in high school, it is less often used in university-level research projects in business areas, although this may vary by institution and subject. For example, referencing within the legal subjects often utilizes footnotes rather than referencing. If you are required to use footnoting for references, you can refer to guides such as *The Bluebook* (1991) for the specifics required.

In most cases, there will be a reference list at the end of the report/project. As was mentioned earlier, there are many different styles of referencing that are used at different institutions, and each system has an extensive style guide identifying how to acknowledge almost every type of material imaginable. Two popular style guides are the *Publication Manual of the American Psychological Association* (APA, 1994) and *The Chicago Manual of Style* (1993). You should refer to the relevant guide to see exactly how materials should be referenced. Within this book, we have used a version of the APA style of referencing.

The format for citing a book is often: Author's Name (year). *Book Title.* City Published: Publisher. For example,

Miller, Kenneth E., and Roger A. Layton (2000). *Fundamentals of marketing, fourth edition.* Sydney: McGraw-Hill.

The format for citing a journal article is often: Author's Name (year). Article Title, *Journal Name,* volume (number): pages. For example,

Waller, David S. (1999). Attitudes towards offensive advertising: An Australian study, *Journal of Consumer Marketing,* 16 (3): 288–294.

Earlier, the use of electronic publications was discussed. There are unique issues associated with referencing these materials. In fact, there are a number of style guides specifically developed to address referencing electronic publications (Tonella, 2000). Some of these are linked to the style guides discussed above (APA, 2000), and others are proposed as independent guidelines (Li & Crane, 1993). As with referencing hard copy material, the critical issue is to ensure that you are as complete as possible so that your lecturer/professor can refer to the original material should he or she wish to do so. One unique characteristic of referencing electronic materials is that the date on which they were accessed is sometimes included, as Web addresses change. For example:

Macdonald, Emma & Sharp, Byron (1996). Management Perceptions of the Importance of Brand Awareness as an Indication of Advertising Effectiveness. *Marketing Research On-Line,* [*Internet*], 1, pp. 1–15. Available from: http://msc.city.unisa.edu.au/msc/JEMS/Pubs/mr_online/aware/aware.html. Accessed on January 10, 2004.

Finally, it is important that you check with your supervisor to find out if there is a particular style that he or she would prefer or one that is recommended by the school. Proper referencing of your project report *is* important, and it does reflect on the quality of the report.

References

American Psychological Association. (1994). *Publication manual of the American Psychological Association, 4th Ed.* Washington, DC: APA.

American Psychological Association (APA). (2000). *Electronic reference formats recommended by the American Psychological Association.* Retrieved May 4, 2000, from http://www.apa.org/journals/webref.html.

The Bluebook: A uniform system of citation, 5th Ed. (1991). Cambridge, MA: The Harvard Law Review Association.

The Chicago manual of style, 14th Ed. (1993). Chicago: University of Chicago Press.

Chittenden, L., & Rettie, R. (2003). An evaluation of e-mail marketing and factors affecting response. *Journal of Targeting, Measurement and Analysis for Marketing, 11*(3), 203–217.

Cooper, H. M. (1989). *Integrating research: A guide for literature reviews.* Newbury Park, CA: Sage.

Cornwell, T. B., & Maignan, I. (1998). An international review of sponsorship research. *Journal of Advertising, 27*(1), 1–21.

Gunn, W. J., & Rhodes, I. N. (1981). Physician response rates to a telephone survey: Effects of monetary incentive level. *Public Opinion Quarterly, 45*(1), 109–115.

Jobber, D., & Sanderson, S. (1983). The effects of a prior letter and coloured questionnaire paper on mail survey response rates. *Journal of the Market Research Society, 25*(4), 339–349.

Kent, M. L. (2001). Essential tips for searching the Web. *Public Relations Quarterly, 46*(1), 26–30.

Levitt, T. (1983). The globalization of markets. *Harvard Business Review, 61*(3), 92–102.

Li, X., & Crane, N. B. (1993). *Electronic style: A guide to citing electronic information.* Westport, CT: Meckler.

Mitchell, R. K., Agle, B. R., & Wood, D. J. (1997). Toward a theory of stakeholder identification and salience: Defining the principle of who and what really counts. *The Academy of Management Review, 22*(4), 853–886.

Perreault, W. D., Jr., & Leigh, L. E. (1989). Reliability of nominal data based on qualitative judgments. *Journal of Marketing Research, 26*(2), 135–148.

Polonsky, M. J., Donoho, C., & Cohen, D. (1996). An international examination of attitudes towards controversial personal selling practices: A comparison of business students in Australia and the U.S. *Journal of International Selling and Sales Management, 2*(2), 93–106.

Rust, R., & Cooil, B. T. (1994). Reliability measures for qualitative data: theory and implications. *Journal of Marketing Research, 31*(1), 1–14.

Sharp, J. A., & Howard, K. (1996). *The management of a student research project.* Hants, UK: Gower.

Sheth, J. N. (1973). A model of industrial buying behavior. *Journal of Marketing, 37*(4), 50–56.

Shosteck, H., & Fairweather, W. R. (1979). Physician response rates to mail and personal interview surveys. *Public Opinion Quarterly, 43*(2, Summer), 206–217.

Tonella, K. (2000). *Karla's guide to citation style guides.* Retrieved May 5, 2000, from http://bailiwick.lib.uiowa.edu/journalism/cite.html.

8

Data Gathering

Data gathering is a very important part of the research project process. It is the fourth step in the research process (Chapter 6), and the type of data gathering method chosen will have a major impact on how activities for the rest of the research project will be undertaken. It can also be the biggest cost (time and money) of the research, so great care should be used when choosing the methodology for your project (Weller & Romney, 1988). You need to ensure that the data collected is focused toward answering your research question. Though extra collected data may be interesting, it may be unnecessary to your core focus. There is a difference between what is nice to know and what you need to know. The relevance of the data collection method will vary based on the question being asked, and some collection methods are more suitable in certain situations than others (Fowler, 1993). This chapter will identify the various approaches to collecting data, both primary and secondary, and will briefly examine some of the advantages and disadvantages of each approach. A more detailed discussion of data methods and analysis will be presented in Chapter 9 (qualitative data) and Chapter 10 (quantitative data).

Factors to Evaluate Data-Gathering Methods

There are many methods used to gather data, each with its own strengths and weaknesses. While planning your research project, if the methodology is not chosen for you, it may be possible for you to use a variety of methods, such as content analysis, surveys, or observation. However, it is important to choose the method that will provide you with the data that best answers your research question/objectives within any limitations you might have (time, cost, research ability, etc.). When you evaluate each methodology to decide on the most suitable to use for your project, there are a number of factors to consider. These include the following:

1. **Validity:** The method chosen must provide data that will measure what you want to measure and provide a valid answer to your research problem. For example, a content analysis is useful when observing how many advertisements have ethnic-looking models, but it will not identify what people's attitudes are toward these models. A methodology should be checked for internal validity (whether the manipulation of the independent variable actually caused the effects on the dependent variable) and external validity (whether the cause-and-effect relationship can be generalized). For example, due to their nature, laboratory experiments have high internal validity and low external validity, whereas field experiments have low internal validity and high external validity (Malhotra et al., 2002).

2. **Reliability:** The method chosen must provide data with consistent results, especially if it is repeated by others. For example, a personal survey of shoppers just before closing time may not provide the same responses as interviewing shoppers at other, more convenient, times. Reliability can also be defined as the extent to which the measures are free from random error. Ways to assess reliability include test-retest, alternative forms of the questions, and internal consistency in regard to how people respond to related questions, such as Cronbach's alpha tests (Malhotra et al., 2002).

3. **Appropriateness:** The method chosen must be appropriate in the context of the project's problem/objectives. Observing what others have done in previous studies on the same topic area may help confirm the most appropriate method (as was discussed in the literature view chapter). For example, a mail survey of managers may be a more appropriate method to gather particular information than undertaking personal interviews with the same managers.

4. **Amount of data:** The method chosen must provide enough quality data for there to be sufficient analysis. For example, this can vary between qualitative and quantitative data, with some quantitative statistical tests needing over 30 responses to be accurate, whereas even descriptive statistics such as percentage might work best with over 100 responses. On the other hand, personal in-depth interviews may need only one or two respondents.

5. **Flexibility:** The method chosen should match the degree of flexibility you require in terms of informational needs. For example, when undertaking exploratory research, you may need a method that provides room for respondents to give answers that the researcher may not have anticipated.

6. **Costs:** The method chosen should not cost you more than you can afford to spend on the project. For example, all methods will have some financial costs, but the purchasing or hiring of specific visual aids can be too expensive for the agreed project budget (Andreasen, 1988).

In addition, hiring people to undertake interviews or simply entering lengthy data from surveys is costly.

7. **Time restraints:** The method chosen should allow you to gather the data, analyze it, interpret the findings, and write a report within the time frame given by your supervisor. For example, if you have a small amount of time, the use of a mail survey might not be appropriate when you consider the slow response rate. However, timing issues will also affect costing issues, and there may be a trade-off between the two.

8. **Potential for errors:** With any methodology, there are a number of sources of potential error that can affect the quality of your research. For example, by using a survey there is a potential for errors based on who you sample and how you obtain the data (i.e., respondent-administered or interviewer-administered). It is important to discuss possible areas that might case errors at the planning stage so that you can try to minimize them when you gather your data. This will be discussed further later in this chapter.

9. **Researcher's ability:** The method chosen must be one that is within your ability to complete. For example, the use of a detailed experiment might provide you with important data, but running the experiment properly may be beyond your current abilities, or you might not be able to properly analyze the data in the way it is required. The same might be true for using complex analysis techniques. For example, structural equation modeling is a tool that requires a sophisticated level of expertise that you might not have. So even though this process was used in other studies, you might be better off focusing on more manageable activities within your level of expertise.

Types of Research Data

As mentioned earlier, there are two main sources of data: primary data and secondary data. A model, based on those found in Malhotra et al. (2002), that sets out the various types of research data is found in Model 8.1. This type of approach is also found in other marketing research texts, such as Hair, Bush, and Ortinau (2003). In the model, the data gathering method to be considered by you (the researcher) is presented in order from left to right across the page. Importantly, secondary data should be undertaken first as it provides invaluable background information for the project. Secondary data can be internal (within the organization) or external (outside the organization). Once these have been considered and utilized within your project, you can evaluate the potential sources of primary data. First, consider qualitative data, as this type of data can be relatively inexpensive to gather and can generate valuable information. Next, evaluate quantitative data methods, such as surveys, observational techniques, and experiments. By evaluating

Model 8.1   Types of Research Data

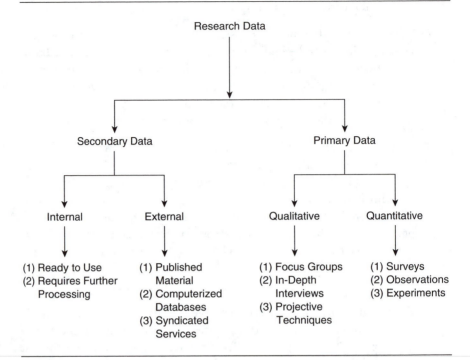

SOURCE: Based on Malhotra et al. (2002).

each potential method, you can then decide which one is the most appropriate method to use in your project. Each of the methods will be discussed in more detail in the following sections.

Secondary Data

Secondary data is information that has already been collected for some purpose other than the problem at hand (Malhotra et al., 2002). When undertaking a research project, it is important to understand the value of secondary data, which may assist in resolving, or partly answering, the research problem, thereby eliminating, or varying, the need for primary data research. As this data already exists, it is often more cost- and time-effective to analyze it before collecting primary data. However, as it has been gathered and reported for another purpose and it may not provide the information necessary to answer your specific research question, some primary data collection may still be warranted.

Nevertheless, secondary data should be examined first, as this can provide background information that can be used for the project, such as defining, refining, and developing various components of the project. It can act "as a solid information base from which information gaps, which can only be filled by fieldwork, can be identified" (Gorton & Doole, 1989, p. 12).

Further, it can serve to better state problems, suggest improved methods or data for the problem, and be a source of comparative data by which primary data can be more insightfully interpreted (Churchill, 2001). What you learn from your search of secondary data sources is presented in the Literature Review section of your project, which was discussed in Chapter 7.

Secondary data can be collected from either internal or external sources.

Internal Data

Internal data is data "available within the organization for whom the research is to be conducted" (Malhotra et al., 2002). Most organizations have large in-house databases with immense amounts of client, product, and sales information that can be utilized in solving many research problems. This can include sales figures, invoices, inventory reports, customer complaints, and product costing, which may be held by the accounting, production, or sales departments. Unfortunately, this can be an underutilized source of important information for many organizations. The data can be "ready to use" in its present form, such as overall sales figures, or may need further processing, such as sales figures for specific products in specific geographic areas. Either way, internal data has the advantage of being relatively inexpensive, assuming that the organization is willing to give you access to it.

Uses for internal secondary data in a research project might include analyzing sales figures for a newly launched product, customer records or complaints, company internal communications, or information technology (IT) access and usage of staff. IT might also assist in broader studies such as examining whether the product life cycle holds across industries.

External Data

Whereas internal data originates from within the organization, external data is "generated by sources outside the organization" (Malhotra et al., 2002). There are three main types of external data available to researchers:

1. **Published materials:** Published materials offer the most extensive source of external data; in fact, searching through this data can be overwhelming if your search is not specific (Sharp & Howard, 1996). Published data may come from individuals, research organizations, industry bodies, professional associations, government departments, and universities. Examples include books, journals, newspapers, magazines, industry reports, and trade literature. Government sources are a very important provider of information, including census data. Appendix 8.1 has a list of some of the statistical bodies in various countries. Of course, a good library is the first stop on your search for relevant published material (Andreasen, 1988).

2. **Computerized databases:** In recent years, there has been a growing use of computerized databases, which provide extensive information for the researcher. These databases can be further classified as online (accessed via modem to the Internet) or offline (accessed via CD-ROM or disk). Both online and offline databases have categories of bibliographic, numeric, full-text, directory, and special-purpose databases. As new technology becomes increasingly part of your daily life, many organizations prefer computer databases to printed data for research purposes (Sharp & Howard, 1996). Searches on computer databases are quicker to perform, thereby enhancing convenience and cost-effectiveness.

3. **Syndicated sources:** Syndicated sources are where market research companies collect and collate pools of data that can be purchased and utilized by other organizations. The data is obtained through various methods including surveys, diary panels, audits, and scanner data (Dillon, Madden, & Firtle, 1993). These services are often able to provide the information needed by an organization at a lower cost than if they conducted primary research themselves.

Uses for external secondary data in a business project include analyzing industry figures for potential growth, census data for relevant demographics, and past academic studies to formulate a conceptual view of the issue and a longitudinal view of database information.

Evaluating Secondary Data

A researcher can utilize either internal or external secondary data, but as all secondary data has been collected for purposes other than the current problem, some questions must be asked to assess the usefulness of the data to the current project's problem. You need to ensure that the methods used in obtaining the data are reliable and valid, that the reason for which the data was collected significantly relates to the present problem, that the data is current, and that the source is credible to ensure accuracy. According to Aaker, Kumar, and Day (2000), some particular questions to be asked when evaluating secondary data include the following:

1. **What was the purpose of the study?** What was the reason the research was undertaken? What was the research problem?

2. **Who collected the information?** Was it collected by a well-known research company or a person who is seen as an authority in the topic area?

3. **What information was collected?** What responses to questions did they collect? What were the main findings?

4. **When was the information collected?** How current is the data? Have conditions changed so much that the information is no longer valid?

5. **How was the information obtained?** What methodology was used to gather the data?

6. **Is the information consistent with other studies?** How do the findings in this study relate to those in other previous studies? Are the results consistent? If not, what makes this study different?

Once the secondary data has been examined, you will be able to determine whether it is sufficient to answer your research question. If the data is not sufficient, you will need to collect the primary data.

Primary Data

Primary data is data gathered that "originated by the researcher for the specific purpose of addressing the problem at hand" (Malhotra et al., 2002). More important, it has the specific purpose of addressing the current research problem. There are many different types of primary data sources, and you must decide which approach is the most suitable method for your research project. Basically, primary data sources can be either qualitative or quantitative.

Qualitative Research

Qualitative research methods are "techniques involving small numbers of respondents who provide information about their thoughts and feelings that are not easily projected to the whole population" (Dillon, Madden, & Firtle, 1993, p. 134). Qualitative methods effectively allow the researcher significant insights into the feelings, such as motivations and attitudes, of individuals who are in their sample group. However, a big drawback is that, as they are based on a small number of respondents, the results cannot be generalized to the whole population. Discussion on analysis of qualitative data is found in Chapter 9. We will briefly discuss some of the available qualitative techniques: focus groups, in-depth interviews, and projective techniques.

Focus Groups

Focus groups involve a moderator listening to a group of targeted participants talk about a particular subject that is of interest. They allow for the collection of more detailed in-depth responses and provide information that would otherwise be difficult or impossible to obtain through more structured methods of interviewing. The unstructured interviewing format allows researchers to be flexible with regard to changing questions asked and aspects of the study design in response to information. The spontaneity and stimulation of the group situation motivates a large number of creative responses and is thus useful in generating new ideas. Focus groups may be more suitable in the early, exploratory stages of a research project, or could be the primary source of data when rich textual data is required.

In-Depth Interviews

In-depth interviews are conducted on a one-to-one basis. The interviews vary in length and can be either highly structured or unstructured. Interviewers often attempt to uncover underlying motivations, prejudices, and attitudes that might not be uncovered in other primary data collection techniques (Durgee, 1986). Unfortunately, it may be harder to compare responses in interviews, as participants may use different terms or expressions to explain the same thing. Interviews are also often expensive, as it takes a long time to conduct, transcribe recordings, and read or analyze the transcripts.

Projective Techniques

Projective techniques are often more "disguised" in terms of their focus and may be in a structured or unstructured format (Malhotra et al., 2002). This method is used to discover respondents' true, and often subconscious, feelings, behaviors, and motivations. The most popular projective methods are word association, sentence completion, and construction or storytelling. Using word or sentence techniques, respondents are asked to respond with the first thing that comes to mind. In construction or storytelling, a cartoon or picture is shown, and respondents are asked to tell a story about it. Respondents' answers are recorded and later analyzed. Projective techniques allow you to delve into the respondents' underlying or subconscious attitudes, feelings, or behavior. However, the process requires you to be a skilled interviewer and information analyst.

Quantitative Research

Quantitative research methods are techniques involving "relatively large numbers of respondents [and are] designed to generate information that can be projected to the whole population" (Dillon, Madden, & Firtle, 1993). The data generated can be projected to represent the population as a whole by using a representative sample (Page & Meyer, 2000) and various statistical analysis techniques, which are discussed further in Chapter 10. Quantitative research aims to recommend a final course of action and can be either descriptive or causal. The main types of quantitative research methods include surveys (personal, telephone, electronic, and mail), observation, and experimentation:

1. **Surveys:** A survey is "a structured questionnaire given to a sample of a population and designed to elicit specific information from respondents" (Malhotra et al., 2002). Surveys are designed to gather information on such things as attitudes, intentions, awareness, behaviors, and motivations. Often, demographic and lifestyle characteristics form part of surveys and may be compared with respondents' attitudes, intentions, as so forth (Fowler, 1993). Surveys are most often direct, with the questions being presented in the same order to each respondent. They can be administered in person, over the telephone, electronically, or by mail:

   a. *Personal surveys* involve asking respondents questions face-to-face. This can be done in-home or by intercept surveys at locations such as shopping malls or on the street. Personal interviews give interviewers the opportunity to have direct contact with respondents so that they can increase the likely response rate, build rapport with the respondent, be reasonably flexible with questions, and use visual stimuli, and so that the questionnaire can be longer and more detailed. However, some disadvantages include a greater possibility of bias, as the interviewer or other environmental variables may influence the way the respondent answers, and the fact that it can be a time-consuming and relatively expensive method. Surveys may be suitable when a visual stimulus is part of the study, such as concept tests, name tests, package tests, copy tests, and in some simulated test-market studies (Dillon, Madden, & Firtle, 1993, p. 172).

   b. *Telephone surveys* involve asking respondents questions over the telephone. These types of surveys are generally popular surveys, as they are the quickest, most cost-effective way of conducting primary research (Payne, 1974). There is less evidence of bias than in face-to-face surveys, an interviewer can spend more time interviewing, and a broad geographical area can be covered relatively inexpensively. However, the disadvantages include the fact that the interview length is generally more restricted, and less flexible, than personal interviews, as the lack of face-to-face contact makes the interview more difficult to undertake and the results less dependable, there is an inability to show visual stimuli, and questions, as well as the survey as a whole, must be kept reasonably short to avoid early termination by the respondent. Telephone surveys are typically used in studies that require national samples and may be appropriate in research involving assessing awareness, attitudes, and usage behavior, and in callback interviews with respondents who were previously contacted through a personal interview or a mail survey. If the topic is particularly focused, the sourcing of an appropriate phone list is essential.

   c. *Electronic surveys* involve electronic media to access respondents to ask questions via e-mail or Web sites on the Internet (Malhotra et al., 2002). These can involve questionnaires written in the body of an e-mail message or as an attachment to a message that explains the questionnaire to the potential respondent. E-mail messages can also be sent to potential respondents with an invitation to link them to a Web site with a more detailed questionnaire. Some of the advantages include the fact that this method is relatively inexpensive, can be highly targeted, and is less intrusive and even interesting for the respondents, and respondents can complete the questionnaire in their own time with a quick turnaround rate (Malhotra et al., 2002). The main disadvantages are that those who respond may not be representative of the whole population, you will not be able to verify who is actually replying and how many times they have replied, and respondents may have security/privacy concerns (Forest, 1999). However, as more people use the Internet and become familiar with completing surveys on the Internet, new possibilities for electronic surveys will increase.

d. *Mail surveys* involve asking respondents questions via a written questionnaire through the mail ("snail-mail"). These involve questionnaires that are composed of a structured (and relatively inflexible) series of questions in written form that are sent to potential respondents and may be answered anonymously. Mail surveys are cost-effective, can reach a wide number and distribution of respondents, may eliminate interviewer bias, and, as there is time to fill out the questionnaire, can yield better-quality data (Erdos, 1974). The main disadvantages are that there is a greater chance of nonresponse than any other method, and the responses are comparatively slow in returning to the researcher. Also, care must be taken in designing the questions, as there is an increased likelihood of ambiguity with the wording of questions and there is a lack of control over who actually completes the survey. Mail surveys provide a method for collecting data in virtually all areas of research, although the disadvantages may rule out studies that need to be done quickly or need a high degree of flexibility or complex visual props. If the topic is particularly focused, the sourcing of an appropriate mail list is essential.

Table 8.1 summarizes the evaluation of various survey methods.

2. **Observation methods:** Observation involves observing and recording people's actions and behaviors to certain stimuli or situations. Observation can be conducted via personal observation, mechanical observation, audit, content analysis, or trace analysis (Malhotra et al., 2002). These methods can be useful in discovering relevant information on what people actually buy, how they act, or how they respond to certain stimuli. Observation is different from surveys, as it can objectively show what people do, not what they say they do. However, one problem with using observation as a means of data collection is that just because you can describe what people do, you can not necessarily explain *why* they do it. Understanding why people

Table 8.1 A Comparative Evaluation of Survey Methods

Criteria	Telephone	In-Home Interviews	Central Location Interview	Computer Assisted Personal	Mail Surveys	Mail Panels	E-Mail	Internet Web
Flexibility of data collection	***	***	***	***	*	*	*	***
Diversity of questions	*	***	***	***	**	**	**	***
Use of physical stimuli	*	***	***	***	**	**	*	**
Sample control	***	***	**	**	*	***	*	**
Control of data collection	**	***	***	***	*	*	*	*
Control of field force	**	*	**	**	***	***	***	***
Quantity of data	*	***	**	**	**	***	**	**
Response rate	**	***	***	***	*	**	*	*
Perceived anonymity of the respondent	**	*	*	*	***	***	**	***
Social desirability	**	***	***	***	*	*	**	*
Obtaining sensitive information	***	*	*	*	***	***	**	***
Potential for interviewer bias	**	***	***	*	None	None	None	None
Speed	***	**	***	***	*	**	***	****
Cost	**	***	***	***	*	**	*	*

*** = High; ** = Medium; * = Low.

SOURCE: Malhotra et al. (2002).

behave a certain way can be the more valued information for the researcher. This is why we do not recommend that you rely solely on observation for solving a research problem. Observation data can be expensive and time-consuming to obtain, but it can be effectively used to expose some myths associated with certain behaviors.

3. **Experimentation:** Experimentation involves the collection of primary data where the researcher changes one variable and measures the effect on the other variable(s). This can be carried out in a laboratory or in the field (Brown & Melamed, 1990). Laboratory experiments use a smaller number of respondents, are generally less expensive, and can be conducted over a shorter time period, but the results may be somewhat artificial, and it is debatable whether laboratory results are representative of a real-world situation. When conducting experiments, the researcher has two main goals: (a) internal validity, to draw valid conclusions about the effects of an independent variable, and (b) external validity, to make valid generalizations to a larger population or setting of interest (Malhotra et al., 2002). Laboratory settings offer greater control for establishing internal validity, whereas field experiments are best for testing external validity. To help overcome this disparity of methods, field and laboratory experiments can be used to complement each other. Experiments can be used to test specific variables, such as new packaging, advertising, or products before they are launched onto a market.

Sampling Methods

When gathering primary data, it is important to look at the issue of sampling—who do we collect the data from, and are they representative of the targeted population? When trying to obtain data by surveys, it may be impossible to contact everyone in the target population, (i.e., perform a census), as it might be too expensive, too time-consuming, or just impossible to physically undertake. Therefore, a researcher can use a sample, which is a subgroup of the population selected for participation in the study. Importantly, if the sample is representative of the target population, then there is no need to spend a lot of effort trying to undertake a census, as the increased numbers would not increase the validity to any significant extent. There are two main types of sampling techniques: (a) nonprobability sampling and (b) probability sampling (Hair, Bush, and Ortinau, 2003).

Nonprobability Sampling

Nonprobability sampling is a technique that does not use chance selection procedures to identify those who will participate; it relies on the personal judgment of the researcher to decide who will be included in the sample. There are a number of nonprobability sampling techniques:

- *Convenience sampling* attempts to obtain a sample of convenient respondents, for example, students.
- *Judgmental sampling* is a technique in which sample members are purposively selected based on the judgment of the researcher; for example, the researchers may seek out respondents whom they feel are part of the target population.
- *Quota sampling* is a restricted judgmental sampling technique in which the first stage consists of developing control categories or quotas of the population and the second stage consists of sample elements being selected based on convenience or judgment. For example, deciding that there will be a quota of 20 respondents aged in their 20s, 20 aged in their 30s, and so on.
- *Snowball sampling* is a technique in which an initial group of respondents is selected randomly, and then subsequent respondents are identified based on the referrals provided by the initial respondents. For example, a sample of respondents is obtained and then asked to survey their family and friends (Malhotra et al., 2002).

Probability Sampling

Probability sampling is a sampling procedure in which each element of the population has the same probabilistic chance of being selected for the sample. There are a number of probability sampling techniques:

- *Simple random sampling* is a technique in which each member in the population has a known and equal probability of selection. Every element is selected independently, and the sample is drawn by a random procedure from a sampling frame. For example, names are written on cards and then selected out of a hat.
- *Systematic sampling* is a technique in which the sample is chosen by selecting a random starting point and then picking every *i*th element in succession from the sampling frame, for example, choosing a name in the telephone directory and then selecting every 10th name afterward.
- *Stratified sampling* is a two-step process that partitions the population into subpopulations, or strata, after which elements are selected from each stratum by a random procedure.
- *Cluster sampling* is another two-step technique by which the target population is divided into mutually exclusive and collectively exhaustive subpopulations called clusters, and then a random sample of clusters is selected based on a probability sampling technique such as simple random sampling (Malhotra et al., 2002).

The advantages and disadvantages of each technique are found in Table 8.2.

Table 8.2   Strengths and Weaknesses of Basic Sampling Techniques

Technique	Strengths	Weaknesses
Nonprobability Sampling		
Convenience sampling	Least expensive, least time-consuming, most convenient	Selection bias, sample not representative, not recommended for descriptive or causal research
Judgmental sampling	Low cost, convenient, not time-consuming	Does not allow generalization, subjective
Quota sampling	Sample can be controlled for certain characteristics	Selection bias, no assurance of representativeness
Snowball sampling	Can estimate rare characteristics	Time-consuming
Probability sampling		
Simple random sampling (SRS)	Easily understood, results projectable	Difficult to construct sampling frame, expensive, lower precision, no assurance of representativeness
Systematic sampling	Can increase representativeness, easier to implement than SRS, sampling frame not necessary	Can decrease representativeness
Stratified sampling	Includes all important subpopulations, precision	Difficult to select relevant stratification variables, not feasible to stratify on many variables, expensive
Cluster sampling	Easy to implement, cost-effective	Imprecise, difficult to compute and interpret results

SOURCE: Malhotra et al. (2002).

Research Errors

Although the issue of errors was mentioned above, an important part of planning your data gathering is trying to minimize the incidence and effect of errors on your research. There are a number of ways that errors can occur, but basically, the total error is composed of two main parts; (a) random sampling error and (b) nonsampling error (response and nonresponse error) (Assael & Keon, 1982; Malhotra et al., 2002). As can be seen in Model 8.2, there are a number of reasons why nonsampling errors may eventuate, and these may be the result of some of your research methods. Thus, you can seek to minimize them.

Random Sampling Error

Random sampling error occurs when the sample members selected for your study "do not represent the population of interest" (Malhotra et al., 2002). Therefore, the responses are not coming from those whom you really want to research. This can be due to carelessness on your part, as it is up to you to select the correct population and sample. It is, therefore,

Model 8.2   Potential Sources of Error

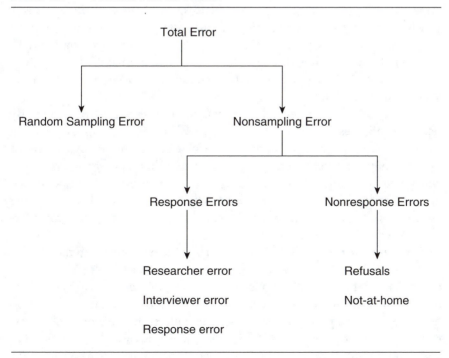

SOURCE: Malhotra et al. (2002).

important that you take care when determining how truly representative the sample is for your research.

Nonsampling Error

Nonsampling errors are those errors that occur that do not relate to the way you select the respondents. These can consist of both response errors (things that affect how people respond) and nonresponse errors (people selected not responding). It can be extremely difficult to completely avoid some nonsampling errors, but they can be reduced with care taken throughout the research process.

Response Errors

Response errors occur "when respondents give inaccurate answers or their answers are misrecorded or misanalyzed" (Malhotra et al., 2002) and can be caused by the researcher, the interviewer, or the respondents.

Researcher errors can include *surrogate information* error, where you ask the wrong question and thus do not get the information needed to answer the research question (e.g., asking about consumer preferences when what is needed is really purchase intention); *measurement error,* which is measuring the information in the wrong way (e.g., using a scale to measure perceptions rather than preferences); *population definition error,* which is the incorrect interpretation of what population is to be researched; *sampling frame error,* which is the difference between the population definition and the sampling frame actually used; and finally, *data analysis error,* which is the incorrect interpretation of the research findings (Malhotra et al., 2002).

Interviewer errors can include *respondent selection,* when you incorrectly select potential respondents to be sample members; *questioning errors*, when you do not ask the questions in the right way (e.g., not probing when needed or not asking the exact wording given in the questionnaire); *recording error*, when you record the incorrect interpetation and/or record respondents' answers incorrectly; and *cheating error,* which occurs when those collecting the data (not you) fabricate, or make up, answers to a part or all of the interview (Malhotra et al., 2002).

Response error can include *inability error,* which occurs when the respondent is unable to provide accurate answers to the question(s) (e.g., due to unfamiliarity, faulty recall, or question content); *unwillingness error,* which occurs when the respondent is unwilling to provide accurate information (e.g., due to trying to provide socially acceptable answers, avoid embarrassment, or please the interviewer); and *bias*, which is caused by factors that you cannot control resulting in respondents changing their answer(s). For example, male respondents might give different answers to a survey depending on whether the interviewer is male or female.

Some of these errors can have a major influence on the quality of your results and can make you project findings invalid. The ways to minimize these errors vary and include checking and rechecking your problem definition, the research objectives, research design, data gathering (especially questionnaire design and interviewing methods), data analysis, and reporting—or each step of the research process!

Nonresponse Errors

Nonresponse errors occur when respondents included in the sample do not respond to the questionnaire or a particular question. This is beyond the researcher's control and is usually due to either a refusal to participate or the respondent not being available, or "not-at-home." If this situation occurs, the researcher must either find some willing respondents in the same sample population, change the sample population, change the wording of any offending or ambiguous questions, or, at worst, cancel the research design and discover another way of obtaining the same data. Usually, the majority of respondents are willing to participate, and those who do not respond have little effect on the result (Malhotra et al., 2002).

Past experiences have shown that it is very unusual to go through a research project process without having some type of data collection error. However, when planning your research, you should attempt to minimize the total error from any source that can affect your research findings.

Conclusion

As has been indicated in this chapter, data gathering is a very important part of your research project. Without gathering the data, there is no way that you can fully answer your research problem and objectives. Therefore, before undertaking your data collection, you must be sure that the method you choose will be the most appropriate to your project and situation. There are a number of valid methods of gathering data that could be valuable to your project, using forms of secondary and primary data and qualitative and quantitative research methods. All data collection methods have different uses, advantages, and disadvantages, so it invariably depends on exactly what the research problem is as to what type or types of data need to be obtained and analyzed to answer it. For your research project, this may mean that you must identify potential approaches and examine the various advantages and disadvantages of each before deciding. The decision of the most appropriate method therefore may or may not be a simple one, depending on your project, but it will be a very important decision.

Appendix 8.1   Statistical Agencies

To assist you with your research, following is a list of some governmental statistical bodies from various countries that can be very useful for up-to-date demographics.

Australia

Australian Bureau of Statistics (ABS)
National Office
Wing 5
Cameron Offices
Chandler Street
Belconnen ACT 2617
AUSTRALIA
Homepage: *http://www.abs.gov.au/*

Canada

Statistics Canada
Tunney's Pasture
Ottawa, Ontario
K1A 0T6
CANADA
Homepage: *http://www.statcan.ca*

European Community

EUROSTAT
Statistical Office of the European Communities
Jean Monnet Building
Rue Alcide De Gasperi
L-2920 Luxembourg
Homepage:
http://europa.eu.int/en/comm/eurostat/eurostat.html

Hong Kong

Census and Statistics Department
Hong Kong Special Administrative Region
21/F Wanchai Tower
12 Harbour Road
Wan Chai
Hong Kong
China
Homepage: *http://www.info.gov.hk/censtatd/*

Indonesia

Badan Pusat Statistik, Republik Indonesia
(Statistics Indonesia of The Republic of Indonesia)
Jl. Dr. Sutomo 6–8

Jakarta 10710
Indonesia
Homepage: *http://www.bps.go.id/*

Ireland

Central Statistics Office
Skehard Rd.
Cork
Ireland
Homepage: *http://www.cso.ie/*

Japan

Statistics Bureau and Statistics Center
19–1 Wakamatsu-cho,
shinjuku-ku
Tokyo 162–8668
Japan
Homepage: *http://www.stat.go.jp*

Malaysia

Department of Statistics, Malaysia
(Jabatan Perangkaan Malaysia)
Jalan Cenderasari
50514 Kuala Lumpur
Malaysia
Homepage: *http://www.statistics.gov.my/*

New Zealand

Statistics New Zealand
Auckland Office
70 Symonds Street
Private Bag 92003
Auckland
New Zealand
Homepage:
http://www.stats.govt.nz/statsweb.nsf

Singapore

Department of Statistics
100 High Street #05–01
The Treasury
Singapore 179434
Homepage: *http://www.singstat.gov.sg/*

South Africa

Statistics South Africa
Private Bag X44
Pretoria
South Africa 0001
Homepage: *http://www.statssa.gov.za/*

Thailand

National Statistical Office Thailand
Larn Luang Road
Bangkok 10100
Thailand
Homepage: *http://www.nso.go.th*

United Kingdom

Office for National Statistics
Homepage: *http://www.ons.gov.uk/*

United States

FedStats Links to statistics and information from more than 70 agencies in the U.S. Federal Government.
Homepage: *http://www.fedstats.gov/*

References

Aaker, D. A., Kumar, V., & Day, G. S. (2000). *Marketing research, 7th Ed.* New York: Wiley.

Andreasen, A. R. (1988). *Cheap but good marketing research, 4th Ed.* Boston: Business One Irwin.

Assael, H., & Keon, J. (1982). Nonsampling vs sampling errors in sampling research. *Journal of Marketing, Spring,* 114–123.

Brown, S. R., & Melamed, L. E. (1990). *Experimental design and analysis.* Newbury Park, CA: Sage.

Churchill, G. A. (2001). *Basic marketing research.* Chicago: Dryden Press.

Dillon, W. R., Madden, T. J., & Firtle, N. H. (1993). *Essentials of marketing research.* Homewood, IL: Richard Irwin.

Durgee, J. F. (1986). Depth-interview techniques for creative advertising. *Journal of Advertising Research, January,* 29–37.

Erdos, P. L. (1974). Data collection methods: Mail surveys. In R. Ferber (Ed.), *Handbook of marketing research* (pp. 2–91). New York: McGraw-Hill.

Forest, E. (1999). *Internet marketing research.* Sydney: McGraw-Hill.

Fowler, F. J. (1993). *Survey research methods.* Newbury Park, CA: Sage.

Gorton, K., & Doole, I. (1989). *Low-cost marketing research—a guide for small businesses, 2nd Ed.* New York: Wiley.

Hair, J. F., Bush, R. P., & Ortinau, D. J. (2003). *Marketing research: With a changing information environment.* New York: McGraw-Hill/Irwin.

Malhotra, N. K., Hall, J., Shaw, M., & Oppenheim, P. (2002). *Marketing research: An applied orientation.* Sydney: Pearson Education.

Page, C., & Meyer, D. (2000). *Applied research design for business and management.* Sydney: Irwin/McGraw-Hill.

Payne, S. L. (1974). Data collection methods: Telephone surveys. In R. Ferber (Ed.), *Handbook of marketing research* (pp. 2.105–2.123). New York: McGraw-Hill.

Sharp, J. A., & Howard, K. (1996). *The management of a student research project.* Aldershot, UK: Gower.

Weller, S. C., & Romney, A. K. (1988). *Systematic data collection.* Newbury Park, CA: Sage.

9

Qualitative
Data Analysis

This is the first of two chapters that discuss ways of examining data. The type of method to be used (quantitative or qualitative) will depend on the research question being examined. Qualitative research will be discussed first and is traditionally used in three different ways. First, qualitative data can be used to define the domain of an issue being examined, which then feeds into the quantitative aspects of the research, as per Churchill's (1979) research paradigm. Second, qualitative research may be the primary data collection method, which is frequently used when the research question requires rich textual data and/or in-depth understanding of issues. For example, examining the various approaches to deal with organizational downsizing might require in-depth interviews with human resource managers to identify their views regarding different alternative practices. Third, qualitative data is sought after quantitative data has been collected and analyzed to assist in understanding the relationships identified. This is especially useful when the resulting findings are unanticipated, and thus, additional insights from participants might assist in understanding the results.

Qualitative research has a strong tradition in the social sciences with extensive theoretical and methodological underpinnings (Marshall & Rossman, 1989; Strauss & Corbin, 1990; Miles & Huberman, 1994; Denzin & Lincoln, 2000). Recent developments and applications in qualitative research show that it is gaining recognition for its unique contribution to the study of some important business questions, and there are even journals that focus on research and methodological issues associated with a qualitative approach (e.g., *Qualitative Market Research*).

As already mentioned, the research questin you pose may require several research methods to be used (Watts, 2000). For example, you might first

Authors' Note: The authors gratefully acknowledge Dale Miller, Griffith University, Gold Coast, for writing this chapter, as well as the valuable ongoing discussions about qualitative research with colleagues, especially Ann Taylor and Dr. Ellen Jordan at the University of Newcastle and Professor Bill Merrilees at Griffith University, Gold Coast.

undertake focus groups (qualitative), which would test ideas that you might use in a structured survey (quantitative). However, increasingly, researchers (students and academics) are using qualitative data collection, such as focus groups after a survey to clarify the survey results (Garee & Schori, 1997). You might even use in-depth interviews to uncover the meaning of document-based research (i.e., what the documents mean in the organizational context) (Zorn & Ruccio, 1998).

Qualitative research methods involve utilizing a diverse range of data including the spoken and printed word, recorded sound and vision, and images, forms, and structures in various media. The critical issue is how to turn this information into meaningful data using various analytical techniques. Because of this, qualitative research interprets the social world using flexible data generation and "to produce rounded understandings on the basis of rich, contextual and detailed data" (Mason, 1998, p. 4). This chapter presents a systematic way of considering, planning, implementing, and evaluating qualitative research. It discusses some of the methods you will find effective in your research projects. A detailed discussion relating to analyzing the qualitative materials used will not be provided, and so you will need to refer to the references provided throughout and at the end of the chapter for more detail on the analysis.

Qualitative Data Collection Methods

You can use various qualitative methods within your research project (Janda, 1999; Dittmar & Drury, 2000; Hamilton, 2000; Kamouche, 1995). The following sections will discuss some of the various qualitative data collection techniques, as well as issues associated with their use.

Focus Groups

To conduct focus group research, you would form a group, or series of groups, comprising individuals who are relevant to your research question. For example, focus groups of existing students might be used to identify how your universities could improve courses. It is important that you use a knowledgeable facilitator to run the focus groups, one who understands the subject area and guides the group through the issue. Exhibit 9.1 provides a checklist for preparing and conducting a focus group (see Morgan, 1997, for a fuller explanation of the processes).

From a research design point of view, you should note that "focus groups are excellent tools for gaining insights about markets, but it should be evident that a group of 10 or so people chosen haphazardly at a single location cannot be expected to reflect the total population of consumers" (Sudman & Blair, 1999, p. 272). It is beneficial to avoid people who know each other, as peer pressure or values could influence their participation, and compensation to

Exhibit 9.1 Focus Group Preparation and Conduct Checklist

Topic	Clearly identify the area for discussion (and the boundaries).
Moderator/ Facilitator	Needs to understand subject matter, to be well-briefed on purpose of the study, to be skilled in group techniques, to have a test run of the questions, to be able to clarify responses and build ideas.
Venue	Comfortable, neutral, quiet, no interruptions, availability of washrooms, suitable for mobility-restricted access, public transport, and parking.
Preparation	Check seating and table arrangements, refreshments, name tags/names plates (first names are usually fine).
Timing	Allow a 10-minute arrival period, so tell people the arrival time is say, 5:50 for a 6:00 start.
Arrival Period	Initial welcome, refreshments, name tags, information sheets, consent forms.
Recording	Scribe with or without audiotape or videotape.
Information Sheet	Explaining purpose of the study, how confidentiality will be managed, where participants can get further information, and where they follow up any concerns/complaints they have.
Consent	Informed consent.
Starting	On time, welcome the group, brief introduction, "The Rules."
Rules	Advised by moderator at the start of the session, usually about one person speaking at a time, all ideas are welcome, nonjudgmental, no right or wrong answers.
Confidentiality	Within the group and by the moderator and scribe.
Running the Actual Group— "The Main Event"	Ask first planned question, model the interactions that are expected. Probe answers, build ideas, listen, involve, and remain nonjudgmental. Manage differing points of view. Ask questions such as: What else? Any other examples? Discipline use of time.
Closure	Ask all participants to think of two key points from the session. Go around the group to hear each response individually. Make a brief summary and conclusion. Thank the group. End on time.
After the Session	Write-up—moderator and scribe to write up separately; have tape transcribed verbatim or in summary form. Find meanings—researcher(s) bring the write-ups together. Identify inputs to next phase. File materials securely.

participants is not essential, although it is sometimes used. Having a neutral and interruption-free venue is preferred. It is also important to have some way of recording the proceedings, such as a scribe or audio or video recordings. When using equipment, it is essential that you know how to use it in advance. You should ensure that the participants understand that they will be recorded. You should also ensure that participants understand how you will use the information collected. For example, will you quote individuals or look for common themes? As is discussed in the ethics chapter, it is essential that you obtain informed consent from all those involved (for specific issues related to unobtrusive research, see Kellehear (1993, 1998).

Conducting the focus group successfully hinges on the role of the facilitator or moderator (McDonald, 1993), and therefore, plenty of training and practice is essential for whomever in your group undertakes this role. This will ensure that the information collected is meaningful and that participants' time is not wasted. When acting as a facilitator, you should not judge, correct, or assert a personal opinion. Rather, your role is to pose questions or open up areas of discussion and elicit information. To do this requires *active* listening, which is a hard-won skill, and means using appropriate prompts and probing (e.g., "How could that be different?" "What else would be important?") rather than judging ("No! That's not right." or "Yes! That's what I wanted!"). Trying to cover too many areas in a short time will possibly result in superficial information and possibly confuse the focus group members. As facilitator you help the group "to reveal previously hidden nuggets" (Murphy, 1997), and a good moderator draws out quiet or shy participants and uses innovative techniques to delve deeper (Greenbaum, 1997). Adding your own views would possibly shift the nature of discussion, and thus you would miss obtaining the information you organized the group for, that is, what the targeted respondents think.

People participating should be relaxed and open, which might be assisted by serving refreshments and keeping things informal. It is also helpful to explain briefly how you will use the data, and it is also important to emphasize confidentiality in terms of the data and that what is said in the room stays in the room. It is also important to explain that there are no right or wrong answers; rather, the idea is to build on each other's ideas, and that only one person should speak at a time. You need to ensure that there is a disciplined use of time, and that the session concludes on time (these usually don't last more than an hour), with suitable thanks to the participants. In this way, people feel able to contribute their views, ensuring that you maximize the applicability of information. For example, if people feel uncomfortable in the group, they may be less likely to contribute openly.

After the session, you and your group members who have acted as the *focus group team* should write up your observations immediately and individually. The initial write-up includes relevant details of participants, facilitator, day/date/time, venue, seating, emerging themes, nonverbal communication, and an evaluation of the process. The ensuing discussion should identify the psyche of the participants, the insights gained, and any surprises or unexpected results. The importance of write-up cannot be overstated; for example, one group we supervised once undertook five focus groups over several days and then went to review the tapes, only to find that each day they recorded over the previous session. They did not write up the sessions right away and lost valuable information.

The focus groups can serve to assist in revising materials to be used in quantitative research, such as survey instruments or semistructured interview questions, and you can also determine if more focus groups are needed.

Focus groups have the benefit of speed and relatively low cost, and also build a synergy of ideas in a dynamic way. Overall, focus groups can be an important element of your research design and can particularly assist clarification of issues for inclusion in surveys and interviews, although it must be remembered that the results from focus groups cannot be generalized to the wider community.

Open-Ended Questions

Open-ended questions are a means of getting the respondents' views, opinions, or descriptions of experiences. Open-ended questions form the basis of focus groups, and semistructured interviews are often used as part of structured surveys, including projective techniques. Any open-ended question must have a specific purpose. It must be worded so that it does not lead the respondent or presuppose the answer. For example, if you are researching promotion and the consumer's perception of bottled water, you could ask a question about what factors influenced purchase rather than whether promotion of the product affected the purchase decision. A checklist for open-ended questions (Exhibit 9.2) suggests that planning and practice will guide their appropriate use.

Open-ended data often help you to understand and explain statistical results; that is, they can add meaning. In some studies, a follow-up focus group or further interview can assist to further clarify meanings.

Semistructured Interviews

Researchers organize semistructured interviews so that they cover a range of questions relevant to the topic at hand, using mainly open-ended

---

Exhibit 9.2   Focus Group Preparation and Conduct Checklist

Are the questions purposeful?   This means you should have a deliberate reason for including each question.

Are they truly open-ended?   Check if you have unintentionally signalled the answer you expect.

Will the intended respondents understand them?   Check that you have avoided any inappropriate or technical language.

Will written or verbal answers be required?   You may choose to have respondents write their answers instead of having them answer verbally after which you then write down or record their answers.

How will answers be recorded?

Written by the respondent?   Alone (e.g., in a mail, fax, or electronic survey) or in the presence of an interviewer?

Directly by an interviewer?   The interviewer can ask direct questions face-to-face, in person, or by telephone or videoconferencing, and can record written answers either verbatim or in summary. Alternatively, with the respondent's permission, the interviewer can record the verbal responses with audio- or videotape.

How will the data be collated and analyzed?

What have you learned in pretests?

questions (Exhibit 9.3). The design of the interview protocol (list of questions) has many parallels with survey construction. The issues are based on a suitable theoretical framework that guides the development of questions or themes to explore in the interview.

Exhibit 9.3   In-Depth Semistructured Interviews Checklist

Structure	Has the structure been planned logically and sensitively? What basis was used for the structure?
Participants	Clarify who is in the sample and on what basis they are to be included.
Interviewer(s)	Confirm skills, practice, and use a "fishbowl" technique for practice so that the observers can give constructive feedback. Decide how many interviewers there will be.
Questions	Prepare the interview schedule. Use a combination of open and closed questions, being sure that there is a clear purpose for each one. Refer also to issues about questions in focus groups.
Decide on Analysis	Is any precoding needed?
Pretest	Did the practice sessions indicate that the questions should be changed to avoid jargon or fuzzy concepts? Pretest the analysis.
Timing/ Appointment	Sometimes it is appropriate to give the interviewee the questions or at least the domain or scope of the interview in advance. Make your appointment in advance and be clear about how much time you are asking the interviewee to have available. Clarify with the interviewee how many interviewers will be attending.
Consent	Ensure that the interviewee gives informed consent.
Confidentiality	Clarify with the interviewee how confidentiality will be maintained.
The Interview	Arrive 5 minutes early and be prepared. Conduct the interview professionally. If there are two interviewers, practice beforehand how you will work as a team and what roles each will have. Explain the purpose of the interview carefully.
Closure	Ask the interviewee if he or she has any other comments. Finally, ask the interviewee to identify the two key points that have come out of the session for him or her. This helps the interviewee to close the interview and to complete his or her own reflections. Explain to the interviewee any next steps such as sending him or her a transcript or summary of the interview to correct any errors of fact. Thank the interviewee for participating.
Transcription	If there are two interviewers, each should write up his or her notes independently. If there is a recording of the interview, you may choose to have a verbatim transcription or a summary prepared, which will require judgement by the person making the summary. Synthesize findings if appropriate at this stage.
Input to Next Phase	Prepare for coding or other analysis.

The semistructured interview differs from the personally administered questionnaire because it gives you an opportunity to gather in-depth responses that reflect the insights of the interviewee. It also allows you to probe into issues and pursue unexpected revelations, hence the term semistructured. For example, you can examine why a person responds in a given way, which cannot be done in a survey. Mason (1998) describes the qualitative interview as a "conversation with a purpose" (p. 43) and strongly suggests that it needs extensive planning.

As well as being adept in designing and asking questions, you also need to be an *active* listener, knowing when to probe answers and when to pause, waiting patiently for the interviewee to think about the question and then respond. Many interviewees find the experience reflective and informative, even gaining new insights themselves as the interview progresses. The interview is an interactive method, so practice is essential to help develop an effective (and efficient) interviewing style.

Semistructured interviews can use one or two interviewers, as long as each has a clear role. Practice is strongly suggested before undertaking an interview. You can record interviews with the informed consent of the interviewee and/or take notes. If two interviewers are being used, the second one can take more extensive notes and ask any clarifying questions. Immediately after the interview, each interviewer should write up his or her own notes and impressions and identify emerging themes.

Analyzing the interview means using coding for themes or content against previously developed coding protocols. The extensive data generated by interviews makes this a time-consuming but worthwhile task. You also might want to use various qualitative software packages to evaluate the data, such as NUD*IST, (Non-numeric Unstructured Data Indexing Searching and Theorizing), but to do this requires transcripts of the responses. Pretesting the entire interview process and analysis is a must. If you plan a series of semistructured interviews, you can make use of a developmental approach in which each interview can build on ideas derived from previous interviews. This approach achieves a cumulative effect rather than a rigid repetition of the interview protocol.

Case Studies

A case study presents the analysis of a study of a single unit, which can be an event (motor racing, athletics carnival), an organization (of any type), or an aspect of organizational function (staff development). It can use single research methods or combinations of qualitative and quantitative methods (Stake, 1994, p. 245). According to Yin (1994, pp. 2–4), the case study "allows an investigation to retain holistic and meaningful characteristics of real-life events—such as . . . organizational and managerial processes."

(Non-numeric Unstructured Data Indexing Searching and Theorizing)

Case-based research can be a very powerful way of examining and "understanding the dynamics present within single settings" (Eisenhardt, 1989, p. 534). It can combine data from a range of qualitative and quantitative sources (Eisenhardt, 1989; Yin, 1994). Research could involve a single case study or a series of case studies built from in-depth interviews and document-based analysis. Case studies can help researchers to formulate larger studies. For example, in a two-stage study of international entrepreneurial activity, Merrilees and Tiessen (1999) used case research–based in-depth interviews with twelve Canadian exporters followed by a comprehensive mail survey of a further two hundred Canadian exporters. Unfortunately, researchers often overlook case research as an option when designing research projects.

Document-Based Research

This type of research is noninterventionist and unobtrusive, and can be very useful for responding to research questions (Kellehear, 1993). The sources of data could be *primary,* such as minute books of boards of directors, letters, original reports, and advertisements, or *secondary,* such as newspaper reports. For example, you might examine advertisements to identify the degree to which they include various characteristics, such as humor, sexist representations, or different types of information.

Document-based studies can contribute to exploring issues as well as building or testing theoretical concepts and models. They are often a foundation for case studies (Miller & Merrilees, 2000) or an adjunct to other qualitative methods such as in-depth interviews. These studies can either be longitudinal or examine an issue at a single point in time. The value of longitudinal studies is that they can show changes or stability over time. To gather data, you need to develop a data collection protocol, similar to the interview or observation protocol, to ensure that you collect the relevant information from each material examined. The data generated can be analyzed either using content analysis (Alison et al., 1998) or thematically (Miller & Merrilees, 2000).

Document selection, like participant selection for interviews or focus groups, must be deliberate and based on the expected contribution it can make. The decision of how many documents to study will depend on constraints such as time, document scope, and availability. If documents seem to be giving repetitive data, the researcher may have reached "theoretical saturation" (Glesne & Peskin, 1992). This means "that successive examination of sources yields redundancy, and that the data you have seem complete and integrated" (Glesne & Peskin, 1992, p. 132). Conversely, when examining documents, gaps in document availability are often noteworthy, as are gaps *within* documents. That is, what is *not* said in the document can be just as important to the research topic as what is said. Such gaps should lead the researcher to critical reflection.

Implementation

The methods for collection and for analysis affect each other, so you must plan with both in mind. It is too late once you have generated the data to regret that you cannot change questions or methodology to analyze it more meaningfully. Pretesting in all phases contributes to the process of research design, development, and implementation. Having the right skills is also critical. For example, practice sessions in running interviews or focus groups will help you to apply theoretical learning and to both pretest your skills and refine your questions. It is difficult for anyone to run groups as a moderator and to monitor the impact of their own actions on the group proceedings; thus, when testing your skills, it may be necessary to have a second person observing you.

The Importance of Training and Pretesting

If the various courses you have taken have not provided you with sufficient training in the methods of data collection, you should seek suitable additional training by:

- **Developing understanding.** To increase your knowledge of the subject and the administration of the methods, you can read and then discuss with experts, such as your supervisor.
- **Practicing the methods.** Do this before starting the actual data collection.
- **Peer review and feedback.** The aim is to build skills and awareness and to improve performance by having your colleagues hear you practice your questioning.
- **Personal reflection** on your own effort. What did you learn? What needs improvement?

Ideally, a program of training in essential techniques and methods should complement your other academic supervision. When undertaking qualitative data collection, you need to watch out that you do not ask questions that are leading or that suggest particular answers that the interviewer wants. You can manage this concern by pretesting interviews, for example, by interviewing members of your group or other friends to see how the questions sound, whether they are understood, and what responses you get. You will soon find the "bumpy" parts of the interview: What doesn't flow? What additional information do respondents seem to want? How long does it really take to conduct the interview, including recruiting, informing the respondent about the purpose of the study, and providing an information sheet? Find out what it is like to be on the other side of the interview—get a colleague to interview *you*, using your interview schedule. They can comment too on their reactions to asking the questions. This is also relevant if there is more than one interviewer.

Inviting people to participate in your study suggests to potential participants that you are a competent researcher. This means you have an obligation to ensure that you are familiar with, and capable in, using the methods you have chosen for data collection. You also have to be competent in the data analysis and interpretation so that you fairly represent the data you have gathered (see Kellehear, 1998 and Mason, 1998).

Analysis and Interpretation

These two words, *analysis* and *interpretation*, are misused frequently as being interchangeable, but they have distinct meanings and roles. Analysis covers the assembling, cleaning, and examining of the data, whereas interpretation is making sense of the data that you have generated. Within this section, some basic issues associated with analysis will be introduced, but specific processes will not be examined in detail. As mentioned earlier, you will need to refer to the various sources referenced here, as well as others provided by your supervisor, to be competent in all aspects of the techniques' use.

A way of analyzing qualitative data is by using *content analysis,* which can be applied to research projects in most business-related disciplines. Content analysis is generally text- or visually based and focuses specifically on analyzing the frequency of particular words or phrases or images. It can be used, for example, to assess the content of advertisements in men's and women's magazines relating to particular research topics. Other examples include studying the change in the portrayal of women as career oriented, or of men as being fashion conscious. Relevant studies in these areas include gender portrayals or stereotyping (Ford et al., 1998). Others include guilt appeals (Huhmann & Brotherton, 1997) and advertising comparisons between business-to-business and consumer services (Turley & Kelley, 1997).

A related technique is *thematic analysis,* by which the researcher may develop an idiosyncratic coding system, usually based on a coding protocol. Coding the data pushes the researcher to engage with the collected material and to seek meaning, connections, and insights. Writers such as Kellehear (1993) and Miles and Huberman (1994) are among those who discuss the many schemas for coding. You are encouraged to investigate and test this part of your study *before* extensive data collection.

How should you interpret your data? Results are meaningless without the researcher's interpretation. Here all the critical thinking skills and synthesizing capabilities of the researcher come into play. The challenge is to interpret what the results mean, not to assume they say what you want them to say. You must keep searching and checking for alternative explanations (disconfirmation). In discussing your interpretation, you need to relate the findings to the research question and the literature (this issue will be discussed again in Chapter 11). Then you can relate the findings to your design, including the characteristics of your sample.

Computer-Aided Qualitative Research

As a student researcher, you have sound reasons to carefully evaluate, and potentially avoid, sophisticated computer-aided qualitative data retrieval systems. The common misperception is that the computer will perform the analysis, whereas essentially the computer program provides a sophisticated storage and retrieval tool (Weitzman, 1999). In the hands of experienced researchers, the retrieval can certainly lead to analysis, but the interpretation of the results comes from the researcher. One of the challenges of some available packages, such as QSR, NUD*IST and Ethnograph, is the precision with which data must be entered into the system for storage and later retrieval (Gahan & Hannibal, 1998). The resources for extensive transcription, whether from audiotapes or printed documents, may not be available to you. Your supervisor will be able to assist you in making more informed decisions about the usefulness of computer-aided qualitative research in particular applications.

The skills and other resources required to use advanced software may be outside the scope of your project. However, Tallerico (1992) gives a concise description of the generic features of computer technology that assist with qualitative research. Tallerico (1992) illustrates the iterative processes involved with a study of the formal and informal interactions in educational administration in which in-depth interviews were used as the main data collection tool. In research projects within business areas, the focus groups or in-depth interviews could be sound methods to pursue, provided suitable means of data analysis are planned well in advance of the data collection, so that enough time can be given to all phases of the project.

Conclusion

This chapter has given an overview of qualitative methods that you can use to enrich your work. Exhibit 9.4 presents a checklist for undertaking qualitative research, and Table 9.1 gives a general overview of qualitative research techniques, analysis procedures, and interpretation. Many sources of further information are readily available, starting with the references at the end of this chapter. There may be many issues to follow up that directly relate to your project. This chapter gives a point of departure so that you have an overview of the issues, ways of generating data, types and methods of analysis, the unique perspectives you can bring to interpretation, and avenues to pursue for further information. The next chapter will discuss quantitative data collection techniques.

Exhibit 9.4   Qualitative Research Checklist

Remember:

Questions that are important and worthy of study.

Unique studies.

Attention to detail in all stages.

Learning *before* doing and *through* doing.

Informed consent of participants.

The data collection is soundly based on literature review and planning.

Analysis—preplanned, pretested, soundly based, thorough, reliable, valid.

Teasing out explanations, alternative explanations and identifying gaps.

Interpretations using the researcher's thoughtful synthesis.

Vivid implications made clear to researchers and practitioners.

Evaluate the entire process, especially the research design and implementation.

Table 9.1   Qualitative Research—An Overview

Data Generation Source	Data Analysis: Type	Data Analysis: Method	Interpretation
Focus groups Survey questions— open-ended In-depth, semistructured interviews Observations Case study Delphi Nominal group Brainstorming Documents Audiotapes, CDs, DVDs, film Visual—print, video, film WWW	**Qualitative** Content analysis Thematic analysis Case study Protocol ⇓ **Quantitative** Options depend on data collection	**Qualitative** Coding Manual Computer-aided storage and retrieval ⇓ **Quantitative** Options depend on data collection	**Researcher-Driven Synthesis**

Resources—A Final Word (or Two)

Library catalogs, online databases, and online search engines can all help the new researcher to locate theoretical papers, critiques, and applied research using the techniques discussed in this chapter. By reviewing the existing literature, you can understand how other researchers have approached similar research topics, what their studies revealed, and what methodological problems they faced.

References

Alison, A., Benjamin, L., Hoerner, K., & Roe, D. (1998). "We'll be back in a moment": A content analysis of advertisements in children's advertising in the 1950s. *Journal of Advertising, 27*(3), 1–9.

Churchill, G. A. (1979). Paradigm for developing better measures of marketing constructs. *Journal of Marketing Research, 29*(1), 23–38.

Denzin, N., & Lincoln, Y. (Eds.). (2000). *Handbook of qualitative research.* Thousand Oaks, CA: Sage.

Dittmar, H., & Drury, J. (2000). Self-image—is it in the bag? A qualitative comparison between ordinary and excessive consumers. *Journal of Economic Psychology, 21*(2), 109–142.

Eisenhardt, K. M. (1989). Building theories from case study research. *Academy of Management Review, 14*(4), 532–550.

Ford, J. B., Vooli, P. K., Honeycutt, E. D., & Casey, S. L. (1998). Gender role portrayals in Japanese advertising: A magazine content analysis. *Journal of Advertising, 27*(1), 113–125.

Gahan, C., & Hannibal, M. (1998). *Doing qualitative research using QSR, NUD*IST.* London: Sage.

Garee, M. L., & Schori, T. R. (1997). Focus groups illuminate quantitative research. *Marketing News, 31*(12), H25, June 9.

Glesne, C., & Peskin, A. (1992). *Becoming qualitative researchers.* White Plains, NY: Longman.

Greenbaum, T. (1997). Internet focus groups: An oxymoron. *Marketing News, 31*(5), 35–36.

Hamilton, K. (2000). Project galore: Qualitative research and leveraging Scotland's brand equity. *Journal of Advertising Research, 40*(1/2), 107–111.

Huhmann, B., & Brotherton, T. (1997). A content analysis of guilt appeals in popular magazine advertisements. *Journal of Advertising, 26*(2), 35–45.

Janda, S. (1999). Using qualitative methods in organizational research. *The International Journal of Organizational Analysis, 7*(4), 379–391.

Kamouche, K. (1995). Rhetoric, ritualism and totemism in human resource management. *Human Relations, 48*(4), 367–385.

Kellehear, A. (1993). *The unobtrusive researcher: A guide to methods.* St. Leonards, Australia: Allen & Unwin.

Kellehear, A. (1998). Ethical issues for the qualitative researcher: Some critical reflections. *Annual Review of Health Social Sciences, 8*, 14–18.

Marshall, C., & Rossman, G. B. (1989). *Designing qualitative research.* Newbury Park, CA: Sage.

Mason, J. (1998). *Qualitative research.* London: Sage.

McDonald, W. (1993). Focus groups research dynamics and reporting: An examination of research objectives and moderator influences. *Journal of the Academy of Marketing Science, 21*(2), 161–168.

Merrilees, B., & Tiessen, J. (1999). Building generalizable SME international marketing models. *International Marketing Review, 16*(4/5), 326–344.

Miles, M., & Huberman, M. (1994). *Qualitative data analysis—expanded sourcebook, 2nd Ed*. Thousand Oaks, CA: Sage.

Miller, D., & Merrilees, B. (2000). Gone to Gowings—an analysis of success factors in retail longevity: Gowings of Sydney. *Service Industries Journal, 20*(1), 61–85.

Morgan, D. (1997). *Focus groups as qualitative research*. Thousand Oaks, CA: Sage.

Murphy, T. (1997). Hurtling the barriers to qualitative research. *Marketing News, 31*(7), 18.

Stake, R. E. (1994). Case studies. In N. Denzin & Y. Lincoln (Eds.), *Handbook of qualitative research* (pp. 236–247). Thousand Oaks, CA: Sage.

Strauss, A., & Corbin, J. (1990). *Basics of qualitative research: Grounded theory procedures and techniques*. Newbury Park, CA: Sage.

Sudman, S., & Blair, E. (1999). Sampling in the twenty-first century. *Journal of Marketing Science, 27*(2), 269–277.

Tallerico, M. (1992). Computer technology for qualitative research: Hope and humbug. *Journal of Educational Administration, 30*(2), 32–40.

Turley, L. W., & Kelley, S. W. (1997). A comparison of advertising content: Business to business versus consumer services. *Journal of Advertising, 26*(4), 39–48.

Watts, B. L. (2000). Mixed methods make research better. *Marketing News, 34*(5), 16.

Weitzman, E. A. (1999). Analyzing qualitative data with computer software. *Health Services Research, 34*(5), 1241–1263.

Yin, R. K.-Z. (1994). *Case study research: Design & methods, 2nd Ed*. Thousand Oaks, CA: Sage.

Zorn, T. E., & Ruccio, S. (1998). The use of communication to motivate college sales teams. *The Journal of Business Communication, 35*(4), 468–500.

10

Quantitative Data Analysis

As with qualitative research, the design of quantitative research depends on the research question, and the feasibility of collecting and analyzing the data. You must plan the analysis at the beginning of the research process. If you have decided to undertake quantitative research, you will usually be gathering information from a "relatively large number of respondents" and performing statistical analysis to generate valuable information that can be projected to the entire population being studied (Malhotra et al., 2002). The analysis is also important, as it aims to assist in recommending a final course of action for decision makers. As was discussed earlier, there are many quantitative data collection methods. These include surveys (personal, telephone, electronic, and mail), experimentation (Brown & Melamed, 1990; Weller & Kimball Romney, 1988), and secondary data (i.e., data collected for other purposes, such as government or industry data). It is critical to consider how you plan to statistically analyze the data you collect to ensure you have the right kind of data for the statistical technique selected.

The empirical examination of information or data can be very complex. It relies on a range of statistical theory as well as intricate mathematical calculations. This chapter does *not* seek to explain the complexities of various quantitative methods; that is, the chapter is *not* designed to cover all possible analytical techniques or to be a chapter on research methods. It is assumed that you have taken at least one quantitative class (business statistics, marketing research, research methods, etc.) in your degree prior to attempting a research project, and you will need to refer back to the texts used in these courses, as well as to specialized texts dealing with quantitative data analysis issues, to learn how to undertake the various techniques discussed.

The focus of this chapter is to provide an overview of a range of quantitative techniques that you *might* want to use in dealing with your research project. The material in this chapter is, therefore, designed to be an overview

Authors' Note: The authors gratefully acknowledge Dr. Christopher D. Hopkins, Assistant Professor of Marketing at Clemson University, for contributing to the writing of this chapter.

of *some* of the more widely available tools that can be used to analyze data and a discussion of when you might use each technique. The complexities of each technique examined will not be provided. A secondary goal of this chapter is to help you to understand the academic works you will most likely read in which these various tools are applied and discussed. The chapter will refer to a range of statistical terms, which is essential for a discussion of the various techniques. These terms are defined in the Glossary, which appears at the end of this chapter.

Statistical analysis provides probabilistic estimates of numerical values that can be extremely useful in decision making and/or understanding your research results. It also enables comparisons to be made between different mean values and testing whether any difference is the result of a chance occurrence or not. It is important to appreciate that statistical analysis does not prove or disprove the existence of relationships and/or hypotheses, but can reject or support their existence.

Statistical analysis is a tool and not an end in itself, as statistical differences identify the existence or nonexistence of mathematical relationships. The managerial implications of any findings need to be considered in light of these relationships. The analysis is, therefore, one piece of information that needs to be considered in light of a range of other information. In some cases, statistical differences may not necessarily suggest differences in managerial action. For example, using a 7-point scale (the higher the response, the more likability), a market research firm might find that consumers have a mean response of likability for Advertisement A of 5.53, but that their mean level of likability for Advertisement B is 5.80. In statistical terms, these two numbers may in fact be different. What is the meaning of this statistical difference for managerial action? The results suggest that consumers like both advertisements, as the mean is above the median point on the scale for both (i.e., greater than 3.5). Though they do like the second advertisement better, there may be many reasons why the firm still chooses to use the first advertisement. The benefit of using the second may be minimal in terms of other effects, for example, purchase intention, and it might be possible that the first advertisement also has a better fit in terms of integrated marketing communication and overall strategy. Thus, managerial implications need to be carefully considered, even when a statistical difference exists.

Hypotheses, Significance, and Errors

After you have defined your research question, you will have to develop a range of propositions, or suppositions, that tentatively explain certain facts or phenomena. For example, you may believe that smaller firms have higher levels of employee involvement (i.e., employees feel more a part of the firm), and there will most likely be a range of academic theory that supports your belief. The question is whether this relationship really exists in the firms being studied.

Your research project is designed around answering your question, but what does answering the question mean? The objective of the project is to provide information that you can then use to support the claim that your proposition is true. Alternatively, it would suggest that you have not found support for your question. In many cases, the results may provide equivocal (unclear) results, as the answer is often not black-and-white.

To statistically evaluate your question, you will usually need to develop and test hypotheses. The testing of hypotheses requires that you determine whether the results you have found did not occur by chance and thus reflect the existence of the hypothesized relationship(s). Statistical evaluation relies on underlying probability theory, as well as what is defined as statistical error. These issues—hypotheses, significance, and errors—will be examined in the following subsections and have also been discussed elsewhere in this book.

Hypotheses

To assist you in answering your question, you will possibly generate a set of propositions, research questions, or hypotheses that can be empirically examined or tested. What this means is that you will be able to collect data from appropriate sources that can be systematically examined using a range of empirical techniques (at least in terms of this chapter), which allows you to evaluate the truthfulness (or validity, to use statistical terminology) of your vision on the population of interest. In the case of the question about employee involvement, the broad research question would be whether there are really differences in the levels of employee involvement based on the size of firms (for example, small and large).

To statistically evaluate questions, you need to put forward a hypothesis, which is an unproven testable proposition or supposition that tentatively explains certain facts or phenomena. It is a statement of assumptions you have about the nature of populations or relationships. In its simplest form, the hypothesis is an educated guess based on the material that you have read. To statistically evaluate the truthfulness of a question, you have to develop a null hypothesis (or statistical hypothesis), which will be used to test your proposition or supposition. In the example about employee involvement, the statistical hypothesis might be that the level of employee involvement does not vary based on the size of the organization.

The idea of hypothesis testing is that the statistical evaluation of your data will seek to ensure that any difference in the variable(s) of interest (in this case, employee involvement levels) that might be found is not simply due to some random error in the data or chance occurrence, but rather is due to the impact of the variable(s) of concern, in this case, organizational size.

The hypothesis that you will seek to test is set up so that it will not be rejected (nullified) purely as a result of random error and is usually expressed in the negative: for example, there is no difference between *a* and *b*, or *a* and *b* are the same (*a* = *b*). Rejecting this statement means that there is some difference between *a* and *b*, that is, they are not equal. In addition to a null hypothesis, you will also develop an alternate hypothesis, which is the opposite of the null hypothesis. Thus, if you reject the null hypothesis, you accept the alternative hypothesis. Within academic literature, a null hypothesis is normally labeled as H_0 and an alternate hypothesis is labeled as H_1. In regard to the question of employee involvement, it might be suggested that, assuming all other things are equal, any difference in employee view on involvement would be due to the size of the organization; thus, organizational size does have an impact on the involvement level of employees. Thus we have the following:

H_0: Employee involvement in small and large firms is the same (i.e., =).

H_1: Employee involvement in small firms and large firms is different (i.e., =).

It should be noted that in this example, the alternative hypothesis does not suggest that employee involvement in large firms will be higher or lower, but rather that they are simply not the same. It would be possible to suggest that they differ in a given way, should you wish to do so, but this is a more specific type of hypothesis (refer to texts such as Malhotra et al., 2002, for a more detailed discussion.).

Errors and Significance

If you flip a coin 10 times, probability theory suggests that on average it should land on heads five times and tails five times. But what if it does not happen this way on the first try? Does it mean that the coin is not balanced? The answer is no, as there is some chance, albeit small (0.001%), that the coin could randomly land on heads 10 times in a row. Thus if 1,000 people were to flip a coin 10 times, at least one person would randomly flip it on heads all 10 times. This is an important fact, as it might be hypothesized that there was no difference in the number of heads or tails flipped over 1,000 times. *But*, what if the first time you tried the experiment, you randomly happened to flip 10 heads? Should the hypothesis be rejected? While you might tend to believe that the hypothesis should be rejected, it should not be, as this is only *one* observation.

When undertaking research, you want to make sure that when you evaluate a hypothesis you do not (a) randomly reject a null hypothesis that is true or (b) accept a null hypothesis that is false. Rejecting a true hypothesis is called Type I error, and accepting a false hypothesis is called Type II error. The two forms of error are complementary, so that the more certain you are that you have not committed a Type I error, the greater the chance is that you have committed a Type II error, and vice versa. In regard to the employee involvement, you would not want to say that there was no difference in employee involvement based on firm size when there was in fact a difference

(Type I error) or that there was a difference in employee involvement based on firm size when there was not (Type II error).

One of the objectives of statistical evaluation and testing is to reduce the possibility of accidentally rejecting a true hypothesis, that is, of committing a Type I error. To achieve this, you will, as a researcher, ask yourself what the degree of error is that you are willing to accept in your research. This might be thought of as the likelihood that you will accidentally reject a valid hypothesis. Traditionally, researchers say that they want to be 95 percent confident that the hypothesis is rejected, which is the same as a 5 percent chance of error or a probability level of 0.05 that the hypothesis is, in fact, correct. However, this is merely a convention used by researchers, and you can use larger or smaller levels of certainty. The range normally is between 90 percent (i.e., a 10 percent chance of error or a probability of 0.1) and 99 percent (i.e., a 1 percent chance of error or a probability of 0.01).

The percentage refers to the fact that 95 percent of the observations will fall within a statistically determined range (we will refer back to this when we discuss confidence intervals) if the null hypothesis is true. This is the same as saying that there is only a 5 percent chance that the measured values will fall outside the relevant spread of observations, and therefore, there is only a 5 percent chance of the null hypothesis being rejected when it is true.

If any statistical evaluation of a hypothesis is to be valuable in assisting you in decision making, then you must know what the likelihood is that you risk rejecting the null hypothesis when in fact the null is true. Your degree of confidence regarding whether your evaluation is correct is referred to as the level of significance. This is the probability that your result did not occur randomly (i.e., that you accept your hypothesis) and will be determined in varying ways based on the specific statistical test to be used.

When you look at statistical results, you need to ensure that you do not confuse an empirical test that is statistically significant and the importance of any relationship identified. When comparing the employee involvement level in small and large firms, you might find that these are statistically different, but what does that mean? In terms of probability, you would have found that the numbers are not the same and that the probability that these different results occurred randomly is small. What the results do not tell you is how important the size of a firm is in regard to affecting employee involvement. Though some types of empirical examination might examine causality, in this case, significance simply says the numbers are *statistically* not the same; the evaluation does not say how important the difference is *or* if managerial actions should vary based on this information. The implications of differences need to be considered within the context of the specific research question being examined (as was discussed earlier). Therefore, you can have a very significant effect, that is, you can be very certain that it has not occurred by chance, and yet the strength or importance in terms of action of the effect can be very small. The evaluation of what this means for managerial decision making must include other situational information as well.

In research, you should select the hypothesis and the level of significance before undertaking the actual collection of data and empirical testing, as you need to ensure that you have the right kind of data and the level of error you are willing to accept. Though in many cases you will find that hypotheses are clearly accepted or rejected, there will be some situations in which this is less clear. For example, you might set a decision rule that you need to be 99 percent confident that the results do not occur randomly, but the analysis suggests that you can only be 95 percent confident that there are statistical differences in the data. Though in one situation you cannot reject the null hypothesis using a 99 percent probability level, you could reject it at a 95 percent significance level. Should you choose to change your decision rule? Is 95 percent confidence sufficient? Though this may make pragmatic sense, many researchers would suggest that this is inappropriate, as the decision rule was set in a given way for a reason. Alternatively, you might collect more data (e.g., increase the sample size), which will affect the statistical results (i.e., the power of the test) and may change the significance. However, this may or may not clarify the situation, depending on whether the new data adds any *different* information.

Empirically Examining Data

The empirical techniques available to you as a researcher are ever increasing. New techniques are being developed, and existing techniques are being applied in new ways. This is accelerated by new computer capacity, with new computers being able to statistically evaluate data in minutes or seconds that previously would have taken days to analyze. In one book, let alone a chapter of a book, it is impossible to cover all the various statistical tools available or the complexities associated with each tool. As we mentioned earlier, the objective of this chapter is to give you some understanding of the ways that you might analyze data, not to detail how you would undertake the analysis or the statistical technicalities of the techniques discussed. There are an increasing number of texts and computer software packages that can be used to assist you in undertaking the analysis and understanding all the nuances of the selected techniques described (Foster, 2002; Sector, 2001).

Deciding which techniques to cover in a chapter on quantitative analysis is no small task. As can be seen in Table 10.1, there are a range of choices, and this table does not cover all possible options or discuss the detailed complexities of each technique. For example, Hair et al. (1998) have spent over 700 pages discussing a range of selected multivariate techniques. In addition, the publishers of this book, Sage, have a whole series (140+ titles and growing) entitled "Quantitative Applications in the Social Sciences" that examines simple and complex aspects of quantitative tools. Though you may not want to understand all possible techniques, the one question that all students undertaking a quantitatively based research project want to know

Table 10.1 Summary of Techniques Discussed in This Chapter

Test/Statistic	Number of Variables	Number of Groups Being Compared	Purpose
Mean	1	N/A	Description of the central tendency of a data set
Variance	1	N/A	Description of dispersion within a data set
Standard deviation	1	N/A	Description of dispersion within a data set
Confidence intervals	1	N/A	Estimate of the range at which a statistic (e.g., mean, variance, standard deviation) should fall
Frequency distributions	1	N/A	Description of the number of times a data item occurs
Cross-tabs	2	2 or more	Description of the relationship between two categorical variables
Pearson product-moment correlation	2	2 or more	Association between two variables
Point biserial coefficient	2	2 or more	Association between two categorical variables
Chi-square test (χ^2)	2 or more	2 or more	Significance between two categorical measures or for the difference in 2 standard deviations
Proportions	1	N/A	Significance between two categorical measures
z-test	1 or 2	2	Mean differences in one or two large (> 30) data sets
t-test	1 or 2	2	Mean difference in one or two small (< 30) data sets
ANOVA	1 or more	2 or more	Means difference test in more than two groups
MANOVA	2 or more	2 or more	Means difference test in more than two groups
Linear regression	1 dependent 1 independent	N/A	The degree to which an independent variable predicts a dependent variable
Multiple regression	1 dependent more than 1 independent	N/A	The degree to which a single dependent variable is predicted by multiple dependent variables
Factor analysis	Multiple related measures	N/A	Places data items into similar heterogeneous groups
Conjoint analysis	1 dependent more than 1 independent	N/A	Assesses how respondents develop attitudes and preferences
Structural equation modeling	Multiple dependent and independent	N/A	Assesses causal effect of multiple independent variables on multiple dependents variables

is which empirical technique is right for their research question. As has been discussed previously, the question drives all aspects of the research. This includes driving any empirical examination and also directs you in regard to the type of data you will need. Though there may be one most appropriate empirical technique for your question, it can only be applied if you have collected the right data. In most cases, there will be multiple techniques that might be used, and thus you do have to make a choice.

There are many ways to classify empirical tests. For the purpose of this book, the following have been chosen to be examined: basic analysis, associations, comparing groups, simple causal relationships, and an introduction to complex analysis. Each of the following subsections will *briefly* overview a set of empirical techniques that you *might* want to use or that is discussed in the literature. This is not a comprehensive listing of all possible empirical tests, but rather, those that students tend to use in their research or that are frequently discussed in the literature. A range of other sources that discuss the complexities of these techniques in more detail, and that provide references to such sources, are referred to in the Further Reading section under the heading "Quantitative Analysis." Once again, the discussion is designed to assist you in determining which technique is the most relevant for your research question. The discussion will by no means make you an expert in the use of these techniques.

Basic Analysis

Before you move on to moderately complex empirical techniques, it is important to undertake some very basic evaluation of the data. Some texts refer to some of these analyses as descriptive analysis and allow you to get a better understanding of the data before undertaking more complex statistical evaluation. The information identified in this descriptive analysis sometimes becomes the basis of more complex analysis.

You will most likely want to examine the *mean* (average) response, assuming you have the right kind of data to start with (i.e., interval- or ratio-valued data), for which a number has meaning beyond any coding value (i.e., parametric data) (Table 10.2). For example, in looking at developing a responsible drinking policy in your university bar, you might want to know the average number of drinks consumed per week by students. This, of course, assumes that you have asked respondents to tell you how many drinks they have in an average week. The mean response has no meaning when you use scales (see Table 10.2 for a brief discussion of scales) that allow people to define a range, such as (a) zero drinks, (b) one to three drinks, (c) four to six drinks, or (d) more than six drinks. When using an interval, the mean response would tell you the average interval, but not the average number of drinks consumed. That is, you would know the range of drinks consumed by the average student, but you would not know the number of

Table 10.2   Summary of Scales

Scale Type	Definition	Example
Nominal scales	"Questions require respondents to provide only some type of descriptor as the raw response."	Gender: (a) Male; (b) Female
Ordinal scale	"Allows a respondent to express relative magnitude between answers to a question."	How important is it that there are examples in this book? (1) Important; (2) Neither important nor unimportant; (3) Unimportant.
Interval scale	"Demonstrates absolute differences between each scale point."	In which category does your average grade fall? (a) Less than 50%; (b) 50%–59%; (c) 60%–69%; (d) 70%–79%; (e) 80%–89%; (f) 90%–100%.
Ratio scale	"Examines absolute point as well as relative distance to other responses."	What is your current age in years?

SOURCE: Adapted from Hair et al. (2003, pp. 380–386).

drinks consumed on average, and given that the last interval is unbounded (i.e., six+), even a guess of the average would be impossible. As a result, when using interval data, you would want to examine the frequency distribution, which tells you how many people responded to each option (as well as the percentage of respondents). This could also be used when you have parametric data asking about the number of drinks compared with the range of drinks consumed.

You may also want to know about how the data is distributed. The *frequency distribution* gives you some general picture about the dispersion, as well as the maximum and minimum response. The frequency is usually not sufficient for you to make empirical statements about the data. If you have parametric data, you will want to know how widely spread the data are using the *variance*, which tells you about the average variation in responses from the mean, which is a statistical manipulation of the variance (i.e., the square root of the variance—*standard deviation*).

Both variance and standard deviation are used when undertaking other statistical evaluations of your data. What the variance tells you is how similar the responses or data are. A small variance indicates that respondents behave similarly, whereas a large variance indicates that there are greater variations in responses. For example, let us assume that the average student consumes five drinks per week and that there is a standard deviation of 1.2 drinks. This means that the students consume a varying number of drinks, but that the average difference to the mean suggests most students consume between 3.8 and 6.2 drinks. So, though there may be some difference in behavior, it is somewhat similar. On the other hand, if the standard deviation were very high, for example, 4.2, this would mean that the students might be expected to consume between .8 and 9.2 drinks. The implication for this is that when undertaking statistical tests, it might be harder to identify statistically significant differences in groups simply because of the higher standard deviation and variance.

It must be remembered that you will rarely be able to collect data from everyone (i.e., the entire population), and typically you are trying to generalize results from a *sample* of respondents from the population. Referring back to the drinking example, would any one class of students be representative of your entire university? There may be a range of differences in behavior based on students' majors or age, and possibly even the time of the class (students taking 8:00 A.M. classes might be different than those taking all afternoon classes). Therefore, you want to know how likely the sample is to be representative of the overall population being examined.

This leads us to one of the more basic statistical tools, *confidence intervals*. A confidence interval provides an estimate of the range in which the mean, or some other measure such as percentage of observations, should fall for a particular population. The range is based on the sample responses collected, the number of observations, and the degree of error that you are willing to accept.

The range of mean values predicted by the confidence interval suggests that you are certain within x percent probability that the population mean of respondents is within the reasonable bounds of the sample mean. Confidence intervals can also be calculated for percentages of respondents answering a given way (e.g., do more than 50 percent of people respond z), although the specific formula used is a bit different.

You can vary the size of the interval by changing the probability that it is correct. A 95 percent confidence level is frequently used, which would mean that you are 95 percent sure that the population mean is within a given range. More generally, this means that you are setting out some bounds within which you are x percent sure that the mean value will fall. As described previously, this will identify how similar the respondents are; that is, a small confidence interval suggests that there are low levels of variation among the sample, whereas a large confidence interval suggests that there is wide variation among respondents. This will give you a feeling for how similar respondents are in a group. Wide variance, for example, in the drinking example, would suggest that there are some students who consume substantially greater quantities than others.

In examining data, you might also want to develop a *cross-tabulation* of results in which you examine responses across two or more variables at the same time. In the case of the drinking question, you could look at the average number of drinks consumed by gender. This is in many ways simply another type of frequency distribution in which there are three columns— one for males, one for females, and one for the total (see Table 10.3). The

Table 10.3   Cross-Tabulations

Average Number of Drinks Consumed in a Week	Female		Male		Total	
Zero	52.6%	10.6%	47.4%	9.6%	100%	20.2%
	21.3%	10	19.1%	9	20.2%	19
One	51.7%	16%	48.3%	14.9%	100	30.9%
	31.9%	15	29.8%	14	30.9%	29
Two	52.1%	12.8%	47.9%	11.7%	100%	24.5%
	25.5%	12	23.4%	11	24.5%	23
Three	43.5%	10.6%	46.5%	13.8%	100%	24.5%
	21.3%	10	27.7%	13	24.5%	23
Total	50%	50%	50%	50%	100%	100
	100%	47	100%	47	100%	94

Where:

Row percentage	Percentage of total
Column percentage	Number of observations in cell

cross-tabulation also usually will provide you with information on the distribution based on the number of drinks (i.e., row percentage), gender (column percentage), and overall (total percentage).

In examining cross-tabulations, you are looking for differences in the percentage responses from those that would be statistically anticipated. An examination of the cross-tabulation provided in the previous paragraph suggests that the sample is evenly balanced between genders, but that drinking behavior by number of drinks consumed appears to vary. The results of the cross-tabulation will provide some valuable information for you, and the next section will discuss some slightly more advanced analysis techniques that can be used based on cross-tabulation.

Basic Associations

The basic descriptive information discussed in the previous section does not really tell you much about how variables relate to one another. Going back to examples discussed earlier in this chapter, if you want to determine if the size of an organization is related to employee involvement in that organization, you might want to determine if there is an association between two variables; for example, do they move together directly (i.e., when one goes up, the other goes up) or indirectly (i.e., when one goes up, the other goes down). Such an examination is valuable, but you should be warned that this does not suggest that organizational size *causes* involvement or that more individual involvement *causes* organizations to be larger. It simply identifies that the two variables move together. Inferring causality from correlations is one basic mistake that students frequently make.

One of the most common tools used to examine associations is a *correlation analysis*. There are in fact several different types of correlation that might be examined, and the most appropriate depends on the type of data that you are going to use. In looking at a correlation, there may be a positive or negative relationship between two variables. The closer the relationship is to 1 or −1, the stronger the relationship; the closer to zero, the weaker the relationship. Most of the time, we are interested in determining whether the correlation between variables is statistically different from zero (i.e., that there is an association). It is possible that because of the statistical complexity of the calculations, a very small correlation between two variables (for example, .05) might be found to be statistically different from zero, but in another case, a larger correlation (for example, .20) might be statistically insignificant from zero. The reason for a lack of statistical significance would relate to the variance in the two variables being examined and/or the number of responses. That is, high variance with low responses might not be statistically significant. The point is that, as with all empirical analysis, you need to be concerned not only with the size of the effect, but also with whether it is statistically significant.

Correlations among variables are also important for another statistical reason. If you have two variables with a statistically significant correlation of 1 (i.e., when one moves up by 1 unit, the other moves up by 1 unit), you in fact might have two variables measuring the same thing. In more complex analysis, this might cause problems with computations and, therefore, is something you need to at least be aware of (see Hair et al., 1998 for a discussion of multicollinearity).

As mentioned earlier, there are a variety of types of correlations that can be used depending on the type of data collected. It is even possible to undertake a correlation analysis when you have data based on different types of scales. One standard correlation technique that is frequently used when you have parametric data (nominal, interval, or ratio scales), for example, if you wanted to look at the relationship between the number of salespeople in a firm and the firm's sales volume, is the *Pearson product-moment correlation*. This type of correlation would also be useful if you wanted to look at organizational size and the level of employee commitment.

In other cases, you will have ranked data (i.e., a form of nonparametric data) and want to see if the rankings are the same. For example, you might want to see if consumers in different segments have the same order of preferences for products in one category. In this situation, you would use a

Spearman rank-order correlation, which examines whether the rankings vary in a similar way. There are also other methods of looking at ranked data, such as the *Wilcoxon signed-rank test.* There is also the *point biserial correlation coefficient,* which allows you to look at correlations between variables that use different types of scales. These more complex tools are useful, but it might be better for you to collect data that allows you to use more readily used techniques, rather than be forced to find a complex technique to deal with the data that you have. Once again this highlights the need to plan your data collection with your analysis in mind.

Cross-tabulations were introduced in the section on basic analysis. These can be examined statistically to identify if the variables are independent using a *chi-square* (χ^2) statistic (see Aaker, Kumar, & Day, 1995). This is slightly different from a simple correlation, as it does not identify the direction or strength of the relationship, but rather whether the distribution of the two variables is independent (i.e., whether there is an association between the variables). Though this is important, if you are trying to make recommendations based on chi-square analysis, it is not really that useful, as you do not know the strength of the relationship or the direction.

At this point, it is important to emphasize once again that you must think about the type of analysis you would like to undertake *before* you collect your data. This is the only way you can ensure that you collect the right data for your research question, and you should also take into consideration your own research expertise and the tools you wish to use. Therefore, from the beginning of the project, you need to make sure that you have the right kind of data for the analysis that you are comfortable with.

Comparing Groups

In many cases, you might want to identify differences, if any, between two or more groups. For example,

- Are there differences in younger and older consumers in regard to a range of issues?
- Are firms that adopt socially responsible practices more profitable than those that do not?
- Do people respond differently to different levels of fear in advertisements?

As with all empirical techniques, the approach you use to compare groups is based on the type of data collected. This discussion will focus primarily on parametric data, although it will begin by discussing one tool that can be used to compare proportions between groups rather than ordinal data.

In some cases, you will not be comparing mean values, but rather looking at whether the proportion of responses differs between two groups. For example, do more alumni from University X support their university's alumni fundraising than do alumni at another university, University Y? Looking at differences in proportions has the benefit adjusting for differences in organization size. For example, if University X has 50,000 students and University Y has 10,000 students, it would be expected that University X would generate more donations through alumni, both in terms of overall dollars and number of donors. However, they might in fact be equally successful in generating donations as a percentage of overall alumni. In this case, you would undertake what is called a z-*test*. This test uses the proportion identified in the two samples and the number of respondents in each group to determine whether there are (or are not) statistically significant differences in the proportions of donors in the two universities. A statistically significant z, based on an examination of a Z table (most computer packages also provide the significance level), would identify whether the groups were statistically different at a given level of significance. It would be up to you to determine the acceptable level, which would usually be 0.05 (or 5%), but could be higher (0.10, or 10%) or lower (0.01, or 1%).

It should be noted that it is also possible to undertake a z-test of proportions in regard to some base level. For example, if University X wanted to see if its letter was effective in generating donations from more than 50% of the alumni, it could undertake a z-test of this as well. Like the comparison between two groups, a statistically significant result would indicate whether it was successful (i.e., more than 50%) or unsuccessful (i.e., 50% or less). If you were looking at comparing proportions across multiple groups, you would use a chi-square test (χ^2), which, as was discussed previously, would show that the variables were (or were not) independent, but you cannot identify the direction of differences when examining multiple groups.

In your research, you might be comparing the mean responses for a variable between two or more groups. When examining mean values between two groups, you use what is referred to as a t-*test,* which provides a t-statistic, which may (or may not) be statistically significant at your selected level of error. Like most empirical tests, computer programs usually provide you with the probability of significance; you can also look this up in an appropriate table. The t-test also identifies the direction of the difference, should it exist, and will not only tell you that two means are different, but also which one is larger. For example, if in your examination of a large sample of male and female levels of satisfaction with work you found that the t-statistic was 1.65, this would indicate that you were 95 percent confident that the responses were statistically different (or $p < .05$ that they are not different). If the t-statistic were 2.326, you would be 99 percent confident that the responses were statistically different (or $p < .01$ that they are not different).

A word of caution about using a t-test must be added here. Students frequently will want to undertake comparisons of many variables between the same two groups. As empirical examination of data is based on probability, you need to realize that if enough comparisons are made between groups, some differences will be expected to occur randomly. In fact, if you compared

20 variables between two groups, you would expect that there would be at least one for which a difference was found simply due to random error (i.e., $.05 \times 20 = 1$). There is a process that can be used to adjust for the fact that you are undertaking multiple tests, a *Bonferroni correction,* which adjusts for the likelihood of accepting that differences exist when there are many tests (Hair et al., 1998). The effect of using this adjustment is that you are being more conservative in your evaluation of differences, and thus greater differences are required to support the idea that statistically significant differences exist.

In some cases, you may want to compare mean values across more than two groups. For example, you might want to examine consumers' attitudes toward three different advertisements. It is possible to use *t*-tests to look at this question, but this would involve you undertaking three pairs of *t*-tests (e.g., Ad1-Ad2, Ad1-Ad3, and Ad2-Ad3). In fact, this type of paired comparison may be valuable, as it will identify whether there are any differences between groups and exactly what those differences are. However, it would also be useful to examine whether attitudes vary across the three advertisements. This type of analysis is undertaken using what is referred to as an *ANOVA (analysis of variance).* A statistically significant F-*statistic* (the test statistic used in ANOVA) is one in which the probability is such that you are sure any difference is not random. This would indicate that attitudes toward the advertisements are different, but it does *not* tell where the difference is. If there were six different advertisements, the interpretation would be the same (i.e., the attitudes of consumers are not the same across the advertisements). But what if you want to know where the difference occurs? The only way to find out how different individual groups are from one another is by undertaking *paired comparisons.* Understanding this subtlety is essential, because if there were six groups, it may be the case that Group 1 and Group 2 are the only ones that are statistically different. The ANOVA would tell you that the six groups are not the same. Undertaking all the paired *t*-tests would tell you exactly where the differences occur.

ANOVA analysis also allows you to look at how multiple individual variables vary between groups. Considering the advertising example, you might want to look at whether the attitudes toward the advertisement differ and whether the attitudes toward the brand differ across the three advertisements, as well as whether there was an interaction between the two attitudes (i.e., does the combination of brand and advertisement matter?). The ANOVA analysis allows you to look at what is called the *one-way effects,* of which there are two in the advertising example—attitude toward the advertisement and attitude toward the brand—as well as the *two-way effect* (i.e., interaction)—attitude toward the advertisement × attitude toward the brand. An F-statistic and probability are generally calculated for each effect. In this way, you can identify whether any variables (one-way or two-way) vary across the groups. Again, any statistical differences indicate that the variables of interest are not the same across the groups, but an ANOVA does not tell you where the differences occur.

When discussing *t*-tests, we mentioned that you might want to compare whether multiple variables differ between two or more groups. This can be done using a *MANOVA (multiple analysis of variance)*. This technique has the benefit of identifying whether a set of variables differs between two groups; thus, you do not have the multiple comparison problem identified earlier. However, a discussion of this and other complex multiple comparisons of means is moving beyond the objectives of this chapter, and if you want to use this, refer to a text on the subject (e.g., Hair et al., 1998).

Basic Causal Relationship

Though the discussion so far has allowed you to look at data empirically, it has not allowed you to identify a relationship in which a movement in one variable causes another to change. Some inferences about causality might have been made when comparing groups—a difference in variables must be attributed to the differences in the groups, and if you could control for all possible variables, then the difference between groups explains the difference in variables. This section will discuss *simple regression* and *multiple regression,* which can be used to examine the causality between dependent and independent variables, that is, whether a change in variable *a* results in a change to variable *b*. Knowing there is a causal relationship will be extremely useful, especially when you are making recommendations, as there is strong support for undertaking some action.

There are many different types of regression analysis, and the technique is indeed a complex tool. For example, within the Sage *Quantitative Applications in the Social Sciences* series, there are more than 15 different volumes focusing on various aspects or types of regression analysis. It is a complex topic, and this brief section of this chapter will describe only the bare bones of two of the simplest types of regression.

A simple linear regression examines how one variable (the independent variable) causes change in another (the dependent variable). Multiple regression analysis is slightly more advanced in that it looks at how several independent variables affect a dependent variable while holding all other variables constant. Therefore, if you want to look at how variables work in combination to affect a dependent variable, you would need to calculate interaction variables. For example, let's assume you are looking at how consumers' purchase intentions change in regard to their attitudes toward the brand and toward the advertisement, both of which the literature has suggested should affect purchase intention. In this case, you could possibly undertake a regression in which purchase intention was the dependent variable and there were three independent variables—attitude toward the brand, attitude toward the advertisement, and a combined (i.e., interactive) variable, attitude toward the brand × attitude toward the advertisement. Though you want to find out whether the three independent variables statistically affect the independent variable, the regression analysis provides a range of other useful statistical information (and tests) that you need to understand if you are to interpret it accurately.

The first question you need to ask yourself is whether the regression equation being examined is actually statistically appropriate. That is, does the regression actually explain anything? To evaluate this question, you will need to examine the regression's F-statistic and associated significance. If the regression's F-statistic is significant (i.e., has a probability level of .05, suggesting that the equation examined is not random), then you can proceed in terms of looking at the specific relationships examined.

A second broad issue to examine is the degree to which the equation specified explains variance in the dependent variable. In looking at this issue, you will want to examine the R-*square (R²)* value and the *adjusted* R-*square* value (which takes into account the number of observations). The higher the R-square value, the higher the variance in the dependent variable. For example, does the regression explain 80 percent of the variance in the dependent variable or 20 percent of the variance? If the equation explains only 20 percent of the variance in the dependent variable, then it means that there are other factors that explain 80 percent of the variance. Because of this, though you may find important relationships between variables (discussed in the following subsection), manipulating these variables will still mean that the dependent variable will change based on other factors.

The next value of importance relates to the independent variable. Statistical software programs will report a coefficient for each independent variable. This number tells you how a 1-unit change in this variable will affect the independent variable. Consider the example of the regression in which the overall profit (in thousands of dollars) of firms in an industry is the dependent variable and the number of salespeople employed by each firm is the independent variable. If the coefficient for salespeople were 12.45, this would suggest that adding one salesperson increases profit by $12,450.

You cannot stop with looking at the coefficient of independent variables alone. The analysis will also report a t-statistic for the coefficient, as well as a probability level, and both the coefficient and the t-statistic need to be considered. The t-statistic and probability are reporting whether you can be confident that the coefficient is statistically different from zero. For example, if the t-statistic were .249 with a probability of .9041, then you would be led to the conclusion that even though the independent variable's coefficient is 12.45, this is not statistically different from zero. In this case you cannot say that adding salespeople (or removing them) will affect profitability, as the coefficient has no statistical meaning, that is, the number of salespeople is not a significant variable in regard to explaining profits.

Understanding the relationships for the empirical results and implications is critical, as you need to know that your regression equation is sound (i.e., the F-statistic is significant), as well as whether any coefficient identified is significantly different from zero (i.e., the t-statistic is significant). Having conclusions or making recommendations based on meaningless information (i.e., non–statistically significant results), is fraught with danger.

Introducing Advanced Techniques

Though it was mentioned earlier that complex evaluation techniques would not be discussed in this chapter, it is important that at least four techniques are mentioned, as these are increasingly being used in the academic business literature. Given that you will most likely be referring to articles using these techniques, it is beneficial to have some idea of what types of relationships the authors are trying to examine. We suggest that you generally not consider using these techniques in your research, unless you have a very solid understanding of the tools and the data analysis is a major component of the subject. Simply using complex tools because they sound interesting is unnecessary; there is no need to crack a peanut with a sledgehammer when less complex approaches work equally well.

When undertaking your project, you may have a number of different variables that do not necessarily measure different things. In some cases, you may have included multiple questions to capture various aspects of one issue (i.e., multidimensional variables). Consider, for example, research looking at service quality. One approach to examining this issue has been to undertake a survey called SERVQUAL (Zeithaml, Parasuraman, & Barry, 1990), which basically asks respondents 22 questions that can be grouped so that they measure five issues associated with service delivery. The question is *how* to group these variables in a way in which you are sure they measure the same thing (i.e., one construct). An empirical approach to this is called *factor analysis*. Factor analysis groups variables based on how they vary, that is, it seeks to empirically group variables that move in similar ways. These variables are then usually added together (aggregated) into one variable (called a composite construct). However, the analysis might also suggest that some variables be omitted from further analysis.

The benefit of developing composite constructs is that you would then have fewer variables to examine. In some ways, it might be suggested that factor analysis is not really data analysis in regard to hypotheses, as it is designed to assist in developing variables for examination. The new variables (i.e., the constructs) would then be analyzed using other techniques discussed elsewhere in this chapter. Factor analysis is not necessarily a pure science, as there are several different approaches to manipulating the data, as well as for identifying what variables should be included in the composite constructs. It could be suggested that the naming of these constructs is purely art, as you would need to develop a name based on some commonality among the variables being aggregated.

Another technique that is frequently used to group data is called *cluster analysis* (see Punj & Stewart, 1983). What this does is group individuals based on their responses rather than group the individual variables. This approach is frequently used to differentiate groups based on how they respond to questions rather than on simple demographic variables. For example, within the research looking at shopping, researchers have identified that people choose to shop for different reasons (i.e., people can be classified as recreational shoppers, value shoppers, convenience shoppers, etc.). These groups were defined by clustering consumers who respond to a set of questions in a similar way (the questions could even be composite variables defined using factor analysis). Researchers could then seek to describe each cluster based on the variables used to define the cluster, as well as other variables. Clusters can also be used as groups from which other analysis, such as ANOVA, can be undertaken. The benefit of cluster analysis is that it allows groupings to be made that might not be clearly definable without complex empirical processes.

In terms of identifying causality, there are a range of complex techniques that are increasingly being used. One such technique is called *structural equation modeling,* and there are in fact several software packages designed specifically to assist with this process. The popularity of modeling has increased as computer capability has increased, because the process requires extensive computer capacity that was previously unavailable. Modeling is, in many ways, an extension of regression analysis. The process allows researchers to identify how variables relate within complex systems; for example, modeling allows for the identification of whether there are direct effects or moderating effects, and as a result moves beyond simple regression, which might not deal with complex interactions among variables easily. Modeling has the benefit of allowing you to test a complex set of relationships among data, representing all independent variables that should affect a dependent variable, in a way that would have been impossible previously. The new software allows you to either develop a model of relationships that can be tested *or* develop a model based on the data included. There are complex processes to refine models, and should you wish to learn more about this, you should refer to one of the texts specifically focusing on the technique you plan to use, as there are differences between approaches. This is a very complex technique, and it is unlikely that you would use it in an undergraduate assignment, but it is frequently used in the literature.

Another complex process that is increasingly being used, especially in choice modeling, is *conjoint analysis.* Individuals, as consumers or managers, are constantly being asked to choose from a range of available options. Within the marketing area, there is great interest in understanding how individuals compare different offerings. For example, how do consumers weigh the following car attributes against one another—low versus medium price, 3-year versus 5-year warrantee, and basic style versus sports model? The problem with this question is that it is difficult to identify the value of each of the attributes in terms of preferences, especially when these three issues may be interrelated. In reality, there are eight different sets of combinations available. Conjoint analysis allows the researcher to actually determine the value of each attribute to the individual and, therefore, allows those developing strategy to better understand how consumers make tradeoffs. The empirical process used for conjoint analysis is complex, and the design of the study to collect conjoint analysis data can also be complex (Louviere, Hensher, & Swait, 2000) and will most likely be beyond many undergraduate student research projects. However, the process is increasingly being used in research, and thus you may come across it in your readings, but like structural equation modeling, it is something that most likely is too advanced for most student projects.

Conclusion

In your research project, you will need to decide what type of analysis you will use to assist you in answering your question. Those described in this chapter and summarized in Table 10.1 might be some of the more relevant. Given that there are many different tools that can be used to answer the same type of question, you need to be able to justify to yourself, your lecturer/professor/supervisor, and possibly the reader, why you chose a specific approach. Choosing the most complex method available is not necessarily the best way to deal with an issue, especially if you do not have the technical expertise to implement the technique selected. The selection of the most appropriate method is a critical issue and affects a range of earlier actions, not just data analysis. The approach used determines the type of data that needs to be collected and, therefore, determines how you ask respondents questions. Because of this, considering empirical analysis is something that should be done carefully. Though we have not focused on them in this chapter, you may need to learn and practice using various statistical software packages to enable you to use the selected tool. Many of these packages are becoming increasingly user-friendly (see Foster, 2002 or Sector, 2001), although the sophistication of the project, the technique selected, and your individual expertise will determine how much training is required.

This chapter has discussed a range of different approaches that can be used to answer different types of questions that are based on an underlying set of statistical principles. Though these have not been discussed in detail within this chapter, it is important that you comply with the basic requirements associated with each specific technique and test. For example, it is suggested that, when undertaking some ANOVA processes, you have at least five observations for each variable. Failure to meet this basic requirement will mean that you are unable to utilize this process. Again, this will affect the way data is collected to ensure, that the minimum requirements of tests are met.

Last, but most important, you need to remember that empirical evaluation of data is a tool, and not an end in itself. The objective of the analysis is to assist you in understanding relationships and answering your research question. It may also assist you in making recommendations about practice. Empirical analysis is based on probability, and therefore, the specific data collected will have a unique distribution, and it may, unfortunately, have inherent flaws. This means that you are never 100% certain (remember Type I and Type II errors) of the results. Though you can blame poor decisions on the numbers, as a researcher, you are responsible for the collection of the data and its interpretation. The adage "garbage in, garbage out" still applies, even if you are undertaking advanced empirical analysis.

Glossary

Alternative Hypothesis (H_1)—The statement that is the opposite of the null hypothesis (H_0). This might suggest that there are in fact differences between groups, whereas the null hypothesis suggests that there are not. Accepting the alternative hypothesis entails rejecting the null hypothesis.

ANOVA (analysis of variance)—A statistical technique for comparing whether mean responses of individual variables vary across more than two groups.

Association—An identification acknowledging that a relationship exists between two variables.

Bonferroni correction—A statistical adjustment used to take into consideration that there are multiple statistical tests being undertaken in regard to the same samples, which adjusts the significance level required.

Causal relationship—A relationship in which a change in one variable results in a change (positive or negative) in another variable.

Chi-square statistic (χ^2)—The statistical test that allows you to determine if two or more variables are distributed as expected, using the results presented in a cross-tabulation. This does not identify direction or strength of relationships, only that variables are not distributed as expected.

Choice modeling—A statistical process that allows you to identify the importance of individual variables in regard to a set of variables.

Cluster analysis—A statistical process that allows you to group *respondents* together based on the fact that they answered questions in a similar way.

Coefficient—A number produced in a range of statistical procedures (regressions, structural equation modeling, etc.) that suggests how independent variables affect other variables. Within a regression analysis, the *t*-test is used to identify whether the coefficient is statistically and significantly different from zero.

Composite construct—A variable that is developed as the result of adding multiple related variables (items) together, also sometimes called a SUMSCORE or composite score.

Confidence interval estimate—A range of numbers within which a population mean should lie; an estimate of the population mean based on the knowledge that it will equate the sample mean plus or minus a sampling error.

Correlation coefficient—A statistical measure assessing whether two variables are associated, that is, whether two variables increase or decrease together.

Cross tabulation—A presentation of two (or sometimes more) variables in a tabular format that identifies the number and percentage response based on the overall sample, row, and column. The chi-square statistic is used to determine if the variables are distributed independently.

Dependent variable—A criterion or variable expected to be predicted or explained by another variable; a variable expected to be dependent on the experimenter's manipulation.

Descriptive analysis—The transformation of raw data into an easily understandable form; it includes a range of basic tools including frequency distributions, mean, variance, and so forth. Examining basic descriptive information is the first step in examining empirical data.

Factor analysis—A statistical process that allows you to group variables together that vary in the same way, which in turn can be used to aggregate these into a new composite variable.

Frequency distribution—A count of the number of responses to a question or the occurrence of a phenomenon of interest.

F-statistic—This statistic is used when undertaking ANOVAs to measure the ratio of within-group to across-group variation; it determines whether there are differences between multiple groups. It does not tell you the direction of differentiation nor where the difference occurs. The *F*-statistic is also used in regressions to determine whether the equation specified fits the data.

Independent variable—A predictor or explanatory variable; it cannot be controlled or is not dependent on other variables.

Interaction effect—When two or more variables interact such that they affect a dependent variable.

Linear regression—A statistical technique in which it is assumed that one independent variable causes, or predicts, another dependent variable and includes some level of random variation (i.e., error). There are a range of statistics that relate to the significance including the coefficient, t-test, F-test, and R-square.

MANOVA (multiple analyses of variance)—A statistical technique for comparing whether sets of multiple dependent variables vary across two or more groups.

Mean—The average response across a sample or population.

Multicolinearity—A situation in which two or more independent variables are highly correlated and thus measure the same thing. Having such variables causes problems for a number of statistical tests.

Multidimensional variables—Sometimes used when discussing composite variables, this is a situation in which one issue is in fact measured using multiple questions that frequently need to be aggregated in some way.

Multiple regression—A more complex version of a linear regression in which there is more than one independent variable and possibly interaction terms as well.

Nonparametric data—This is data for which descriptive statistics have no meaning and that requires you to use different types of statistical tests, which usually mirror those used for parametric data.

Null hypothesis (H_0)—The statement that we are testing. It is usually suggested that there are no differences between variables or groups. Accepting the null hypothesis entails rejecting the alternative hypothesis.

One-way effects—This term suggests that the independent variable directly affects the dependent variable in a situation that includes a single dependent variable and single, multilevel, independent variables.

Parametric variables—Variables which the distribution associated with the data can be described by a mean, variance, and standard deviation.

Pearson product-moment correlation—This is a statistical measure that can be used to determine the degree to which two parametric variables are correlated.

Population—All possible members of the group being investigated.

Probability—The likelihood that an event will occur. Within empirical analysis, it relates to the likelihood that an event occurred (or did not occur) randomly.

Qualitative—This is rich data that is recorded without using scaled responses and is usually collected using techniques such as open-ended questions (see Chapter 9 for discussion of techniques).

Quantitative—This is data that has various numeric properties and allows for statistical testing of various types described within Chapter 10.

Rejecting—Deciding whether the statistical results, using the relevant decision rule, indicate that the null hypothesis should be assumed to be incorrect at the specified level of significance.

Responses—How individuals answer the questions asked.

R-square (R^2)—This statistic tells you the percentage of variance that is explained by a linear or multiple regression. It can be adjusted to take into account the number of variables being used (i.e., the adjusted R-square).

Sample—The set of respondents that you examine; a subset of a larger population. It is desired that the sample be representative of the population of interest.

Spearman rank-order correlation—A statistical tool that is used to determine the degree to which two nonparametric (ranking) variables are correlated.

Standard deviation—The square root of the variance. This statistic is used extensively to assist in understanding the spread of response and is used in many of the empirical tests.

Statistically significant—A decision rule that is used to determine whether the result of the test being examined (i.e., hypothesis) is rejected or not. This takes into account the level of error that you are willing to accept (i.e., the likelihood that the results occurred randomly).

Structural equation modeling—A statistical technique that allows you to examine how independent variables interact and affect one or more dependent variables. The technique can be undertaken using one of the many statistical software packages available that is specifically designed to undertake this type of analysis.

t-test—A statistical test that determines whether two mean values are statistically significantly different, or in a regression, whether the coefficient is statistically significantly different from zero.

Two-way effect—Interactions between variables; the concept is often used in ANOVAs examining multiple independent variables. The situation includes a single dependent variable and multiple, multilevel, independent variables.

Type I error—The likelihood that a true null hypothesis will be rejected.

Type II error—The likelihood that a false null hypothesis will be accepted (failure to reject a false null).

Variance—The degree to which responses on average differ from the mean (i.e., average value).

z-test—A statistical test used to examine if proportions are statistically significantly different from one another.

References

Aaker, D. A., Kumar, V., & Day, G. S. (1995) *Marketing research.* New York: Wiley.

Brown, S. R., & Melamed, L. E. (1990). *Experimental design and analysis.* Newbury Park, CA: Sage.

Foster, J. J. (2002). *Data analysis using SPSS for Windows: A beginners' guide.* Thousand Oaks, CA: Sage.

Hair, J. F. J., Anderson, R. E., Tatham, R. L., & Black, W. C. (1998). *Multivariate data analysis.* Englewood Cliffs, NJ: Prentice Hall.

Hair, J. F., Bush, R. P., & Ortinau, D. J. (2000). *Marketing research: A practical guide for the new millennium.* Boston: Irwin McGraw-Hill.

Hair, J. F., Bush, R. P., & Ortinau, D. J. (2003). *Marketing research: Within a changing information environment.* Boston: McGraw-Hill/Irwin.

Louviere, J. J., Hensher, D. A., & Swait, J. D. (2000). *Stated choice methods: Analysis and application.* Cambridge, UK: Cambridge University Press.

Malhotra, N. K., Hall, J., Shaw, M., & Oppenheim, P. (2002). *Marketing research: An applied orientation.* Sydney: Pearson Education.

Punj, G., & Stewart, D. W. (1983). Cluster analysis in marketing research: Review and suggestions for application. *Journal of Marketing Research,* May, 134–148.

Sector, P. E. (2001). *SAS programming for researchers and social scientists.* Thousand Oaks, CA: Sage.

Weller, S. C., & Kimball Romney, A. (1988). *Systematic data collection.* Thousand Oaks, CA: Sage.

Zeithaml, V. A., Parasuraman, A., & Barry, L. L. (1990). *Delivering service quality: Balancing consumer perceptions and expectations.* New York: The Free Press.

Further Reading

Qualitative Analysis

Chisnall, P. M. (2000). Goodthinking: a guide to qualitative research. *Journal of the Market Research Society, 42*(2), 247–249.

Denzin, N., & Lincoln, Y. (Eds.). (1998). *Collecting and interpreting qualitative materials.* Thousand Oaks, CA: Sage.

Greenbaum, T. L (2000). Focus groups vs. online. *Advertising Age, 71*(7), 34.

Kassarjian, H. H. (1974). Projective methods. In R. Ferber (Ed.), *Handbook of marketing research* (pp. 3.85–3.100). New York: McGraw-Hill.

Morgan, D. (1988). *Focus groups as qualitative research.* Newbury Park, CA: Sage.

Skinner, D., Tagg, C., & Holloway, J. (2000). Managers and research: The pros and cons of qualitative approaches. *Management Learning, 31*(2), 163–179.

Stewart, D. W., & Shamdasani, P. N. (1990). *Focus groups: Theory and practice.* Newbury Park, CA: Sage.

Sykes, W. (1990). Validity and reliability in qualitative market research: A review of the literature. *Journal of the Market Research Society, 32*(3), 289–328.

Sykes, W., & Warren, M. (1991). Taking stock: Issues from the literature on validity and reliability in qualitative research; another day, another debrief: the use and assessment of qualitative research. *Journal of the Market Research Society, 33*(1), 3–17.

Quantitative Analysis

Specific Statistical Tests

Howell, D. C. (1987). *Statistical methods for psychology*. Boston: Duxbury Press.
Turner, J. R., & Thayer, J. (2001). *Introduction to analysis of variance*. Thousand Oaks, CA: Sage.

Cluster Analysis

Aldeberfer, S., & Blashfield, R. K. (1984). *Cluster analysis*. Thousand Oaks, CA: Sage.
Milligan, G. W., & Cooper, M. C. (1985). An examination of the procedures for determining the number of clusters in a data set. *Psychometrika, 50*(2), 159–179.

Correlations

Chen, P. Y., & Porotic, P. M. (2002). *Correlation: Parametric and nonparametric measures*. Thousand Oaks, CA: Sage.

Confidence Intervals

Smithson, M. (2002). *Confidence intervals*. Thousand Oaks, CA: Sage.

Factor Analysis

Cattell, R. B. (1979). *The scientific use of factor analysis in behavioral and life sciences*. New York: Plenum Press.
Kim, J. O., & Mueller, C. W. (1978). *Factor analysis: Statistical methods and practical issues*. Thousand Oaks, CA: Sage.
Nunnally, J. C., & Bernstein, I. H. (1994). *Psychometric theory*. New York: McGraw-Hill.

Multiple Regression

Allison, P. D. (1998). *Multiple regression: A primer*. Thousand Oaks, CA: Sage.
Klahanie, L. H. (2001). *Regression basics*. Thousand Oaks, CA: Sage.

Nonparametric Statistics

Gibbons, J. D. (1992). *Nonparametric statistics: An introduction*. Thousand Oaks, CA: Sage.

Structural Equation Modeling

Bollen, K. A., & Long, J. S. (1993). *Testing structural equation models* (pp. 1–9). Newbury Park, CA: Sage.
Diamantopoulos, A., & Siquaw, J. (2000). *Introducing LISREL: A guide for the uninitiated*. Thousand Oaks, CA: Sage.

11

Establishing Recommendations

Y ou may think that once you have analyzed the data, you are basically finished with the project, but this is not the case. Once the analysis is complete, there are still several critical steps that need to be undertaken in completing your research project. These tasks include describing the results, discussing and interpreting the results, identifying any limitations to the research, and, of course, making recommendations for practice and possibly for theory. Each of these tasks is very different, and the importance of each aspect will vary depending on the focus or emphasis of your research.

After you have collected and analyzed the data, this information must be summarized into a meaningful format. In many cases, you will be expected to discuss what the results mean, as well as give some advice to the reader based on the research findings. One objective of most research projects is to sharpen your analytical and communication skills. No matter what you have personally discovered and understood about your research findings, you must be able to clearly communicate these findings to the reader. Activities associated with the communication of your findings are, therefore, extremely important in being able to complete the project. Communication crystallizes certain points identified in the research, clearly recommends particular courses of action, and concludes the report. If the report is concerned with making some sort of business decision, then the appropriate course of action should also be recommended, which is supported by your research findings. You might also be asked to make suggestions for further research, which demonstrates an understanding of where your work fits in with the general discussion of your research question. It is critical that, as a researcher, you understand the differences among describing the results, discussion/interpretation, and making recommendations based on your work; we have found that many students confuse these issues.

Describing the Results

Describing the results is just that, a description of what has been found in your research. As you are the one who actually undertook the research, you will have a much better understanding of what the data and findings mean, and this needs to be effectively communicated to the reader. The description of the results is essential, as it explains the findings in a way that is meaningful to the reader. This moves beyond the simple reporting of information, to communicating the information in a meaningful way. This type of explanation allows the reader to understand the later sections of the report.

In some cases, your research will be focused on a simple description of a phenomenon, for example, the number of employees who are satisfied with their jobs, factors that have been identified as leading to work-related stress, or the percentage of consumers favorably disposed to a given advertisement. In fact, if you undertake descriptive research, your primary focus would be to describe a specific situation at a point in time (Hedrick, Bickman, & Rog, 1993). In other cases, you might be describing more complex issues of your research, such as two variables that are correlated, indicating that they move together.

All types of research involve some description of the results, but the emphasis of this description will vary depending on the type of project. If you are undertaking exploratory research, most of the emphasis is on explaining a specific issue, for example, how consumers believe that a given product can be improved. In a project with this focus, you would be identifying the various areas in which consumers believe an improvement could take place as well as documenting the types of people with given views. As this type of question is exploratory, the data would most likely not allow for complex analysis and may not in fact be generalizable to all consumers, but rather something that could be used to develop a more detailed descriptive or causal type of research finding (Churchill, 2001).

The description of the results is an important part of the overall research process, with the goal being to summarize the data in a meaningful way. The description can be used in a number of ways. For example, researchers tend to describe the sample that has been used in terms of demographic characteristics (e.g., "45 percent of respondents were middle managers, 20 percent senior managers, and 35 percent chief executive officers/presidents"). This type of description is factual in nature and might be important when you are trying to demonstrate that the sample is representative of a wider population, if that is important to your project.

The description can also be used to explain the results of an analysis, which allows the reader to understand the type of analysis undertaken. For example, "Ergeneli and Arikan (2002) found that the mean response of males 40 to 49 to specific ethical issues was 3.811, whereas the mean response for females in this age-group was 4.401. A comparison of the mean values gave a t-value of 2.67, with a probability of 0.104. The results indicate a difference in the views of these two groups." In this example, the researchers report what was found and do not attempt to interpret the findings, with no expansion on the interpretation or implications. Describing these results is critical, as it allows readers to identify the mean values of males and females as well as to see whether there is a statistical difference. After reading a description such as this, your reader would be able to follow the flow of the logic behind the discussion that follows.

Discussion and Interpretation

The description of data and results will take you only so far in terms of understanding and solving business problems, but it is necessary to allow readers to understand where your interpretation comes from. The discussion and interpretation of the results is a higher-order examination of the data. In this section, you would focus on the meaning of results, rather than a simple reporting of the results. In many cases, you will link this discussion back to the theories identified in the literature review section and identify whether your findings are consistent with previous published studies or not. If the results are consistent, it will make it easy to link your work to theory. On the other hand, if your results are different from previously published research, you will be forced to attempt to explain why your results are different.

Following through with the example used previously, would an organization understand what the information means? The results above indicated that females in the 40 to 49-year-old category believed that the activities described in the research were more unethical than did their male counterparts (i.e., the *t*-test was significant at the $<.05$ level). Even though this is the case, the results for this age-group suggest that both groups generally believe the issues examined were inappropriate (i.e., the mean value is above 3, which is the midpoint of the scale, on which 5 indicates that respondents strongly disagree with the unethical practice being described). This example suggests that females are more sensitive to ethical issues. This is consistent with the broader ethical literature, and is discussed as such within Ergeneli and Arikan's (2002) work. In this way, the researchers have integrated their work with the previous literature in the area. They (as well as you in your research) are giving the results more meaning and framing their work in the broader area of study. In the context of the ethical behavior example, this tends to strengthen the reader's belief that the findings are indeed valid and reliable.

Research Implications

The description and interpretation of the results might not clarify what these results mean in practice, and this needs to be explained to the reader. While undertaking a major research project, there may be certain issues that you have uncovered that are related to the topic area and that you believe are important to the reader for the understanding of the findings. These issues may relate, or confirm, issues that were first discussed in the literature review, or they may have been generated from the research. The final section of a report may focus on discussing these issues, particularly in regard to what insights and implications for practice have been gained from the findings. However, the importance of implications is, of course, dependent on the focus of the research project.

Following through with the Ergeneli and Arikan (2002) example, researchers might want to discuss the implications of having a gender-balanced sales force. For example, this approach might have some positive implications for organizations if the values of female salespeople rub off on others and, therefore, make the overall organization more ethically sensitive. On the other hand, it might be the case that female salespeople feel pressured to adopt less ethical orientations in order to compete in the organization, if, in fact, less ethical practices do lead to increases in short-term sales. In this case, female staff might face internal personal conflict between their own values and those of the organization, which could result in higher female turnover or other human resource problems. One broad implication of this result is that firms need to realize that there is a potential problem in having mixed-gender sales forces, and they should be in a position to deal with the problem if the second situation arises.

In some types of projects, it may also be important for you to understand the implications of your work for future research. For example, if your project is exploratory in nature, the results will have real implications in terms of the focus or scope of follow-up research for the organization. In this situation, the findings might suggest some prioritization of issues for further research. For example, a project looking at exporting certain products may focus on legal issues, economic issues, cultural issues, and market characteristics as points of discussion and identify which are most important for the firm or situation that you are examining.

Most important, the issues identified may generate and describe alternative solutions to a problem, as was described previously. This may help you to formulate certain suggestions, explain the rationale, and lay the foundations to propose the final recommendations for the report, which will assist organizations in dealing with the issue being addressed. It may be difficult for the reader to understand why a particular course of action was recommended without some discussion of the issues and implications of the research. However, before the recommendations are made, some indication of potential limitations to the results should be mentioned.

Limitations

The Limitations section presents to the reader some of the unforeseen problems or issues that arose during the research process or reasons that the results are not as conclusive as you would have hoped. No matter how careful you are, there will always be some issue(s) that will limit or affect the adoption of the results. It is, therefore, important to evaluate your research work and identify these limitations. Limitations should not be perceived as failures in your research skills, or as an opportunity to identify every fault or error in the research. In many ways, the Limitations section can be a positive part of a research project report, as it shows that you can look objectively at your research, justify why the process and results are still applicable/valid, and identify areas that may be improved with further research. For example, issues that limit the research could be the use of student respondents, low response rates, response rates heavily weighted to a particular gender or age-group, mistakes with particular questions, or certain questions not being asked. However, if further research were to be undertaken, extra care could be made to ensure that each of these problems does not occur again. Further, the Limitations section can play an important role in tempering the overall tone of the research findings and providing more thoughtful or sober recommendations. The following section will discuss some broad guidelines for designing recommendations.

Recommendation Guidelines

In developing the Recommendations section, it is your job to explain how your results will assist in future business activities or in developing/examining theory in the future. This section is important, as it will demonstrate that you have the ability not only to undertake research but also to interpret the results in a meaningful and practical way. As a future manager, you will be expected to use information to aid in decision making (Malhotra et al., 2002). Discussing how research will direct future activities is a core aspect of this.

The importance of making recommendations within a research project cannot be overestimated, although, as with all issues discussed within this book, its weighting will vary based on the focus of the project. The recommendations set out the actions, or alternative actions, that could be implemented based on the findings of your research and analysis of previous research. This might include strategic plans, the time frame, responsible parties, and so forth, to deal with the issue. In many cases, your lecturer/professor/supervisor may use this as one of the main criteria to evaluate the assignment and award a grade to your report. If, after you have carried out your research, you cannot crystallize your thoughts and make clear, actionable recommendations, your performance will most likely be graded poorly. The ability to identify the implications of research is a key ability for managers to have, and this is one reason that you have most likely been assigned a research project. Translating the information from your project and the related literature into meaningful directions or actions demonstrates that you have mastered these critical-thinking and problem-solving skills.

Having said this, it is important to remember that in most cases, you are undertaking the role of an external investigator who might not necessarily have a comprehensive understanding of the broader business environment in which your question was examined. For example, a study looking at satisfaction of an existing customer service process might not necessarily take into consideration broader changes in technology and how these affect the organization. Making recommendations is fine, but managers will need to use this information in line with other information that they have. The point is that though recommendations are extremely important, it is the manager's job not to blindly follow recommendations without taking his or her own specific situation, knowledge, and experience into consideration.

These are a few points you should consider when making your final recommendations:

1. Clearly State Your Recommendation

Write your recommendation as a sentence or a statement. You could even write it in bold or italics so that the reader is clear on the main thrust of the recommendation. This should then be supported by a clear rationale that draws on all relevant information (i.e., research results, previous literature, and theoretical suppositions). In making these recommendations, it is important to identify the positive *and* negative implications of undertaking change. This information is critical in evaluating alternative options if they exist.

2. Be Specific for Each Recommendation

Focus each recommendation around one particular topic, issue, or problem. Sometimes, students try to provide detailed, wide-ranging recommendations that relate to a number of topics, but these types of recommendations can be too vague or unclear and are extremely difficult to support in a concise way. Therefore, it is important to be clear and specific in relation to each issue. There may, however, be several interrelated actions that need to be considered, and if this is the case, a clear linkage between each point is essential. In this way, there is clear communication of the implications of each issue as well as some broad strategic focusing that encompasses more than one issue.

3. Recommendations Must Link Back to the Objectives and the Research Findings

It should be clear that the recommendations relate to the original objectives of the study. They could then provide an action-oriented answer to the objectives and a conclusion to the study. The recommendations must also be generated only from what you have found after undertaking your research, and so be justified by your findings. A common trap is identifying issues that might be considered that are completely unrelated to the project research. It is fine to identify broader interrelated issues that might be considered, in terms of both actions and future research, but it would seem inappropriate to bring in unrelated ideas that cannot be linked to the current research or literature. It is very confusing from the reader's point of view when the findings and recommended course of action are unrelated. From an assessment perspective, this shows a lack of focus and raises questions related to the appropriateness of the original research question.

4. Be Action-Oriented

In relation to your business problem or objective, the reader should be clear on what course of action you are recommending. This should include the roles of the key players, the desired time frame, and relevant information about the various pros and cons of the course of action, particularly if caution should be taken. What do your recommendations mean in the context of the research? What does this mean in practice? Even if no action is recommended, a rationale for this should be explained and the current course of action confirmed.

Future Research

For some projects, it is important not to simply end with the Recommendations section, but to look ahead to other issues raised in the research that could be worthy of further research. No research project can cover *all* aspects of a chosen topic, and the research may uncover new possibilities for areas of future research. The Further Research section is not meant to downplay the current research or indicate that you will do this research, but to suggest, in the light of the current research, that this is a topic worthy of more research. Some of the new possibilities for further study may include focusing on a different country, market, industry, company, management level, or group. It may be that a particular issue identified in the research needs more attention by managers, or that a certain line of questioning or research methodology should be used to develop further understanding of the topic. It might involve undertaking a different research design to include more complex relationships or variables, or to examine the phenomenon from a different perspective to delve into the area more deeply.

The aim, therefore, is to identify how this research can serve to further expand the body of knowledge in the topic area. This might be especially important if the research project is designed to prepare a student for more advanced research, as identifying where a project fits within existing literature needs to be complemented by understanding how it can assist in further developing theory as well, although, as has been mentioned, the importance of this will vary based on the project's focus.

References

Churchill, G. A. (2001). *Basic marketing research*. Chicago: The Dryden Press.

Ergeneli, A., & Arikan, S. (2002). Gender differences in ethical perceptions of sales-people: An empirical examination in Turkey. *Journal of Business, 40*(3), 247–260.

Hedrick, T. E., Bickman, L., & Rog, D. J. (1993). *Applied research design: A practical guide*. Newbury Park, CA: Sage.

Malhotra, N. K., Hall, J., Shaw, M., & Oppenheim, P. (2002). *Marketing research: An applied orientation*. Sydney: Pearson Education.

PART III

Communicating the Results

12

Presenting the Results

An important part of writing your research project is the presentation of the results, particularly the statistical findings. Once you have conducted the research and turned the raw data into useful information, the results must be presented in a clear form that communicates to your audience. In the past, some students have undertaken research on an interesting topic, chosen a valid method to gather the data, and been meticulous in data collection and analysis, but failed to clearly present and communicate the results. The analysis and formulation of the recommendations is not the end of the research process for your project, as it is vital that your results and findings, which support your final recommendations, are clearly communicated to your reader/audience. No matter how much work you have done beforehand, a poor presentation of your results will give the impression that the overall project is of poor quality.

The two main ways of summarizing and communicating your findings are through (a) a written report and (b) an oral presentation. Your research results should be presented in a way that is concise, provides the maximum amount of information, and reinforces key points. This part of the book looks at "Communicating the Results," with this chapter examining the range of approaches to present your results, particularly the statistical findings. The following chapters will discuss how to best present your research in written reports (Chapter 13) and in oral presentations (Chapter 14).

Ways to Present Research Findings

For both written and oral presentations, it is important to present your research findings in a clear, logical way. This can be done by using various visual aids, such as tables, charts, graphs, pictures, and maps, which can increase clarity of communication and impact (Takeuchi & Schmidt, 1980). There is no standard format for using these visual aids, as requirements may differ depending on the type of methodology used, the value of the data obtained, and the writing style of the researcher. There are, however, a few common elements to assist in the effective communication of research findings. Some of the main elements include the following:

1. **Visually Clean Presentation.** Whatever visual aid you use, it must clearly and unambiguously communicate the main points you want to send to your reader/audience (Zeisel, 1985). Some graphs, for example, may look cluttered when you include all the information that might be required, so a numeric table may be the best form for that data.

2. **Reader-Friendly Format.** The aid chosen should be easy to follow to better facilitate understanding of the data. This means that aids should be well-designed and labeled so that the reader/audience will comprehend the message of the graph at a glance. Varying typography and the use of white space can also contribute to the readability and understanding of the data.

3. **Suitable Presentation for Type of Data.** The aid used should be suitable for the type of data to be presented. For example, if there is a large amount of complex data, a numerical table could be used to clearly summarize it, whereas a line graph may be used to depict results from a longitudinal study.

4. **Appropriate Number of Visual Aids.** The use of visual aids should be done sparingly to emphasize particular results, especially those that answer specific research problems/objectives or hypotheses. Too many visual aids can reduce their impact and clutter the look of the report or interfere with the flow of the presentation.

5. **Appropriate Use of Visual Aids.** The use of devices is to emphasize particular results; therefore, it should supplement the written text and not replace it (Sudman & Blair, 1998). There still needs to be a discussion to clarify and focus specific aspects of the findings.

6. **Undistracting Presentation.** In some cases, your material will be too detailed, and the audience will be focusing on understanding the visuals, rather than on the implications associated with the information being provided.

The following section will discuss the use of the main visual devices: numerical tables, charts and graphs, pictures, and maps.

Numerical Tables

Numerical tables are excellent visual tools for concisely and effectively presenting large amounts of statistical data (Sudman & Blair, 1998). A tabular presentation can clearly show the actual statistical figures rather than graphical comparisons, which is an advantage of some charts and graphs. Further, they can present basic tabulations of data or complex analysis, depending on the type of information you want to convey. This can be displayed as in the following examples of tables, which may be helpful to you when you are creating your own tables for your project results.

Tables 12.1 and 12.2 basically present the same results: the demographics from a sample surveyed for a project. Each table has the characteristics gender, age, and type of study, but the main difference is the amount of detail presented. In Table 12.1, the characteristics are presented representing the total sample with overall number and percentage calculated. In Table 12.2, the sample data has been presented with a cross-tabulation comparing the scores of each characteristic with the gender. This can be very useful if your study is looking at gender as a key variable or if you have noticed in your analysis that gender is a significant factor. If, however, gender is not of interest in your study, the use of Table 12.1 would be valid.

Similarly, Tables 12.3 and 12.4 show the same data: the results of a Likert scale from a questionnaire that analyzes people's attitudes toward political advertising. In Table 12.3, there is a summary of the results, with a copy of the statement presented to the sample, the number of people who responded, the mean score, and standard deviation. This table presents a general

Table 12.1   Demographics (A)

	Number	*Percentage*
GENDER:		
Male	68	52.7%
Female	61	47.3%
	129	
AGE:		
19	23	17.8%
20	29	22.5%
21	26	20.2%
22	24	18.6%
23	2	1.5%
24+	25	19.4%
	129	
STUDY:		
Full-Time	110	85.3%
Part-Time	18	13.9%
Not Stated	1	0.8%
	129	

Table 12.2   Demographics (B)

	MALE *Number (%)*	*FEMALE* *Number (%)*	*TOTAL* *Number (%)*
GENDER:	68 (52.7%)	61 (47.3%)	129
AGE			
19	7 (10.3%)	16 (26.2)	23 (17.8%)
20	15 (22.1%)	14 (23.0%)	29 (22.5%)
21	13 (19.1%)	13 (21.3%)	26 (20.2%)
22	16 (23.5%)	8 (13.1%)	24 (18.6%)
23	1 (1.5%)	1 (1.6%)	2 (1.5%)
24+	16 (23.5%)	9 (14.8%)	25 (19.4%)
	68	*61*	*129*
STUDY:			
Full-Time	53 (77.9%)	57 (93.4%)	110 (85.3%)
Part-Time	14 (20.6%)	4 (6.6%)	18 (13.9%)
Not Stated	1 (1.5%)	0 (0%)	1 (0.8%)
	68	*61*	*129*

Table 12.3   Attitudes Toward Political Advertising (A)

Statement	*Number*	*Mean*	*Standard* *Deviation*
1. The most effective way to reach voters is to appeal to their emotions.	129	2.23	.94
2. Political advertisements exert a great deal of influence on voters.	128	2.52	.98
3. People obtain a lot of information on issues from political ads.	128	3.33	1.06
4. Political ads are guided by the same principles of successful advertising.	127	2.47	1.01
5. Advertising a politician is the same as advertising a product.	129	2.60	1.12

NOTE: 1 = Strongly Agree; 3 = Neither; 5 = Strongly Disagree.

overview of the response to the statements. Table 12.4, however, presents more detailed information about the responses by including the number of people who responded to each option in the 5-point scale. Both tables are quite acceptable, depending on what you want to present to your reader/ audience and the detail they may require.

Table 12.4   Attitudes Toward Political Advertising (B)

Statement	1 (SA)	2 (A)	3(Neither)	4 (D)	5 (SD)	Mean (St.D.)
1. The most effective way to reach voters is to appeal to their emotions.	30	52	36	9	2	2.23 (.94)
2. Political advertisements exert a great deal of influence on voters.	16	56	33	20	3	2.52 (.98)
3. People obtain a lot of information on issues from political ads.	5	27	32	49	15	3.33 (1.06)
4. Political ads are guided by the same principles of successful advertising.	22	48	36	18	3	2.47 (1.01)
5. Advertising a politician is the same as advertising a product.	22	45	30	27	5	2.60 (1.12)

NOTE: 1 = Strongly Agree; 3 = Neither; 5 = Strongly Disagree.

Below are some important features regarding numerical tables that should be followed when creating tables for your project results (Luck & Rubin, 1987; Malhotra et al., 2002):

1. **Numbering.** Each table in your results should be numbered consecutively for easy referencing and to show its position within the report.

2. **Title.** Each table should be given a brief title that clearly describes what information it is presenting.

3. **Headings.** Each row and column should have a heading so that there is no doubt what the figures represent.

4. **Unit of Measurement.** The units of measurement should be stated unless they are obvious (e.g., US$, 000, and %).

5. **Arrangement.** The data should be clearly arranged in a way that will best display the most significant aspect of the data.

6. **Order.** Where possible, rows or columns should be arranged in some order, for example, a natural order (1, 2, 3), alphabetical order, ascending order of magnitude, or a logical order.

7. **Totals.** Totals should be clearly shown. Depending on the data being presented, the totals should be presented at the bottom, or possibly at the side, of the table.

8. **Calculations.** The calculations in the table must be correct and verified before presenting the results. Often, simple mistakes are made

in addition when transferring data to a table, which can reflect poorly on your research.

9. **Source of Data.** If you are using secondary data, the original source of the data should be cited. This is not necessary if the table is based on primary data.

10. **Visually Emphasize Items.** Certain figures in your table can be emphasized to assist in communicating particular results. This can be done by using footnotes or contrasting typography with bold, italics, shading, and so forth.

APA Style

The American Psychological Association (APA) (http://www.apa.org) has a publication manual that provides a comprehensive reference guideline for using APA style, organization, and content. A summary of the guide can be found in Degelman and Harris (2000). Regarding instructions on the formatting of tables and figures, the APA's publication manual (1994) provides details on pp. 253–255. For an example of an APA-formatted table, go to http://www.vanguard.edu/psychology/table.pdf.

Though some guidelines suggest that tables and figures appear at the end of research, within your work, it is generally better for tables to appear within the body of the paper, which adds to the impact and communicates findings more readily. Therefore, it is worthwhile to discuss this with your lecturer/professor/supervisor before deciding where to place tables and figures (Degelman & Harris, 2000).

Charts and Graphs

Graphical presentations are a very effective way to visually display a large range of data (Zeisel, 1985). As visual communication can greatly increase the clarity of explanation and the impact of the findings, the use of charts or graphs can greatly assist the reader/audience to detect, interpret, and retain important information. According to Griffiths, Stirling, and Weldon (1998, p. 196), "[e]xcellence in statistical graphics consists of complex ideas communicated with clarity, precision and efficiency." Therefore, it is important that the visual device chosen best represent the data in an objective manner and not distort it. Simplicity is the key for designing the right visual aid (Gallant, 1998). Examples include bar charts, pie charts, and line graphs.

Bar Charts

Bar charts can be used to show the value, or breakdown, of a variable. They can be presented vertically or horizontally, with each bar representing a variable

(Sudman & Blair, 1998). They can show absolute values, make comparisons, and emphasize differences or change. An example of a bar chart using the data from Table 12.3, item 1 is found in Exhibit 12.1.

Pie Charts

Pie charts use a circle, or "pie," that is segmented so that each section represents a percentage associated with the value of a specific variable (Malhotra et al., 2002). These are very useful for showing an overall breakdown of variables within a population. However, they are not useful when trying to present relationships with other variables or over time. As a guide, a pie chart should not have more than seven sections (Tufte, 1983). An example of a pie chart using the data from Table 12.3, Item 1, is found in Exhibit 12.2.

Line Graphs

Line graphs show the connection of a series of data points using continuous lines (Malhotra et al., 2002). These are useful when showing the movement of one variable relative to another, particularly when representing growth, trends, or rates of change. They can also show several variables on the same graph, thereby revealing any potential relationships (Sudman & Blair, 1998). An example of a line graph using the data from Table 12.3, Item 1, is found in Exhibit 12.3.

Exhibit 12.1   Bar Chart Showing Data From Item 1 of Table 12

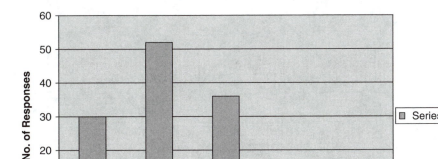

NOTE: 1 = Strongly Agree; 3 = Neither; 5 = Strongly Disagree.

Exhibit 12.2   Pie Chart Showing Data From Item 1 of Table 12.3

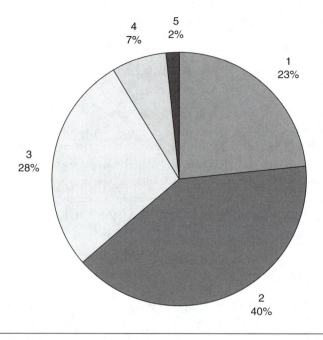

NOTE: 1 = Strongly Agree; 3 = Neither; 5 = Strongly Disagree.

Exhibit 12.3   Line Graph Showing Data from Item 1 of Table 12.3

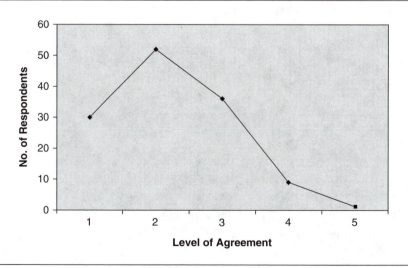

NOTE: 1 = Strongly Agree; 3 = Neither; 5 = Strongly Disagree.

As mentioned earlier, it important that the visual aid chosen best represent the data in an objective manner. From the examples above, using a bar chart, pie chart, and line graph, which do you think is the most effective for presenting the results of Item 1 from Table 12.3: "The most effective way to reach voters is to appeal to their emotions"? There is no one right answer, but it is important that the audience can follow the discussion.

Pictures

Pictures can be an important visual aid by showing an example of the product, label, workplace, or something relevant to the project. They can help with understanding and acceptance from the reader/audience, who can actually see what the research's focus is. They can also provide a temporary break to the reader/audience from reading the complicated text of your report (Ehrenborg & Mattock, 1993). You do need to make sure that pictures are clear and are used to highlight specific points. Too many pictures might distract the audience and clutter the oral and written presentation.

Maps

Maps may be instrumental in illustrating the geographic location of the area studied in the research or the sample areas in relation to each other (Luck & Rubin, 1987). Mapping can also display different market characteristics across several geographical boundaries, which can assist in positioning (Malhotra et al., 2002). When looking at perceptual mapping, this visual depiction sometimes makes it easier for you and the audience to visually see how products or attributes relate to one another. On the other hand, perceptual maps are sometimes considered to be confusing, especially when used in regard to multiple variables.

Conclusion

The presentation of the research results, particularly the statistical findings, is a very important part of your research project. The use of visual aids, such as numerical tables, charts and graphs, pictures, and maps, can play an important part in your written report and oral presentation. It is, therefore, vital that you choose the device that will best communicate your results. The old adage that a picture is worth a thousand words is very true, but this requires that the pictures be clear to the reader; otherwise, this material confuses the key points and detracts from the reader's understanding the implications of the work.

The next two chapters will continue discussing the presentation of your research project in written reports (Chapter 13) and oral presentations (Chapter 14).

References

Degelman, D., & Harris, M. L. (2000). *APA style essential.* Retrieved February 28, 2004, from http://www.vanguard.edu/faculty/ddegelman/index.cfm?doc_id=796.

Ehrenborg, J., & Mattock, J. (1993). *Powerful presentations: 50 Original ideas for making a real impact.* London: Kogan Page.

Gallant, J. (1998). Say it simple, stupid. *Network World, 15*(22), 50–51.

Griffiths, D., Stirling, W. D., & Weldon, K. L. (1998). *Understanding data: Principles & practice of statistics.* Sydney: Jacaranda Wiley.

Luck, D. J., & Rubin, R. S. (1987). *Marketing research.* Englewood Cliffs, NJ: Prentice Hall.

Malhotra, N. K., Hall, J., Shaw, M., & Oppenheim, P. (2002). *Marketing research: An applied orientation.* Sydney: Pearson Education.

Sudman, S., & Blair, E. (1998). *Marketing research: A problem-solving approach.* Burr Ridge, IL: McGraw-Hill.

Takeuchi, H., & Schmidt, A. H. (1980). New promise of computer graphics. *Harvard Business Review, Jan.-Feb.,* 122–131.

Tufte, E. R. (1983). *The visual display of quantitative information.* Cheshire, CT: Graphics Press.

Zeisel, H. (1985). *Say it with figures.* New York: Harper and Row.

13 Writing the Report

One of the most important aspects of a student's research project is communicating what was done and the results of the project. In the classroom setting, effective communication will determine a student's grade. In the business world, it may mean getting ideas accepted by supervisors or even initially gaining employment (Anonymous, 1992). The importance of written communication has been recognized across a wide range of business disciplines. For example, in one study, employers identified that they wanted to find marketing students with solid communication skills, both oral (ranked 2 out of 29 skills examined) and written (ranked 17 out of 29 skills examined) (Borin & Watkins, 1998). In the accounting area, written communication was deemed to be the most important skill students can have, even more important than accounting ability (Maupin & May, 1993). Even in technically based business areas, such as information technology, writing skills are essential for success (Jacobs, 1998). Thus, effective communication is essential in all business disciplines. However, poor communication is a problem not only for students but also for business, as it has been suggested that poor written communication costs business enterprises $1 billion annually (Hansen, 1993). Thus, improving report-writing skills will assist students and the firms that hire them.

Even if students undertake a research project in a systematic fashion, their recommendations may be ineffective if they do not clearly and concisely communicate what they have done and what it means. The specific requirements of this communication, whether it needs to be presented orally or in a written form, will depend on the subject requirement and/or the type of project that is being undertaken.

Though oral presentations are extremely important, these will be discussed in detail in the next chapter. The objective of this chapter is to discuss the process of writing your research. A range of practical issues associated with presenting the written project material will be discussed, including some suggestions for writing the report, determining the type of report required, and structuring a written report. As with all chapters, it is not possible to provide a comprehensive discussion of every facet of business and report writing, but there are a number of texts that discuss these topics in detail (Lesikar, 1972; Sussams, 1991; Turk & Kirkman, 1989), and there are also checklists that discuss a range of issues associated with writing various types of reports as well (Armstrong, 2003). This chapter will identify and discuss the various components of a written report and provide some guidelines that will enable students to write more effective reports that reflect their research activities.

Written Communication

Effective writing is something that does not come easily to all students, but it is a skill that is increasingly being included in business curricula (Williams, 1996). In many cases, a business degree will have a business communication subject that focuses on specific writing situations, such as memo writing or crisis communication, although, as was identified in the introduction to this chapter, broader communication skills are important for all business students (McNerney, 1994). Though students are traditionally asked to write essays, these types of assignments are different from reports. Essays often require students to simply explain what they have read or have been taught, whereas a student research project usually needs to focus more on systematically explaining to others what was done, why it was done, what the results mean, and what the implications are for business or theory (depending on the focus of the report). Though there are differences between academic and professional writing styles (Garay, 1995), many of the broad principles are the same (Lesikar, 1972).

It has been suggested that there are seven steps to writing user-friendly reports (Leach, 1993). These include the following:

1. *Decide what information should be included and what should be omitted.* Though some student reports seem to progress logically, others often wander through the discussion without much focus; therefore, narrowing the focus is important. For example, within the literature review, one cannot trace the development of all theories related to the topic. So the review must focus on the best way to explain how the students' work relates to previous research.

2. *Identify who the audience is.* As will be discussed later in the chapter, different audiences want different things. This will be true when writing for a class, as each lecturer/professor/supervisor wants students to adopt a different focus. The same will be true in business, where reports written for accountants and those written for engineers may need to communicate the same information differently.

3. *Organize the materials to make it easy for the reader to follow.* This means not only summarizing the key points but also explaining to the reader what will be discussed later in the report.

4. *Clearly ensure that you explain the five W's—who, what, where, when, and why.* This sets the scene for the reader and helps him or her to understand the context in which the report is written, that is, who the report is written for, what was done, where it was done, and why it was done.

5. *Keep it simple.* Unnecessary complexity makes reports more difficult to understand (Suchan, 1991).

6. *Be specific.* The reader does not necessarily have as much information as the writer does, and therefore, the report should clearly explain the discussion.

7. *Revise and proofread.* Writing reports is a complex process that frequently requires several drafts (Straub, 1991). This ensures that the report is clear to the reader, as a confusing structure or poor grammar distracts the reader from the message you are trying to communicate.

There are, of course, other sets of tips for clearer report writing. For example, one business-writing consultant suggests the use of the following nine-point checklist covering a range of issues to improve business writing (Anonymous, 1995):

1. Early in the introduction, summarize the goal and conclusion of the report.

2. Use simple words and phrases.

3. Eliminate useless words; the shorter the better.

4. Speak in the active rather than the passive voice.

5. Avoid long sentences, as shorter sentences are easy to follow.

6. Paragraphs should be short and include one or two ideas.

7. If there are a number of points, number them rather than write them as a paragraph.

8. Use highlighting, bolding, or boxes to emphasize key points, and point them out to the reader (this may be more appropriate in business reports).

9. Try to make the report easy on the eye, reducing orphan words or single lines on one page.

Scott Armstrong (2003), a leading business academic, has suggested that business reports need to consider nine issues as well (in his complete checklist he has a range of sub-points as well). His nine points are the following:

1. Target market—make sure you write information targeting the audience.

2. Source—identify who you are and any limitations associated with the project (i.e., a second-year business-student project might have very different depth than a final-year MBA student project).

3. Guides to the reader—this includes a clear discussion of how the project will address the issue being considered. It includes a table of contents, summaries of sections, and so forth.

4. Recommendations—these need to clearly identify the benefits or pitfalls of corporate actions.

5. Arguments—there needs to be sufficient discussion of material to ensure that the reader understands how you arrived at your conclusions as well as ensure that there is a clear demonstration of understanding of the complexity of issues examined.

6. Exhibits—materials should be presented in a way that makes them visually easy to follow.

7. Style—you need to write in a way that is balanced and makes it easy for the reader to follow issues.

8. Format—the material needs to have a logical flow and be easy to follow.

9. Rewrite—the report needs to be crafted in such a way that it flows and is interesting to read.

These lists suggest that report writing, academic-type research, or business reports need to be considered and planned before the writing starts. You should not sit down and "just do it," as there are a number of communication issues that need to be carefully considered. Addressing these issues may take almost as much time as undertaking the research, and it is, therefore, essential that you allocate time to drafting *and* revising your reports.

In terms of actually writing the report, it is important to plan a structure that enables you to include all key information, remembering who you are writing it for. This means that you might want to think of your audience as the customer, to whom you are selling your ideas. It is important that any written report satisfy the customers' informational needs (Huettman, 1996; Armstrong, 2003), as well as the requirements of the assessment task.

When to Write?

You need to plan your research and associated report so that it achieves the objectives of the project and communicates to the audience what has been done. The writing needs to be expressed in a convincing fashion such that it not only reflects the project process but also supports all arguments and recommendations. You, therefore, need to consider how this can be done *before* you begin writing your final report. In fact, you should plan the research report, at least the broad structure and length of sections, early on in the project to ensure that all necessary activities are undertaken and the project is not too lengthy.

One general question that you need to ask is whether you should wait until all work associated with the research is completed before beginning to write it up. Like most questions asked in this book, there is no clear-cut answer. In some situations, you would be well advised to ensure that you write up sections as you progress throughout the research process. This approach has the advantage of removing the burden of writing up the whole report just before the submission deadline. There are frequently unforeseen delays that push the writing closer and closer to the deadline, and unfortunately, many students may actually wait until a few hours before the deadline to print out the full report for the first time, which leaves them with very little time for proofreading and revising.

Writing as the research progresses also ensures that you don't forget important information. For example, if you undertake a focus group, it is imperative that it is written up soon after it is completed, as it may take a while to transcribe and analyze the discussions. Finally, writing parts of the report as you progress through the process ensures that all information is appropriately included in the project. Consider a focus group, for example; if you do not write it up soon after it is completed, there is a good chance that key information will not be incorporated into a follow-up survey design or interview schedule. Because of this, key issues may be omitted, resulting in significant gaps in the information collected during the course of the project. This problem can be so severe that in some cases, students actually cannot answer their research question.

Though there are benefits to writing up sections of the report during the research process, there are a number of sections that may not be written until the project is completed. It is assumed that things such as the recommendations and implications can only be written at the end of the research process, but other areas such as the literature review may also only be finalized at the end of the project. The reason for this is that while you go through the research process, you frequently identify new pieces of literature and thus are continually updating this material. Having said this, you may wish to have a draft of the literature review section that is continually updated throughout the research process. In this way, some sections may evolve throughout the research, which is different from waiting until the end of the project to write it up, whereas other sections may be finished early in the process.

Types of Reports

You need to be able to write all information (literature review, analysis, implications, and recommendations) in a way that effectively communicates with your specific target audience. This will vary depending on whether the report is aimed at a lecturer/professor/supervisor (i.e., an academic-type report) or designed to communicate with a client, real or hypothetical (i.e., a business-type report). Different target audiences want, or may need, to be addressed in different ways, and may even be interested in different types of informational emphasis. For example, if the research were a small part of a course, your instructor most likely would want to know that you understood and used the literature appropriately. However, if the research is the primary assessment in a course, your instructor would most likely not only be concerned that you understood and applied the literature, but also that the research followed an appropriate structure and resulted in reasonable conclusions. On the other hand, if the research project is undertaken for a client (real or hypothetical), the report might be very different, as many clients want student researchers to focus on the implications of the research and not the nuances of theory or methodology, although it would be assumed that these were appropriately undertaken.

It is, therefore, very important that before you begin writing your report, you know what type of report is required, who the reader or audience of the report will be, and what sorts of things they will expect the report to cover. The type and focus of the report required will, therefore, determine the structure of your report, the style in which you write, and the amount of detail required within each section. These factors will vary within undergraduate reports, but will also vary in relation to master's and MBA theses (Sharp & Howard, 1996; Jankowicz, 1995). Within this chapter, more comprehensive academic-type reports and, to a lesser extent, business-type reports will be discussed. The components will, however, vary depending on the course and lecturer/professor/supervisor. It is, therefore, important to identify the specific requirements of your subject.

The two types of reports are substantially different in relation to the language used, structure, and focus. Thus, you cannot necessarily just cut down an academic report to make it a business-type report (Krajewski & Smith, 1997; Lesikar, 1972; Thomas, 1994). If you have to write both a business and an academic report for one research project, we would suggest based on past experience that you would most likely be better off writing the two reports as separate documents. This will ensure that each report clearly targets the desired audience and specified objectives.

An Academic Report

This report has an academic focus, which is designed to identify that students can undertake research in a systematic fashion. The final report is frequently lengthy, as it usually includes detailed discussion of the literature, methodology, data analysis and interpretation, implications, references, and possibly appendices. Though an academic-type report may discuss the managerial findings, these are usually not the emphasis of the report, although this will vary by subject and institution.

The academic report will tend to focus more on the theoretical grounding, methodology, and academic implications of your research project. The report should, therefore, display your ability to deal with all relevant academic issues and communicate the research you have undertaken in a formal way. It might be suggested that the structure of your research project follow the structure of an academic journal article, although the standard would most likely be less rigorous. Therefore, it is very worthwhile for you to study the style of writing, structure, and presentation of several research articles before you begin writing your academic report.

A Business Report

The term *business report* may be somewhat misleading, as within this broad category there are a range of varying types of business reports (Sussams, 1991; Bentley, 1992). There are detailed internal reports within organizations, and there are external-based consulting reports undertaken by independent bodies for firms as clients. Even within consulting reports, there can be a high degree of variation, with some consulting reports providing detailed discussion of issues and others serving more as a summary of information. These latter reports tend to be very brief, with statements predominantly made in short one- or two-sentence paragraphs or with unpunctuated "dot points." For example,

> As outlined in our proposal, we have undertaken our assessment with reference to four broad variables:
> - Environmental policy issues
> - Organization issues
> - Environmental issues
> - Awareness and understanding

Within the context of this section, the discussion will not refer to these consulting-type reports, but will focus on more structured and detailed business-type reports, which may be internal or external documents. One way for you to think about these business reports is that they are designed to be read by managers within the organization who are less familiar with the issue, but who are responsible for making a strategic decision based solely on the report. Therefore, these reports need to clearly discuss the critical issues, highlighting what the course of action would mean for the organization.

Business reports, therefore, have a heavy managerial focus when explaining the problem, how it was examined, and appropriate implications for business practice. This is not to suggest that students should omit all discussion of past research, project objectives, methodology, analysis, and so forth. The discussion of these materials should be abbreviated and must be clear and concise, so that managers evaluating the situation will have sufficient confidence in your recommendations to act on them. The client should agree with the logic used to develop recommendations and conclusions, based on the written presentation of material.

As was discussed earlier, writing up the report (business or academic) is a process that involves a number of drafts and revisions. However, for the most part it is the reader's evaluation of the final project report that determines the student's grade. If the report is unclear, contradictory, inconsistent, or confusing, the reader may assume that poor communication means the overall research process is flawed (i.e., it is a poor research project), and this may occur even if the results are conclusive. Anything that distracts the reader from your message should be eliminated. It is, therefore, essential that you spend a reasonable amount of time and effort producing the written project.

Structure of a Project Report

When writing a research report, one of the most important features it should have is a clear and logical structure. Though the two types of research report, business and academic, have different foci, the structures of the various types of reports overlap to such an extent that it would be repetitive to discuss each separately. Table 13.1 lists all of the possible sections that might be included in a business or academic research report, as well as identifying the likelihood that each section will be required in either report, but the specific requirements will vary based on the requirements of the subject.

The Title Page

All reports include a title page, and though it may seem to be a minor component, it is important to ensure that the title page is error-free. We are all familiar with the phrase "first impressions last," and therefore, a mistake on the front of the report reflects poorly on the report as a whole, and particularly, on its writers. It may also encourage readers to unnecessarily look for or focus on other errors or typing mistakes. The title page should include the title of the project, all of the names of those in the project team, who the report is written for, and the date it was submitted. Some institutions may require other information, such as a signed statement of contribution, but this would usually only be required in longer academic reports that are part of a master's thesis. As with all components, you need to be sure that you follow the requirements of the subject or the institution.

Table 13.1   Structure of a Project Report

	Business	*Academic*
Title Page	Usually	Usually
Acknowledgments	Sometimes	Sometimes
Table of Contents	Usually	Usually
List of Tables, Figures, Exhibits, and/or Appendices	Sometimes	Sometimes
Executive Summary	Usually	Usually
Introduction	Usually	Usually
Research Objectives	Rarely	Usually
Background	Usually	Usually
Literature Review	Unlikely	Usually
Methodology	Usually	Usually
Analysis/Results	Sometimes	Usually
Limitations	Usually	Usually
Implications/Discussions	Usually	Usually
Recommendations	Usually	Sometimes
Conclusion	Sometimes	Usually
Further Research	Rarely	Usually
Bibliography	Usually	Usually
Appendices	Sometimes	Sometimes

Acknowledgment

This statement is sometimes used in an academic report and would be unlikely to appear in most traditional business reports, although it may be appropriate in some cases within business-type projects. The objective of the acknowledgment is to thank those who were particularly helpful in the undertaking of the project. In a higher degree, the acknowledgment is used to thank the student's supervisor, administrative people who assisted, organizations that funded the work (if applicable), and, in some cases, friends and family, as well.

If students choose to include an acknowledgment, it is important that they thank any organization that assisted in the research. This might include an organization that funded the work or that allowed the students to examine its employees. Though such a statement seems to be unnecessary, it recognizes this support, and the firm or organization will see that its assistance was both appreciated and formally acknowledged, should the students give the organization a copy.

Table of Contents

All reports require a contents page of some description. It serves an essential function, allowing the reader to see, at a glance, the structure of the report and what information is included and where it appears in the report. This is important, because readers can turn to sections that are of particular interest to them, should they wish.

There are two broad approaches to designing the table of contents section. The first approach gives the reader broad headings and would most likely be appropriate for short reports. However, a brief table of contents may be insufficient if the research report is lengthy or covers a number of important issues. In these cases, it may be more appropriate to give the reader a more detailed table of contents, which would be similar to an outline of the report (see Exhibit 13.1). The benefit of using a detailed table of contents is that it clearly identifies what appears in the report and where it appears.

Exhibit 13.1   Types of Tables of Contents

Brief	Detailed
1. Introduction	1. Introduction
2. Methodology	1.1. Objective
3. Results	1.2. Background
4. Etc.	1.3. Rationale
	2. Methodology
	2.1. Brief Overview of Literature
	2.2. Interviews
	2.3. Focus Groups
	2.4. Survey
	2.5. Analytical Tools Used
	3. Etc.

Lists of Tables, Figures, Exhibits, or Appendices

Some academic and business reports will include a list of tables, figures, exhibits, and/or appendices. Whether these are included will depend on the specific report and the requirements of the subject. When such a listing is provided, the information should be listed in chronological order with the title of the figure, table, or exhibit, and the page number on which it appears. The titles should be the same as those appearing in the body of the report and should be of sufficient detail that the reader knows what information is contained within them.

In long reports, it is likely that a list of tables and/or appendices may both be included. However, brief business reports might not contain either type of list. Consider, for example, an applied business report that has a table on each page with a few "dot points" highlighting key issues. In this case, a list of figures would be overkill. Longer business reports frequently cover a complex range of issues, and in these cases, it may be beneficial to include a list of tables, especially if the tables provide summaries or key information presented in the report that serves as a basis for recommendations made in the report. For example, a demographic breakdown of the industry might be included if it is essential to discussions in the report.

Though appendices are often important in business reports, a listing of these is less likely to be needed. If there are only one or two appendices, these should be included in the table of contents, rather than in a separate section of the report. If, however, there are a number of appendices, it may be beneficial to list these in the table of contents as "Appendices" and include a detailed breakdown in a separate listing.

Executive Summary

The executive summary is normally included in both academic and business reports. It is usually found at the very beginning of the report, before the introduction and sometimes even before the table of contents. The idea behind an executive summary is to do just that, to summarize the paper for the executive, or other reader, who in some circumstances wishes to read an overview of the report before deciding if he or she should read the whole report. Though this seems to suggest that it is only important for business reports, concisely summarizing the material is a skill that is essential for communication in business, and its inclusion is good practice for you (Loehr, 1995).

The executive summary provides the reader with a brief summary of the whole report, including what the report is about, how the information was obtained, *and* the final recommendations. Therefore, it needs to provide sufficient detail that the reader would be encouraged to read the entire report. In this way, an executive summary is different from an introduction, which simply introduces the reader to the topic and does not outline the important findings.

Introduction

All reports will include an introduction section of some description. The exact composition will vary, and within business research reports, the introduction might include the material discussed in the research objectives and/or background sections. The body of the report begins with the introduction, which sets the scene for the whole report. It establishes a rationale for the project by explaining who prepared the report (this may occur more frequently in a business report), why the topic is being examined, and what approach was undertaken to obtain the necessary information.

The introduction also frequently sets out the structure of the report, telling the reader what will be discussed within each section. In this case, the introduction expands on the table of contents, which only provides titles of sections. The introduction provides a solid beginning for the whole report by clearly stating what the report is about, thereby preparing the reader for what will follow. For example, this is what was done in the Chapter 1 ("Introduction") of this book.

Research Objectives

To help guide you and the reader, it is essential that there is a concise statement of the overall research problem along with the research objectives and/or research hypotheses to be examined. It is very important to tell the reader exactly what the aims of the project are (i.e., to address the research objective). This section will most frequently occur in an academic-type report and would be included in the introduction of a business-type report.

Having clear, easily understood, and reachable objectives allows you to maintain focus and provides those evaluating the report with a way to determine if you accomplish what you said you would. The process of setting objectives was presented in Chapter 6 and will not be discussed here, but it is important that you clearly set out research objectives. Throughout the report, it should be clear that the activities you undertook actually assist you in answering your research question(s). If any activity does not achieve that objective, it is unlikely that it should be included in the main body of the report, if at all.

Background

There will be some discussion of the background to the project in all reports. Within academic-type reports, this might be a separate chapter or be included in the introduction, whereas in most business-type reports, this would be included in the introduction. The background section sets the context of the study. For example, it might explain the development of the industry or the firm being examined, or how the problem being research has evolved. This brings the reader up to date on the issues to be examined. It is, however, different from the literature review, which focuses more on the development of the theory to be examined within the project. However, depending on the topic, the background section could be combined with the literature review.

The discussion of the background might also position the problem within the context of broader issues. In this way, the reader gains an understanding of why you have focused on this particular issue.

Literature Review

The literature review was discussed in Chapter 7, and most people believe that it is an essential part of the research process. It is unlikely that there will be a formal discussion of the literature within a business-type report. However, it is very likely that there will be a comprehensive literature review within an academic-type report. The literature review serves several roles. As was discussed in Chapter 7, it provides you with a solid theoretical grounding for your topic. Based on the literature, you should understand what has been done previously in your topic area and thus will not reinvent the wheel. In addition, you can use the literature to develop the focus of your report, design research tools, and even broadly compare your results to others' results. These activities are essential for all types of reports, although they will most likely only be explicitly discussed in academic-type reports.

The presentation of the literature in the report tells the reader how theory relates to the student researchers' topic and/or methodology. It should serve to provide some rationale for the research questions and or hypotheses. For example, "The previous research suggests that these relationships exist in Europe, and so this project aims to identify whether these relationships exist in the United States." In this way, you are using the literature to develop and support your ideas, suppositions, and arguments. Readers usually will be more comfortable with what you have done if there is some supporting logic for your activities based in the literature.

The question arises of how much literature should be included, both in terms of areas and depth. There is no firm answer to this question, and for the most part, it will be impossible and unnecessary to cover everything (i.e., do not try to be exhaustive). You should include sufficient material to demonstrate an understanding of the previous work and discuss it in a way that complements your research activities (i.e., you should be comprehensive). This ensures that the reader knows what has happened "so far" in this topic area and why your project research is worthwhile in relation to examining theory.

Methodology

All reports will contain some description of the methodology used in the project. In most academic-type reports, this will be covered in its own section, but in many business-type reports, it may be covered elsewhere. The methodology section provides the reader with a road map of what was done and why. In this way, the reader understands how the data were collected and analyzed. This section has important relevance, because if readers do not understand what was done and why, they may be less likely to agree with the results, implications, or recommendations.

When presenting a detailed description of the approach or approaches used for the research, you may want to consider how these will assist you in undertaking a more effective study. This means explaining why specific techniques will provide the best information and why the selected approach is the most appropriate. For example, "We want to examine organizational strategy development and thus will survey the CEO/President, who is the key decision maker in the strategy development process. This approach has been used extensively in other studies examining similar topics (for examples, see Smith, 1998, and Jones, 1990)."

The methodology section also provides a rationale as to why specific empirical methods are being applied. For example, "Given that we are comparing the behavior of two subsamples (i.e., large and small firms), we will use a set of paired t-tests. These are deemed most appropriate because they enable comparisons of multiple variables to be examined (Sage, 1996). This approach is most frequently used in the literature (SPSS, 1988) and enables us to compare our results with previous research such as the work of Bloggs (1998)."

This type of discussion should be provided for each activity, even if you are employing a multiple-stage research design. This means that the reader should not be left in any doubt regarding the data collection or analysis, and it also has the advantage that it forces you to think about what you are doing and why. This is one section that might be important to write up early on in the research process, rather than trying to justify things after they are completed.

Analysis/Results

All reports should have a section that explains the analysis or results. In business reports this section might be combined with the implications and discussion sections, although it could be a separate section as well. The role of an analysis/results section is to provide the data analysis (i.e., it presents the findings) and *describe* the results, rather than *explaining* what the results mean. For example, "The factor analysis of the data identified the following four factors with an eigenvalue of greater than 1.0, the standard cut-off for this type of work (Hair et al., 1995). (See Table I for the rotated factor loadings.) An examination of the variables within each factor resulted in them being named in the following way: Factor 1, Factor 2, Factor 3, and Factor 4."

The analysis needs to be such that the information is clearly presented and described. There are texts, such as Huck, Cromier, and Bounds (1974), that focus on assisting students in describing the results of various types of data analysis techniques. As was discussed in Chapters 11 and 12, this material needs to be clear and concise, as well as enable readers to follow the implications and discussion sections. For example, "The t-value of 4.7 with a p-value of <.01 identifies that there are statistical differences between the two samples. What this difference means will be discussed in the following section of the report."

Implications/Discussion

All reports will have sections examining the implications and/or discussing of the results, although some reports may combine the implications/discussion section with the results/analysis section. In the implications/discussion section, you will pull together your work and explain to the reader what the findings mean and whether the research questions, hypotheses, and so forth. were answered. In this way, you are expanding on the material in the analysis/results section by adding more commentary.

For example, "The results of the t-test identify that there are statistical differences between the two subsamples ($t = 4.17$, $p < .01$). In this case, larger organizations are more likely to have structures in place to develop corporate policy. This is consistent with the literature, which suggests that larger firms have more resources available to develop structured systems. It may therefore suggest that smaller firms develop polices in a more ad hoc fashion, although this was not explicitly examined and might be examined in the future."

However, the discussion might also explain alternative explanations for the results. For example, "A factor analysis identified four factors rather than the three factors examined in previous research. This might suggest that the issue being examined is more complex. Alternatively, it might suggest that the dimensions do not hold across countries, as the earlier studies were undertaken in Australia, rather than the U.S. The study did not examine this possibility."

The discussion section explains what the results mean in the context of the research objectives and tries to rationalize any inconsistencies with the support of the literature. This discussion will be used when you are making recommendations, as well as identifying limitations and opportunities for future research. Clearly explaining the results reinforces that the ideas discussed are not simple supposition, but are supported by the literature and the results of the research. *If* used effectively, you will then have the ammunition to support the recommendations that you make later in the report.

Limitations

All reports should include a limitations section. In the context of your research, it is almost certain that some unforeseen problem will arise or that the results will not be as conclusive as one would have hoped. Therefore, you need to objectively evaluate your work and identify things that may limit the wholehearted adoption of your results. Such limitations should not be seen as failures, as (a) these are student research projects, which are undertaken as a learning process; (b) there are frequently methodological problems that arise in all research (e.g., low response rates); and (c) mistakes or errors sometimes occur (e.g., a question was omitted from the survey and one research question cannot be examined).

Having a limitations section does not mean that you should attack every part of your research, but rather it is designed to assess the research, admit any limitations, and justify why the process and results are still applicable or valid. It also provides the opportunity to temper the overall tone of what has been done and to suggest areas for further research.

Recommendations

Most business reports will have recommendations, but these may not be part of all academic-type reports (the establishment of a recommendations section was discussed in Chapter 11). The recommendations are action-orientated suggestions made by you after having thoroughly analyzed and discussed the data. The recommendations are designed to provide some guidance for organizational actions based on your research. For all intents and purposes, the recommendations tell businesses what you believe is the most appropriate course of action; that is, after analyzing the results, this is what you believe they should do. This does not imply that these are actions that should be followed blindly, as any issues identified in the limitations section may require that managers proceed with caution.

In many cases, you may provide a set of alternative courses of action. This is especially relevant to business reports that need to take into consideration a range of constraints on the organization. For example, it would be unwise to suggest that a firm that is having cash-flow problems undertake cash-intensive strategies, unless you also identify how the cash-flow problem can be addressed. One of the most frequent problems experienced by students when making recommendations is that they forget to consider the bigger picture.

The recommendations should be based on the material within the report. Students frequently make rational suggestions that seem to appear from nowhere and are not supported by their results *or* the literature. In these situations, the question must be asked why you undertook the research if you were not going to use this information. This is not to suggest that a research project might not be used to verify that a given strategy or action is appropriate, but in this case, the research objective clearly sets this as the projects' focus.

For example, "The project examined whether increased training in the sales area will improve performance, as is suggested in the literature. It found that within the context of the study, this relationship did exist and thus the firm should develop additional training programs for sales staff." Thus, the project is testing common sense and does *not* simply assume that this relationship holds.

When making recommendations you need to clearly state what you believe should be done and why. However, you generally should not include information that is not discussed elsewhere in the report to justify your position. If other information is important, it should be included elsewhere in the body of the report. In the final analysis, one of the most critical ways to evaluate your report is to ask if the reader would agree with the recommendations based on what was presented. If the answer is yes, then you most likely have constructed a well-written report. If the answer is no, there are most likely flaws within the report that could have been addressed by clearer communication or a more appropriately designed research project. Having said this, no amount of drafting and redrafting will be able to fix a report based on a flawed research approach. The trick is to identify the flaws as limitations and make sure that any recommendations consider these limitations.

For example, "The results appear to suggest that more training will improve performance. However, given the limitations with the study design, the firm should undertake additional research to identify the specific types and programs that would be most appropriate." In this way, you can make it more difficult for readers to disagree with the recommendations, but it does identify that results and the associated recommendations are far from conclusive.

Conclusion

Not all reports will have a specific conclusion section, as some may combine this section with the recommendations or with the discussion/implications sections. The conclusion ties the report together and shows that the report has a clear, logical flow with a beginning, middle, and end. Some authors in the communication area suggest that the role of the conclusion is to "present a section that repeats succinctly the logical outcome of all that has gone before" (Turk & Kirkman, 1989, p. 65). In this case, the conclusion section will not necessarily be lengthy, given that all the information is discussed elsewhere in the report.

However, if a project report simply stops without a conclusion section, readers may wonder if this is actually the end of the report or if something has been left out. The conclusion section should state that this is the end of the report. It also allows one last opportunity to reinforce the main points of the report and encourage the acceptance of the recommendations. That is, it is also one last chance to sell what you have found.

Future Research

One issue that might only be focused on in academic-type reports is the future research section, which also may be combined with the conclusion section. These opportunities can arise for a number of reasons. First the limitations may provide a range of future research opportunities. For example, "The study used a student sample as a proxy for the wider population, and future research could sample the wider community." The findings themselves might point to opportunities for future research for example, "The findings were not conclusive, which might be explained by differences within the sample, and therefore may warrant further examination. Future research might examine this issue further by attempting to segment the population based on demographic factors." There may also be natural extensions to the work; for example, "This research examined these relationships in one industry, and future research could determine if these relationships are generalizable across industries."

The purpose of the future research section is partly to demonstrate that you not only understand what you did, but also see how your work fits in with the wider development of the area. Though for the most part you are not expected to push the frontiers of knowledge, all research does advance knowledge to varying degrees.

References

All reports should identify the full reference of any materials cited within the report, and for the most part these materials will have been mentioned in the background, literature review, or methodology sections. Including the full bibliographical reference is designed to allow readers to refer to these original materials, should they wish to do so. In some cases, readers may look at the references to identify the significance of a given referenced work. For example, are students using evidence from a scholarly journal, such as *Administrative Sciences Quarterly,* or are they basing their arguments on something from a less auspicious source, such as the *National Enquirer.* This is not to suggest that newspapers, magazines, and/or Web pages are not useful materials to reference, but the reader needs to be able to identify the source of materials cited.

In terms of writing up a reference section, the specific format has been discussed in Chapter 7. One key is to make sure that a consistent referencing format is used and that all materials cited in the paper are included in the references section. In addition, it is important that names and dates are accurately documented. Sloppy referencing may make the reader question other aspects of your work, and as such may make arguments, conclusions, and recommendations less convincing.

Appendices

Appendices may be used in both academic-type and business-type reports. Appendices may include a range of information that is unnecessary to the main argument in the report. This might include more detailed discussions of issues overviewed in the report or material that is too technical for inclusion in the body of the report (Sussams, 1991; Turk & Kirkman, 1989). For example, details of complex statistical analysis may be more appropriate for an appendix than for the body of a business-type report. Appendices may also include a range of materials related to the data collection, such as the survey instrument or any other materials that were distributed to respondents. For example, if people were shown pictures on which they commented, these pictures would be included in an appendix.

You may also include supplementary tables, figures, or diagrams in an appendix. However, this should only be done if these materials are not frequently referred to in the body of the report, unless they are included in an appendix because they are lengthy. Having information that is core to your argument in the appendix makes it difficult for readers to follow, as they would have to flip back and forth in the report. Though technically this should not distract readers, anything that makes the report harder to read may distort the communication or at least get in the way of effective communication. Also, an appendix should not become a "dumping ground" for unrelated material distantly related to the research, printouts of raw data, or statistical tests that are not even included or discussed in the body of the report. The evaluation of a report is based on the content, not just the size.

Conclusion

It is extremely important to have a well-written project report that clearly and logically explains what was done, why it was done, and what it means. This chapter has not only discussed the sections that might be included in such a report but also provided some suggestions for the written report. Though there is no one structure that achieves the objects of all types of reports, it is important that your written communication follow some basic guidelines, which have been described for academic and business reports.

It is important to ensure that the wording of the report is direct, unambiguous, and straight-to-the-point and the structure is clear and logical, all of which makes the report easy to read. Sentences and paragraphs need to make sense and be well structured.

Make sure that the writing style suits the focus of the project, as academic-type and business-type reports should differ significantly (Jankowicz, 1995). If readers are technical, be more technical in your language; if they are action-oriented, explain the recommended tactics in more detail. Use language suited to the readers so that they will understand at the level required.

You need to consider the length of the report. How long does each section need to be? No one wants to read a 100-page report if the information could be efficiently presented in 50 pages. You can't bore someone into implementing your recommendations, and long reports are more likely to lose readers. Of course, in addressing length, you also need to check the requirements of your instructor.

We hope you have found your research project interesting, *but* it is equally important that you make the report interesting for the reader. One way to make the body of the report interesting to read is by breaking up the report with headings and subheadings. Though changing font sizes and emphasis may also be useful, be careful that you comply with the requirements of your courses and that when you change the font or layout, there is a reason. Visual aids such as pictures, tables, graphs, and diagrams should also be used where appropriate, although these too should only be used to make a point, rather than simply because they look pretty. Ways to present the results are discussed in Chapter 12.

In Exhibit 13.2 is a final checklist for student researchers to use when writing their reports, although other checklists may be valuable as well (Armstrong, 2003). Though these questions seem fairly simplistic, it is amazing how frequently student researchers forget to identify these issues early on in the writing of the report. Asking yourself these questions early on will not only prevent your rushing around at the end of the project process but should also ensure that more time is allocated to the important task of actually writing the final report.

Exhibit 13.2   The Final Checklist

1. What is the type of report that is required?
2. What is the required length of the report?
3. When is the report due?
4. What is the planned structure of the report?
5. Who is responsible for writing each section?
6. When will draft chapters be available for proofreading?
7. Is the draft report clear and consistent?
8. Do the final recommendations make logical sense?
9. Who is responsible for the final printing, collating, and delivery of the final report?
10. Is there to be an oral presentation of the report findings?

References

Anonymous. (1992). Writing skills that spell employment. *Baylor Business Review, 10*(2), 20–21.

Anonymous. (1995). Tips for effective business writing. *Supervision, 56*(6), 13.

Armstrong, S. J. (2003). *Checklist for writing management report.* Retrieved December 12, 2003, from http://www.marketing.wharton.upenn.edu/ideas/pdf/Writing%20Management%20Reports.pdf.

Bentley, T. J. (1992). *Report writing in business.* London: The Chartered Institute of Management Accounts.

Borin, N., & Watkins, H. (1998). Employers evaluate critical skills of today's marketing undergraduates. *Marketing Educator, 17*(3), 1–6.

Garay, M. S. (1995). Meeting workplace needs in an introductory business writing course. *Business Communication Quarterly, 58*(1), 35–41.

Hair, J. F., Anderson, R. E., Tatham, R. L., & Black, W. C. (1995). *Multivariate data analysis with readings.* Englewood Cliffs, NJ: Prentice Hall.

Hansen, R. S. (1993). Clear, concise writing is especially important for marketers. *Marketing News, 27*(19), 20.

Huck, S. W., Cromier, W. H., & Bounds, W. G., Jr. (1974). *Reading statistics and research*. New York: Harper and Row.

Huettman, E. (1996). Writing for multiple audiences: An examination of audience concerns in a hospitality consulting firm. *Journal of Business Communication, 33, July*, 257–273.

Jacobs, P. (1998). Strong writing skills essential for success, even in IT. *Infoworld, 20*(27), 86.

Jankowicz, A. D. (1995). *Business research projects*. London: Chapman & Hall.

Krajewski, L., & Smith, G. (1997). From letter writing to report writing: Bridging the gap. *Business Communication Quarterly, 60*(4), 88–90.

Leach, J. (1993). Seven steps to better writing. *Planning, 59*(6), 26–27.

Lesikar, R. V. (1972). *Report writing for business*. Homewood, IL: Richard D. Irwin, Inc.

Loehr, L. (1995). An integrated approach to introducing research methods in required business and technical writing courses. *Business Communication Quarterly, 58*(4), 25–27.

Maupin, R. J., & May, C. A. (1993). Communication for accounting students. *International Journal of Educational Management, 7*(3), 30–38.

McNerney, D. J. (1994). Improve your communication skills. *HR Focus, 71*(10), 22.

Sharp, J. A., & Howard, K. (1996). *The management of a student research project*. Aldershot, UK: Gower.

Straub, J. T. (1991). Memos and reports: Write them right the first time. *Supervisory Management, 36*(7), 6.

Suchan, J. (1991). The high cost of bureaucratic written communications. *Business Horizons, 34*(2), 68–73.

Sussams, J. E. (1991). *How to write effective reports*. Hants, UK: Grower.

Thomas, S. G. (1994). Preparing business students for real-world writing. *Education & Training, 36*(6), 11–15.

Turk, C., & Kirkman, J. (1989). *Effective writing: Improving scientific, technical and business communication*. New York: E. F. Spon.

Williams, J. (1996). Top business schools see value of communication skills. *Communication World, 13*(8), 36–38.

14

Oral Presentations

This chapter will examine a range of issues relating to presenting your results in an oral presentation. An oral presentation may not be essential for all research projects, but is often required. If you have to give an oral presentation, you need to clearly explain your research in a way that is appropriate for the assigned requirements and the audience. You also need to provide support for the arguments presented. In business, some managers are too busy to fully read a written report and so will make a decision partly based on an oral presentation (Waller, 1998). Such a presentation can be used to outline the research problem, methodology undertaken, main findings, and recommendations. It is a very effective tool to reinforce key elements of the research project. Like your written report, the oral presentation is an opportunity to sell your findings, and clear communication is critical.

Oral presentations are in an audiovisual manner (unlike written reports), which attracts the audience's attention to what is being communicated. Effective presentations, academic or business, require preparation and share some important elements. Some people, such as Scott Armstrong (2003), a highly regarded academic, suggest that there are several main phases of the presentation that need to be considered. These include the following:

1. Activities before the talk that set the stage

2. During the talk, activities that include issues such as (a) organization of materials; (b) visuals used; and (c) oral communication issues

3. Ending activities, which round off the presentation

4. Post-presentation activities (such as sending or distributing summaries) that further emphasize the material

The following discussion will expand on the issues that relate to giving an oral presentation.

Before the Presentation

For an effective presentation, you must undertake some groundwork before you begin the actual presentation. Only a skillful communicator with a lot of experience in public speaking can successfully ad lib a presentation or speech. In the case of a presentation of research findings, it is very important that you prepare before you present, as you do not want to miss critical issues or fail to present your work effectively. In fact, the smaller the amount of experience you have with oral presentations, the greater the amount of preparation that may be needed. Some things you will have to address are the following:

1. Know Your Audience

It is *vital* that you know about your audience before you begin your presentation (Warne & White, 1986). Some of the things you should try to discover are who your audience is, what they already know about your topic, what they want to know about your presentation, and what they need to know from your presentation. By answering these types of questions, you can better focus your presentation and pitch it at the level, and with the right language, that will satisfy the audience's requirements. This can result in the best use of your presentation time and reduce any misunderstandings between you and your audience. Within your assigned topic, some of the questions may be easily addressed, and the answers will equally affect on your presentation style and coverage of the material.

2. Know Your Surroundings

This can be difficult for some people, who may not know where they are making their presentation, but it can be helpful to go to the room before you present to get a feeling for its physical surroundings. To be comfortable in the room you are going to present in, it might be a good idea to see the layout of the room, find out where you will be positioned, and test the sound, overhead projector, PowerPoint system, and so forth. This is especially important with the increased use of multimedia materials. For example, if you develop a PowerPoint presentation using a version that is more advanced than the version on the computer you are supposed to use, you might have a problem. Being more confident in your physical surroundings can assist you in being more confident in your oral presentation.

3. Plan Your Presentation

Planning your presentation is extremely important, because a planned presentation is a good presentation, and you must know about what you are presenting. You should thoroughly plan the structure of your presentation (see below), what is to be said (and by whom if it is a group presentation), what is to be shown in a visual format, and how long it will take to present it. Planning and understanding all areas of your presentation can reduce any nervousness about giving the presentation and make you more confident in what you are saying. However, even if you plan, you may need to be flexible. For example, if one person in your group goes on too long, it might require adjustments in others' materials. According to Warne and White (1986), "planning begins with your purpose" (p. 7), so from the start you should be very clear in what the purpose of your presentation is (e.g., to entertain, inform, teach, or persuade). Your lecturer/professor/supervisor should help you in planning your presentation.

4. Practice Your Presentation

As the saying goes, "practice makes perfect." You may not end up with a perfect presentation, but by practicing your public speaking skills and specific presentations, the result will definitely be a more effective presentation. You can practice in front of family or friends who will give you feedback as well as experience with the content of what you are saying and the timing of the presentation. Some people may find it more comfortable to practice by themselves, which can be done in front of a mirror or into an audio/video recorder. Again, being more familiar with what you are going to say will give you more confidence and help reduce nerves.

The Presentation

In business, there are a number of different types of presentations (e.g., impromptu, from memory, and scripted) that can be made for various situations (e.g., a staff member leaving, a new product launch, imparting consumer information, and revealing research results). When it comes to the actual presentation of your research, there are a number of skills that can be used that will assist in an effective oral presentation. These can relate to the presentation content and the presentation style.

1. Presentation Content

An important part of an oral presentation is the content of what is being communicated. While planning what will be in the content of your presentation, there are a number of things to keep in mind, including the following:

Structure the Presentation

Make sure that your presentation has a planned structure, with a clear beginning, middle, and end that flow in a logical way. Explain to the audience what you are going to talk about; give them the information they want to hear (e.g., the overview, results, and recommendations of the project); and then conclude by summarizing what you have told them. Malhotra et al. (2002) describe this as the "tell 'em" principle:

1. Tell 'em what you're going to tell 'em.

2. Tell 'em.

3. Tell 'em what you've told 'em.

Make it simple, easy to understand, and within the time limit. To do all this effectively and professionally, it cannot be done without a planned structure. You might even want to have one of your first overheads communicate this to the audience. A possible structure for your business project presentation is found in Exhibit 14.1.

Exhibit 14.1   Presentation Structure

1. Introduction
   Introduce speaker(s) and the structure of the presentation

2. Research Problem
   Basic background to the topic
   Research problem, objectives/hypothesis

3. Research Design
   Explain methodology in nontechnical terms
   Data collection

4. Results
   Data analysis
   Tables with results that answer the research objectives/hypothesis
   Interpretation

5. Recommendations
   Clear recommendations that answer the research problem

6. Conclusion
   Summing up and emphasizing the main points

7. Thank audience and ask for questions

You should also be aware of the concentration curve, which states that memory retention is greatest at the beginning and end of any presentation (Ehrenborg & Mattock, 1993). This is particularly true for any talk over 5 minutes long. It is, therefore, important that you plan a strong beginning and end with an emphasis on the most important information. Ways to try to create some extra peaks of attention include voice loudness, pitch, and so forth; equipment changes; body language and position; involving the audience; telling a joke or story; and keeping a clear, flowing structure (Ehrenborg & Mattock, 1993).

Beware of the Beginning

The beginning, or introduction, of your presentation is very important and can set the scene for the rest of your presentation. You should use the time carefully to get the audience's interest regarding the project. Two things you should *not* do in the introduction stage are to begin with an apology for what you are about to say, or to begin with a joke or story that may not be funny or could embarrass or offend some audience members. You should be professional at all times during the presentation (Ehrenborg & Mattock, 1993).

Prepare the Ending

The end of your presentation is just as important as the beginning. By the end you should have achieved your purpose, satisfied the audience's basic informational needs, summed the main points, and pointed to future action or future research. After a great deal of effort working on your project, it is not appropriate to leave the ending of your final presentation as a spur-of-the-moment grab for words (Warne & White, 1986). The ending is your last chance to sell your work and thus is an opportunity to emphasize issues of importance. Everything should be planned from beginning to end.

Be Visual

Visual aids can assist in effective communication during oral presentation, as (a) people are visually minded; (b) memory retention is increased; (c) visualization encourages organization; and (d) misunderstandings are less likely to occur (Luck & Rubin, 1987). Visual aids also have the effect of diverting the audience's attention away from the speaker to the visual (illustration, graph, or slide), thereby giving the speaker a few moments in which to relax, gather thoughts, and prepare for the next point (Elliot & Windschuttle, 1999). Designing overheads that communicate information in a visually appealing way is important.

Therefore, to help in the explanation of the project results, or to emphasize particular points, it is worthwhile to use visual aids. These can include overheads, slides, PowerPoint presentations, flip charts, chalkboards, whiteboards, magnetic boards, videos, and practical examples. However, if you use these devices, make sure that they *assist* in presenting the results and are not interfering in, or diverting attention away from, the communication of the intended ideas. Problems can occur, for example, when the information is too cluttered or too small to be read by the audience, and where there are too many information-packed slides, or too few to keep up with the spoken information. Do *not* just photocopy or cut and paste sections of your written report onto an overhead. Presentation slides should be developed specifically to communicate the key issues.

Discussion of the ways to present the results is found in Chapter 12. Though you do need to present the findings, you need to present all the associated information as well. Visuals are a tool that allows you to emphasize things as well as lead the audience through the discussion. You, therefore, need to make sure that you stick to the key issues, as you can distract the audience by trying to discuss every issue in minute detail.

2. Presentation Style

Once the content of your presentation has been planned and prepared, effort must be made to ensure that your presentation style effectively communicates your message. Even if you have all the information necessary in your presentation, your overall presentation could be ruined by poor presentation style. Improving your public speaking and presentation skills can increase the effectiveness of your presentation. The following are some suggestions to improve the presentation style for your oral presentation and prevent it from becoming an embarrassing mess.

Don't Read

Reading your presentation word-for-word is very boring for the audience. Reading hinders the communication process and can stop any eye contact, which is important for holding people's attention. Knowing your material before the presentation and being confident with what you are going to say and when you will say it can reduce the dependence on reading (Waller, 1998). If you need help with remembering information, then use palm cards or visual devices (e.g., overheads, PowerPoint slides, or other devices mentioned above) with the main points written to assist your presentation. Thus, you need to remember to communicate the key points to your audience; don't read to them. You do need to be careful that you also do not try to put too much information on overheads, which can result in reading these to the audience. Overheads should be designed to display key points that guide you through the presentation. If you know your topic, you should be able to expand on these points, thereby making the presentation more interesting.

Speak Up and Be Clear

Your audience must be able to hear and understand what you say, so it is important to speak up clearly. Everyone in the room should be able to hear you. Speaking quickly or mumbling will only distract the audience. The loudness of your voice may have to differ depending on whether you are presenting in a classroom or a lecture theater, and whether you have a microphone or not. It may then be important, as mentioned above, to visit the room first to test the physical surroundings.

Use Your Voice

It is important for a presenter to use his or her voice. There are a wide range of voice qualities involved in oral presentations, including speed, pitch, loudness, and rhythm. To communicate effectively, the speaker must control all these aspects of his or her voice. For example, to communicate less anxiety when speaking, a speaker should lower the pitch, slow down the pace, and use subtle pauses between key points (Elliot & Windschuttle, 1999).

Use Your Body

Body language features, such as position, posture, gestures, facial expressions, and eye contact, may influence the audience's perception of both you as a speaker and the presentation of the results. It is important for you to express confidence in what you have done. Therefore, you should stand erect with head out, avoid hiding behind objects, keep gestures to a minimum but use them effectively to emphasize points, establish various eye contact points, and dress professionally (Ehrenborg & Mattock, 1993).

Be Interested/Enthusiastic

Show that you are interested in your project results and get the audience interested too. This interest and enthusiasm will also encourage you in your presentation style. After undertaking all the project research activities, no matter what the final results, you do have something interesting to tell others—so tell them! Try to keep the audience awake, attentive, and involved. Unfortunately, being monotone in your voice and unenthusiastic about the project will quickly be communicated to your audience.

Support Activities and Materials

Students frequently look to differentiate themselves and their presentations. This can be done in various ways. For example, students may dress up to support the theme of the presentation or seek to get audience participation. These activities are generally fine, as long as they do not distract from the presentation and are used to support the material being presented. Therefore, asking people what their favorite sporting team is might be relevant in a presentation on customer loyalty if it linked up with the teams' performance later in the presentation, whereas asking something that does not add to the presentation could seem to distract the audience and take up time, which is usually limited.

The same caution needs to be raised with using video materials within a presentation. Though short "grabs" or advertisements as examples may highlight points, showing a 10-minute video in a 20-minute presentation would usually be unwarranted. This would reflect 50% of the presentation and, therefore, its importance should be commensurate with the time allocated.

A second issue within supplementary materials relates to the question of whether you should distribute materials before or during the presentation (distributing at the end of the presentation will be discussed later). Distributing materials before or during the presentation could be valuable, especially if there are detailed tables that will be discussed, and make it easier for the audience to follow the material. On the other hand, distributing the report, a set of PowerPoint notes, or other supplementary information could serve to distract the audience. In some cases, the audience spends the time reading this other material rather than paying attention to the presentation, thereby reducing the benefit of presenting material.

Be Positive

You should be positive about your results, even if the final results do not give clear findings. Do not be negative, even as a joke, as this can make the audience negative toward your project and you as a researcher.

Keep to Your Time Limit

The audience will loose interest if the presentation is too long and does not hold their interest. Keep to the point, while providing the main information required by the audience, and aim to be finished within your time limit to leave time for questions. You cannot bore someone into understanding, let alone implementing, your recommendations.

Be Professional

It is important that you present in a formal fashion. While you may not have to present in business attire, it always seems that when students take themselves more seriously, it usually translates to the audience taking the presentation more seriously. Other issues to consider here relate to how members of your group behave when they are not presenting. If they appear to be disinterested (i.e., talking among themselves), how can you expect the audience to be interested? Your mannerisms are equally important, so things such as chewing gum or being disorganized distract from what you are saying. Other issues, such as using a phrase too frequently, can also distract in this regard. For example, an audience can get distracted when the presenter frequently says "Umm." Though this phrase is frequently used when people are nervous, it is a stylistic issue that you should seek to eliminate.

Wrapping Up

The oral presentation has the benefit of going beyond the written words, as well as being flexible in activities. There are two final activities associated with the oral presentation that frequently occur at the end, that of dealing with questions and distributing supplementary materials. These two issues will be discussed below.

Dealing With Questions

One key benefit of an oral presentation is that you can directly deal with issues that are not clear to the audience right away. For example, though the material is clear to you, it might not be clear to the audience. In some cases, you are in fact graded on how well you deal with questions. If you are given the choice of dealing with questions during the presentation or at the end, we suggest that you deal with questions at the end. The main reasons for this are that questions might fluster you or others in your group and they also take up time (i.e., disrupt your rhythm). Therefore, dealing with questions at the end allows you to present the material as you intended. The only negative with this approach is that if an essential point is not understood, it could detract from the remainder of the presentation. It is important to realize that questions are not necessarily an indication that there are problems with the presentation or report, but could be an indication that you have stimulated the audience's interest.

Given that there will most likely be questions, you need to consider how these will be dealt with. This is especially important when there is a group presentation and questions may relate to different individuals' sections. Should the individual that presented the material deal with the question or possibly should others in the group respond? This will partly depend on how sections to the presentation are allocated. For example, the presenter might not have worked on the section of the research related to the question and, therefore, someone else might be better able to respond.

You should consider what questions people might ask, as in some cases it may be clear from your presentation that people might want more information about specific issues. For example, in past presentations, some groups have prepared additional overheads that they use to further explain points they believe may be asked about in question time. This does not mean the points were not covered well in the presentation, but that more depth is needed to explain the issue to some members of the audience. The type of audience might also indicate whether they will ask certain types of questions.

Another problem that frequently arises in presentations of research is that someone will ask about an issue that you did not consider. This sort of question often is difficult to address off the top of your head, although thinking on your feet is a valuable skill to have. You need to be careful that questions about unanticipated issues do not result in you or others in your group getting overly defensive. If you believe that the individual has not understood a point, then it is important to clarify the matter. This should be done is a civil and objective fashion; that is, do not attack the person. In some cases, the question asked might relate to an issue that was not considered in the research or that you do not know the answer to. There is nothing wrong with identifying that this is the case and that the issue should be taken into consideration in the future. It is impossible to cover everything in one research project or the presentation of that research. If the person's question identifies an error, you should also recognize that. In this case, you do need to also consider if the issue would affect the material presented. In some cases, these corrections may be typos. For example, in one place you mention you interviewed 20 people and in another it is 25. However, if the problems are more fundamental, then it may not be as easy to answer them off the top of your head. Ideally, these errors will not occur, but admitting something is wrong is often better than trying to defend the error.

Distributing Support Materials

The issue of supplementary materials was discussed in regard to the beginning or during the presentation itself, and though it was suggested that these might serve as a distraction, at the end of the presentation these same materials might serve to reinforce the points made in the presentation—timing is everything. At the end of the presentation, you might want to distribute an executive summary, PowerPoint notes, or even the full report. These materials distributed at this point can be taken away and be referred to later. Some students have distributed other materials, similar to promotional materials. For example, a group discussing a brewery gave each person one of the company's beers at the end. In another situation, students distributed brochures about the organizations the presentations were about. However, if there are several presentations in a row, materials distributed might distract the audience from listening to these other presenters. It should be noted that in a business presentation in which there is a client, distributing materials at the end to reinforce what you have said is exceptionally valuable.

If you wish to distribute materials at the end, it might be beneficial to ask your lecturer/professor in advance to ensure that he or she does not believe it will distract from other groups. You should also make sure you have materials for everyone, especially if it is something everyone might want. Failing to have enough in a real business presentation would potentially alienate members of the organization if they did not receive the material. You should also stay well away from anything that might be offensive to anyone.

Conclusion

For your research project, an oral presentation may play an important part in the assessment. Whatever its role in your project, it is still an effective tool to reinforce key elements, such as the problem, methodology, main findings, and recommendations. It is vital that you clearly explain your project to a given audience and provide them with the information they require. To make sure that you have an effective presentation, you *must* plan the presentation with a clear, logical structure and be confident with your content and in your presentation style.

Often, students have complained that they are too nervous when presenting. Nervousness is not a completely bad thing, as it helps produce adrenaline, which can assist in your presentation delivery. However, at its worst it can affect the overall communication of ideas, as well as embarrass you and the audience. There may be a few ways to reduce nervousness before public speaking, such as breathing deeply and relaxing muscles, but, as mentioned above, one practical way is to thoroughly plan and understand all areas of your presentation so that you are confident in what you will say. Remember, the presentation will be over before you know it, so it is important to give it your best shot!

References

Armstrong, S. J. (2003). *Checklist for making oral presentations.* Retrieved December 13, 2003, from http://www-marketing.wharton.upenn.edu/ideas/pdf/Armstrong/Checklist_for_Oral_Presentations.pdf.

Ehrenborg, J., & Mattock, J. (1993). *Powerful presentations: 50 Original ideas for making a real impact.* London: Kogan Page.

Elliot, E., & Windschuttle, K. (1999). *Writing, researching, communicating: Communication skills for the information age, 3rd Ed.* Sydney: McGraw-Hill.

Luck, D. J., & Rubin, R. S. (1987). *Marketing research.* Englewood Cliffs, NJ: Prentice Hall International.

Malhotra, N. K., Hall, J., Shaw, M., & Oppenheim, P. (2002). *Marketing research: An applied orientation.* Sydney: Pearson Education.

Waller, D. (1998). *How to prepare a promotional plan.* Sydney: Irwin/McGraw-Hill.

Warne, C., & White, P. (1986). *How to hold an audience—without a rope.* Sydney: AIO Press.

15 Concluding Remarks

ormer students have mentioned to us that they usually enjoyed the opportunity to undertake a research project and that it was a very rewarding experience. They have indicated that they have benefited from working in groups, being able to apply theory to practice, researching a topic of interest to them, honing their ability to solve real-world problems, formulating realistic recommendations from research data, and presenting the findings in a written and oral form. Students frequently comment that this has allowed them not only to draw together everything they learned over their various subjects but also to exercise skills such as leadership, team building, data analysis, report writing, and improving general confidence to an extent that they would not normally obtain from other subjects.

Former students have suggested the following benefits of undertaking a research project:

> "finding out how the Real World really operates," "being able to complete a practical assignment which is worthwhile to an organization," "application of theory and knowledge learned throughout the degree," "learning experience—research, topic area, business environment," being able to "see the immediate use of the work," and "the ability to use my business skills learned during my course in a practical manner and in an area of interest to me."

Some students have reported that they have taken their research report with them to job interviews. They believe that this has given them a competitive advantage over others, as they have been able to demonstrate that they can work as part of a team and solve complex problems, and, to some extent, link theory to practice. The tangible outcome of the research (i.e., the report) is therefore often very important to students, as it is a concrete demonstration of their abilities.

However, the research process can be difficult and requires a great commitment of time and effort. There will be periods of "ups" and "downs" where you will need to motivate yourself, and possibly other group members, until the job at hand is finished and the project is successfully completed.

Hints for Those Undertaking a Project

While the process described in this book will assist you in completing your research project, we know from past experience that there are a number of key issues that need to be addressed and clarified. Addressing these points will enable you to complete your business project more effectively.

1. **Overall project objectives.** You need to be clear as to exactly what the overall objectives of the project are. Whenever possible, the focus of the project should be integrating theory into practice, which will allow you to demonstrate that you have the ability to work in teams and can use theory to solve realistic complex business problems in a systematic way. The objectives of the type of projects described in this book are *rarely* to undertake publishable research, provide professional consulting advice, or produce a comprehensive business plan. Clarify with your lecturer/professor/supervisor if there is any uncertainty regarding the goals, as this will affect the focus of your work.

2. **Clear planning.** It is important that you, and any other students if it is a group project, plan and understand all of the various activities related to the project, and that your supervisor(s) understands your project's goals as well. It is very important to have an agreement that covers all key project activities, explaining exactly what is expected. This may begin in the form of a detailed subject outline, and be developed with the written research proposal. The sooner you understand the objectives, what is expected, the planned activities, and who will do what, the better you will be able to develop your project. By planning and keeping focused, you will ensure a smooth flow of activities throughout the project. Chapter 6 discusses the importance of planning.

3. **Choosing topics.** One key step to ensuring that the subject runs smoothly is for you to formalize your topic as soon as possible. It is important that your topic is of interest to you, applies theory to practice when possible, and is achievable within the time and financial constraints, given *your* specific level of expertise. Trying to take on a huge project will put unnecessary strain on you and will often result in refocusing the work halfway through or not completing the task as comprehensively as anticipated. Thus, you might not be able to answer the question you set for yourself. Chapter 2 assists you in choosing your topic.

4. **Supervisor's support.** Do not be afraid to ask for clarification, advice, or assistance from your supervisor(s). At times, you will need extensive

support and interaction, such as in the development stage. At other points in time, such as for the literature review, you may need less involvement. It is your supervisor's responsibility to help you to complete your project successfully, and you should take advantage of his or her knowledge and experience. Chapter 3 discusses the role of the supervisor.

5. **Human intervention.** If proposed student projects involve intervention in human activity (surveys, focus groups, interviews, etc.), it is essential that you understand your ethical responsibilities in regard to dealing with subjects or potential subjects. The potential for harming subjects should be avoided at all costs, especially given that the focus of the project is education and learning rather than pure research. Chapter 5 discusses ethical considerations.

6. **Being equitable.** It is important to be equitable during the research process. This can mean giving a fair time to each stage of the project (e.g., not spending a long time on choosing a topic and a short time on data analysis), or that each group member does his or her fair share of work (e.g., not having one group member be a "dead weight" that does no work). This can be achieved with the help of good planning and a common goal of successfully completing the project.

7. **Being flexible.** While the process is fairly structured, it is important that there is a degree of flexibility. Flexibility refers to the development and management of the project. Often, selected topics are initially too broad or are beyond the necessary scope and must be refined. Changes can sometimes even occur during the implementation of projects (e.g., when a manager in a firm agrees to work with a group, and then changes his or her mind or leaves the position). In this situation, you will need to either find alternative firms willing to support the project or look for new ways to implement the project. Therefore, you need to be able to see how things might be recast or redeveloped throughout the research process.

8. **Learn from the project.** Remember that the focus of the project is for education and learning. It is important to view the project as an opportunity to exercise some valuable skills. When (not if) mistakes are made, we hope that you will be able to learn from your mistakes and continue to develop your project to completion.

Finally, we encourage you to make the most of your opportunity to complete your research project and develop a range of skills as discussed in the book. The development of "soft skills" (such as group work, critical thinking, oral communication, etc.) will be important not only in your academic studies but also when you are looking for a job and in the workforce. The research and associated report will potentially serve as tangible indications of what you can do. Given the competitive employment market, being able to demonstrate your skills will assist you in differentiating yourself from others. From our experiences, we believe that research projects are very worthwhile, educationally and developmentally, and many of the students we have supervised feel the same way. We wish you well in your endeavors, and remember to try to enjoy the research process.

Index

About the Authors

Michael Jay Polonsky is the Melbourne Airport Chair in Marketing within the School of Tourism, Hospitality and Marketing at Victoria University, Melbourne, Australia. Prior to taking up this position, he was an Associate Professor at the University of Newcastle, and he has also taught at Charles Sturt University (Australia), Massey University (New Zealand), the University of the Witwatersrand (South Africa), and Temple University (United States). He has a PhD from the Australian Catholic University, two master's degrees—from Rutgers University–Newark and Temple University—as well as a BS from Towson State University.

Michael's areas of research include environmental marketing/management, stakeholder theory, ethical and social issues in marketing, cross-cultural studies, and marketing education. In 2001, he won the Vice-Chancellor's Citation for Excellence in Research within the Faculty of Business and Law. He has published extensively across these areas, including coediting three books, one of which was recently translated into Chinese; authoring or co-authoring 11 book chapters; authoring or coauthoring 70 journal articles; and presenting more than 100 presentations at national and international conferences. Some of his works appear in *Marketing Theory, Advances in International Marketing, Journal of Market Focused Management, Journal of Marketing Communications, European Journal of Marketing, Business Horizons, Journal of Marketing Theory and Practice, Journal of Business Ethics, Journal of Macromarketing, Journal of Marketing Management, International Journal of Nonprofit and Voluntary Sector Marketing, Business Strategy and the Environment, International Journal of Retailing & Distribution Management, Journal of Organizational Change Management, Journal of Business and Industrial Marketing, International Marketing Review, International Journal of Advertising*, and *Journal of Advertising Research*.

He has also undertaken a range of administrative roles for conferences and journals, which include serving as guest editor for issues of the *European Journal of Marketing* on stakeholder theory, *Journal of Marketing Theory and Practice* on the business of nonprofits, *Journal of Business Research* on the unintended consequences of marketing, and *Asia-Pacific Journal of Marketing and Logistics* looking at cross-cultural issues.

David S. Waller is a Senior Lecturer in Marketing at the University of Technology, Sydney, Australia. David was born and raised in Sydney and, after working in the banking and film industries, taught at a number of universities in Australia, including the University of Newcastle, the University of New South Wales, and Charles Sturt University, Riverina. David has a BA from the University of Sydney, a Master's of Commerce from the University of New South Wales, and a PhD from the University of Newcastle. His research interests include advertising agencies, agency–client relationships, controversial advertising, international advertising, and marketing education.

David has published in a wide range of areas relating to advertising and marketing communication. He has authored and coauthored a number of articles that have appeared in various journals including *Journal of Advertising Research, Journal of Consumer Marketing, Journal of Marketing Communications, International Journal of Advertising, European Journal of Marketing, Marketing Intelligence & Planning, Journal of Marketing Education, Asia-Pacific Journal of Marketing and Logistics, Asia-Australia Marketing Journal, Asian Journal of Marketing, Australasian Journal of Market Research,* and *Journal of Business Ethics.* David is also a regular presenter at marketing educators' conferences in Australia and New Zealand. His workbooks, *How to Prepare a Marketing Plan* and *How to Prepare a Promotional Plan,* are being used by marketing and advertising students at tertiary institutions in a number of countries.